The Gospel Chronicle

Seventy Weeks of Messiah

Daniel 9:20-27

Redaction

A Chronological Study
Attesting Gospel Unity

- collated by-

G.L. Kirschke

a disciple of Jesus Christ

As received from the

AMEN

Revelation 3:14-22

www.witnessground.org

All scripture is chosen from the 1611 bible heritage

Deluxe Hardcover Edition

MMXVIX

GIVEN FOR FAITHFUL CONSIDERATION

TO ALL DISCIPLES OF JESUS CHRIST

WHO CHOOSE THE LIBERTY OF EXILE

WITHIN THE CONGREGATION OF THE

ONLY LIVING GOD JEHOVAH-SHALOM

Judges 6:21-24

THE GOSPEL CHRONICLE: REDACTION

Subtitle: Seventy Weeks of Messiah

Copyright © 2019 by Witness Ground Publications

ISBN: 978-1-7325845-3-2

First Printed Edition: December 2017

First Printed ISBN Edition: December 2018

Deluxe Hardcover Edtion: February 2019

Standard Softcover Edition: February 2019

Printed in the United States by Witness Ground Publications

0   9   8   7   6   5   4   3   2

Available Editions:

Hardcover:

    The Gospel Chronicle: Narrative

        ISBN: 978-1-7325845-1-8

    The Gospel Chronicle: Parallel

        ISBN: 978-1-7325845-2-5

    The Gospel Chronicle: Redaction

        ISBN: 978-1-7325845-3-2

    The Gospel Chronicle: Redaction – SE

        ISBN: 978-1-7325845-4-9

Softcover:

    The Gospel Chronicle: Narrative

        ISBN: 978-1-7325845-5-6

    The Gospel Chronicle: Parallel

        ISBN: 978-1-7325845-6-3

    The Gospel Chronicle: Redaction

        ISBN: 978-1-7325845-7-0

    The Gospel Chronicle: Redaction – SE

        ISBN: 978-1-7325845-8-7

Irregular Symbols Key

¶   Paragraph breaks as found in the gospels.

[ ]   Capitalization was changed, punctuation or a conjunction added.

•   Switch between gospel sources (also identified by text color change).

•••   End of chapters as found in the gospels.

- -   Section title is extracted from the gospels text.

{ }   Alternate readings between the gospels, that could not be merged.

/   Division between gospel sources in alternate readings brackets.

* *   Added clarification of ambiguous text.

Ω   End of section.

ΑΩ   End of chapter.

The Gospel Chronicle

REDACTION

THE GOSPEL CHRONICLE: REDACTION

CONTENTS

Redaction Introduction

Have you wished that you could read the four narrative gospels as one single story? Were you ever troubled by your efforts to compare similar sounding events amongst them? Did you ever wonder why these accounts were never combined into a single biography? I did. I struggled with seeing how these four separate accounts of Jesus' life could be merged together to tell a more complete story. They each seem to seal up Jesus' life in their own account; and of course whenever I attempted to compare their similar parts I encountered frustration with the pieces that read differently. So I struggled.

Then God challenged me. I had this unexplainable urge or perhaps obsession to pursue the study which has become The Gospel Chronicle. That was in 1998. The path I have walked from then to now has indeed been a challenge, and it changed me. I believe better.

The Redaction is a very unique work. This is the part of the Gospel Chronicle that combines the separate gospel accounts in the Parallel into a singular text of the Narrative. It shows the reader how the Narrative was made from the Parallel. It it is the second step of the work, but is likely to have the least interest to the casual reader. Its purpose is to extract a comprehensive account of the ministry of Jesus Christ, allowing the removal of the duplicate material while maintaining the maximum content possible from the four narrative gospels.

According to the website, www.biblebelievers.com, the four raw gospel narratives of Matthew, Mark, Luke and John in the King James bible contain approximately 82,600 words altogether. The finished Narrative of the Gospel Chronicle contains approximately 73,200 words. Deleting only the shared content, the total word count for the gospels was only reduced by approximately 9,400 words or 11.5%. This high retention of content in the Gospel Chronicle is very surprising when compared against the Synoptic Gospels theory. From the Synoptic perspective, approximately 75% of Mark, 45% of Matthew and 40% of Luke are considered shared or synoptic content and the gospel of John is considered to contain too little shared content to be included. What does this mean? The Synoptic perspective basically tells us that we can effectively remove 40-75% of the content from two of the three synoptic gospels depending on which gospel is granted priority. But from a chronological perspective less that 12% of the combined content can be removed. These two results cannot be reconciled; they are too different. But how can there be such a large difference, when both perspectives have the same goal of comparing the gospels to each other?

Before investigating further let's first level the field and remove the gospel of John so that both perspectives contain only three of the four gospels. Adjusting the numbers to exclude the book of John, approximately 18,600 words should be subtracted from the total starting word count. The new word count for total gospel words is approximately 64,000 words, reducing by 22.5% of its total. As John is considered to have too little shared content to include in the Synoptic Gospel theory, then we shall subtract the same word count from the Gospel Chronicle Narrative, reducing it to 54,600 words or about 25.5%. The 3% difference should approximately represent how much John might contribute to the Synoptic theory should John have been icluded. Now as before let's subtract the narrative word count from the total gospel word count. The result is now 10,000 words for a difference of only 600 words between the John inclusive and John exclusive word count. This increases shared content amongst the three remaining gospels to 17.5%, a 5.5% increase. An expected result if the gospel of John contributes more shared content than previously understood. All considered these compared percentages remain drastically lower than the 40-75% shared content suggested by the Synoptic perspective. The difference is clear. But why is there such a large difference in these numbers? Could it be because the gospels contain a much broader array of differing content than has been previously suggested?

The difference lays in the definition of shared or synoptic content. Observing the Synoptic Gospel theory in practice, shared content is determined primarily by whether an event in one gospel sounds similar to an event in another gospel. This seems practical, but quickly becomes very subjective, leading to a multitude of gospel harmonies which largely disagree on the specific arrangement of the four gospels' events. One example that stands out is the passages in Matthew and Luke that Jesus teaches the Beatitudes.

In Matthew, Jesus goes up into a mountain and his disciples (not necessarily his Apostles) follow him and are taught of him up in the mountain. This event is called by most theologians the Sermon on the Mount. But this can be problematic as the Synoptic Gospel theory tends to link this event recorded in Matthew to another recorded in Luke. But there are glaring differences. In Luke, Jesus also teaches the Beatitudes, but Luke tells us that Jesus is standing in a plain (not a mountain), and looking around upon his disciples, Jesus teaches the surrounding multitudes. Clearly this event in Luke cannot also be called the Sermon on the Mount, because there isn't a mountain involved.

Yet strangely from a synoptic perspective, these events are considered the same, which opens the gospels up to the claim that they are contradicting each other. But this does not have to be how these events are viewed. From a chronological perspective, these events are seen as separate and sequential. First Jesus' disciples (whether there be two or one hundred.) follow Jesus up into a mountain and are taught of Jesus. Then after three chapters of dialog Jesus ends his teaching and he and his disciples depart, coming down from the mountain. It is at this point that we can insert the account in Luke, where Jesus and his disciples (his followers that went after him into the mountain,) now coming down, enter into a plain area where the rest of the multitude that chose not to follow Jesus into the mountain are gathered and Jesus looks knowingly upon his disciples, repeats only a brief part of the message that he taught his disciples up in the mountain. These are related but separate events.

This example illustrates how with the synoptic perspective we can be given the perception that the gospels contradict one another, when it is simply an error of our own making. Alternatively, the chronological perspective subordinates shared or synoptic content as a secondary filter rather than the primary filter. Taking the same passages and chronologically aligning them into sequence, offers a glimpse into bigger story with multiple stages, purposes and participants. The chronological perspective sweeps away contradiction, allowing a deeper look into Jesus' ministry.

After nearly 20 years, the Gospel Chronicle is complete. It is my hope that everyone that receives it will benefit from its contents as much as I have in compiling and collating it. It is by no

Redaction: Introduction

means my intention that anyone should let this work supersede the separate gospel accounts on which it is based; but rather to be a help toward better understanding the interrelationship of the four narrative gospels to each other.

- G.L. Kirschke,

December 2, 2017

Chapter 1

CALL HIS NAME IMMANUEL

Isaiah 7:14-16

Redaction: Call His Name Immanuel

MATTHEW	MARK	LUKE	JOHN

MATTHEW	MARK	LUKE	JOHN

- The Generation -

Matt 01:01-17 • Mark 01:01 • Luke 01:01-04 • John 01:01-05

¶ T[he] book of the • beginning of the • generation of • [the] gospel of Jesus Christ, • the son of David, the son of Abraham • the Son of God; • [forasmuch] as many have taken in hand to set forth in order a declaration of those things which are most surely believed among us, [e]ven as they delivered them unto us, which from the beginning were eyewitnesses, and ministers of the word; [i]t seemed good to me also, having had perfect understanding of all things from the very first, to write unto thee in order, most excellent Theophilus, [t]hat thou mightest know the certainty of those things, wherein thou hast been instructed. •

¶ I[n] the beginning was the Word, and the Word was with God, and the Word was God. The same was in the beginning with God. All things were made by him; and without him was not any thing made that was made. In him was life; and the life was the light of men. And the light shineth in darkness; and the darkness comprehended it not. • Abraham begat Isaac; and Isaac begat Jacob; and Jacob begat Judas and his brethren; [a]nd Judas begat Phares and Zara of Thamar; and Phares begat Esrom; and Esrom begat Aram; [a]nd Aram begat Aminadab; and Aminadab begat Naasson; and Naasson begat Salmon; [a]nd Salmon begat Booz of Rachab; and Booz begat Obed of Ruth; and Obed begat Jesse; [a]nd Jesse begat David the king; And David the king begat Solomon of her *that had been the wife* of Urias; [a]nd Solomon begat Roboam; and Roboam begat Abia; and Abia begat Asa; And Asa begat Josaphat; and Josaphat begat Joram; and Joram begat Ozias; [a]nd Ozias begat Joatham; and Joatham begat Achaz; and Achaz begat Ezekias; [a]nd Ezekias begat Manasses; and Manasses begat Amon; and Amon begat Josias; [a]nd Josias begat Jechonias and his brethren, about the time they were carried away to Babylon: [a]nd after they were brought to Babylon, Jechonias begat Salathiel; and Salathiel begat Zorobabel; [a]nd Zorobabel begat Abiud; and Abiud begat Eliakim; and Eliakim begat Azor; [a]nd Azor begat Sadoc; and Sadoc begat Achim; and Achim begat Eliud; [a]nd Eliud begat Eleazar; and Eleazar begat Matthan; and Matthan begat Jacob; [a]nd Jacob begat Joseph the husband of

Redaction: Call His Name Immanuel

MATTHEW	MARK	LUKE	JOHN

Mary, of whom was born Jesus, who is called Christ. So all the generations from Abraham to David *are* fourteen generations; and from David until the carrying away into Babylon *are* fourteen generations; and from the carrying away into Babylon unto Christ *are* fourteen generations.

Ω

MATTHEW	MARK	LUKE	JOHN

- A People Prepared -

Matt • Mark • Luke 01:05-80 • John

¶ T[here] was in the days of Herod, the king of Judæa, a certain priest named Zacharias, of the course of Abia: and his wife *was* of the daughters of Aaron, and her name *was* Elisabeth. And they were both righteous before God, walking in all the commandments and ordinances of the Lord blameless. And they had no child, because that Elisabeth was barren, and they both were *now* well stricken in years. And it came to pass, that while he executed the priest's office before God in the order of his course, [a]ccording to the custom of the priest's office, his lot was to burn incense when he went into the temple of the Lord. And the whole multitude of the people were praying without at the time of incense. And there appeared unto him an angel of the Lord standing on the right side of the altar of incense. And when Zacharias saw *him*, he was troubled, and fear fell upon him. But the angel said unto him, Fear not, Zacharias: [F]or thy prayer is heard; and thy wife Elisabeth shall bear thee a son, and thou shalt call his name John. And thou shalt have joy and gladness; and many shall rejoice at his birth. For he shall be great in the sight of the Lord, and shall drink neither wine nor strong drink; and he shall be filled with the Holy Ghost, even from his mother's womb. And many of the children of Israel shall he turn to the Lord their God. And he shall go before him in the spirit and and power of Elias, to turn the hearts of the fathers to the children, and the disobedient to the wisdom of the just; to make ready a people prepared for the Lord. And Zacharias said unto the angel, Whereby shall I know this? [F]or I am an old man, and my wife well stricken in years. And the angel answering said unto him, I am Gabriel, that stand in the presence of God; and am sent to speak unto thee, and to shew thee these glad tidings. And, behold, thou shalt be dumb, and not able to speak, until the day that these things shall be performed, because thou believest not my words, which shall be fulfilled in their season. And the people waited for Zacharias, and marvelled that he tarried so long in the temple. And when he came out, he could not speak unto them: [A]nd they perceived that he had seen a vision in the temple: for he beckoned unto them, and remained speechless. And it came to pass, that, as soon as the days of his

MATTHEW	MARK	LUKE	JOHN

ministration were accomplished, he departed to his own house. And after those days his wife Elisabeth conceived, and hid herself five months, saying, Thus hath the Lord dealt with me in the days wherein he looked on *me*, to take away my reproach among men. And in the sixth month the angel Gabriel was sent from God unto a city of Galilee, named Nazareth, [t]o a virgin espoused to a man whose name was Joseph, of the house of David; and the virgin's name *was* Mary. And the angel came in unto her, and said, Hail, *thou that art* highly favoured, the Lord *is* with thee: [B]lessed *art* thou among women. And when she saw *him*, she was troubled at his saying, and cast in her mind what manner of salutation this should be. And the angel said unto her, Fear not, Mary: for thou hast found favor with God. And, behold, thou shalt conceive in thy womb, and bring forth a son, and shalt call his name JESUS. He shall be great, and shall be called the Son of the Highest: [A]nd the Lord God shall give unto him the throne of his father David: And he shall reign over the house of Jacob for ever; and of his kingdom there shall be no end. Then said Mary unto the angel, How shall this be, seeing I know not a man? And the angel answered and said unto her, The Holy Ghost shall come upon thee, and the power of the Highest shall overshadow thee: therefore also that holy thing which shall be born of thee shall be called the Son of God. And, behold, thy cousin Elisabeth, she hath also conceived a son in her old age: [A]nd this is the sixth month with her, who was called barren. For with God nothing shall be impossible. And Mary said, Behold the handmaid of the Lord; be it unto me according to thy word. And the angel departed from her. And Mary arose in those days, and went into the hill country with haste, into a city of Juda; [a]nd entered into the house of Zacharias, and saluted Elisabeth. And it came to pass, that, when Elisabeth heard the salutation of Mary, the babe leaped in her womb; and Elisabeth was filled with the Holy Ghost: And she spake out with a loud voice, and said, Blessed *art* thou among women, and blessed is the fruit of thy womb. And whence *is* this to me, that the mother of my Lord should come to me? For, lo, as soon as the voice of thy salutation sounded in mine ears, the babe leaped in my womb for joy. And blessed *is* she that believed: [F]or there shall be a performance of those things which were told her from the Lord. And Mary said, My soul doth magnify the Lord, [a]nd my spirit hath rejoiced in God my Saviour. For he hath regarded the low estate of his handmaiden: [F]or, behold, from henceforth all

MATTHEW	MARK	LUKE	JOHN

generations shall call me blessed. For he that is mighty hath done to me great things; and holy *is* his

name. And his mercy *is* on them that fear him from generation to generation. He hath shewed strength

with his arm; he hath scattered the proud in the imagination of their hearts. He hath put down the

mighty from *their* seats, and exalted them of low degree. He hath filled the hungry with good things;

and the rich he hath sent empty away. He hath holpen his servant Israel, in remembrance of *his* mercy;

[a]s he spake to our fathers, to Abraham, and to his seed for ever. And Mary abode with her about

three months, and returned unto her own house. Now Elisabeth's full time came that she should be

delivered; and she brought forth a son. And her neighbors and her cousins heard how the Lord had

shewed great mercy upon her; and they rejoiced with her. And it came to pass, that on the eighth day

they came to circumcise the child; and they called him Zacharias, after the name of his father. And his

mother answered and said, Not *so;* but he shall be called John. And they said unto her, there is none of

thy kindred that is called by this name. And they made signs to his father, how he would have him

called. And he asked for a writing table, and wrote, saying, His name is John. And they marvelled all.

And his mouth was opened immediately, and his tongue *loosed,* and he spake, and praised God. And

fear came on all that dwelt round about them: [A]nd all these sayings were noised abroad though out

all the hill country of Judæa. And all they that heard *them* laid *them* up in their hearts, saying, What

manner of child shall this be! And the hand of the Lord was with him. And his father Zacharias was filled

with the Holy Ghost, and prophesied, saying, Blessed *be* the Lord God of Israel; for he hath visited and

redeemed his people, [a]nd hath raised up an horn of salvation for us in the house of his servant David;

[a]s he spake by the mouth of his holy prophets, which have been since the world began: That we

should be saved from our enemies, and from the hand of all that hate us; [t]o perform the mercy

promised to our fathers, and to remember his holy covenant; [t]he oath which he sware to our father

Abraham, [t]hat he would grant unto us, that we being delivered out of the hand of our enemies might

serve him without fear, [i]n holiness and righteousness before him, all the days of our life. And thou,

child, shalt be called the prophet of the Highest: [F]or thou shalt go before the face of the Lord to

prepare his ways; [t]o give knowledge of salvation unto his people by the remission of their sins,

MATTHEW	MARK	LUKE	JOHN

[t]hrough the tender mercy of our God; whereby the dayspring from on high hath visited us, [t]o give light to them that sit in darkness and *in* the shadow of death, to guide our feet into the way of peace. And the child grew, and waxed strong in spirit, and was in the deserts till the day of his shewing unto Israel.

Ω

MATTHEW	MARK	LUKE	JOHN

- God with Us -

Matt 01:18-02:18 • Mark • Luke 02:01-38 • John

¶ Now the birth of Jesus Christ was on this wise: When as his mother Mary was espoused to Joseph, before they came together, she was found with child of the Holy Ghost. Then Joseph her husband being a just *man*, and not willing to make her a publick example, was minded to put her away privily. But while he thought on these things, behold, the angel of the Lord appeared unto him in a dream, saying, Joseph, thou son of David, fear not to take unto thee Mary thy wife: [F]or that which is conceived in her is of the Holy Ghost. And she shall bring forth a son, and thou shall call his name JESUS: [F]or he shall save his people from their sins. Now all this was done, that it might be fulfilled which was spoken of the Lord by the prophet, saying, Behold, a virgin shall be with child, and shall bring forth a son, and they shall call his name Emmanuel, which being interpreted is, God with us. Then Joseph being raised from sleep did as the angel of the Lord had bidden him, and took unto him his wife: And knew her not till she had brought forth her firstborn son: •

¶ A[nd] it came to pass in those days, that there went out a decree from Cæsar Augustus, that all the world should be taxed. (*And* this taxing was first made when Cyrenius was governor of Syria.) And all went to be taxed, every one into his own city. And Joseph also went up from Galilee, out of the city of Nazareth, into Judæa, unto the city of David, which is called Bethlehem; (because he was of the house and lineage of David:) [t]o be taxed with Mary his espoused wife, being great with child. And so it was, that, while they were there, the days were accomplished that she should be delivered. And she brought forth her firstborn son, and wrapped him in swaddling clothes, and laid him in a manger; because there was no room for them in the inn. And there were in the same country shepherds abiding in the field, keeping watch over their flock by night. And, lo, the angel of the Lord came upon them, and the glory of the Lord shone round about them: [A]nd they were sore afraid. And the angel said unto them, Fear not: [F]or, behold, I bring you good tidings of great joy, which shall be to all people. For unto you is born this day in the city of David a Saviour, which is Christ the Lord. And this *shall be* a sign

Redaction: Call His Name Immanuel

MATTHEW	MARK	LUKE	JOHN

unto you; Ye shall find the babe wrapped in swaddling clothes, lying in a manger. And suddenly there

was with the angel a multitude of the heavenly host praising God, and saying, Glory to God in the

highest and on earth peace, good will toward men. And it came to pass, as the angels were gone away

from them into heaven, the shepherds said one to another, Let us now go even unto Bethlehem, and see

this thing which is come to pass, which the Lord hath made known unto us. And they came with haste,

and found Mary, and Joseph, and the babe lying in a manger. And when they had seen *it*, they made

known abroad the saying which was told them concerning this child. And all they that heard *it*

wondered at those things which were told them by the shepherds. But Mary kept all these things, and

pondered *them* in her heart. And the shepherds returned, glorifying and praising God for all the things

that they had heard and seen, as it was told unto them. And when eight days were accomplished for the

circumcising of the child, his name was called JESUS, which was so named of the angel before he was

conceived in the womb. And when the days of her purification according to the law of Moses were

accomplished, they brought him to Jerusalem, to present *him* to the Lord; (As it is written in the law of

the Lord, Every male that openeth the womb shall be called holy to the Lord;) [a]nd to offer a sacrifice

according to that which is said in the law of the Lord, A pair of turtledoves, or two young pigeons. •

¶ N[ow] when Jesus was born in Bethlehem of Judæa in the days of Herod the king, behold,

there came wise men from the east to Jerusalem, [s]aying, Where is he that is born King of the Jews?

[F]or we have seen his star in the east, and are come to worship him. When Herod the king had heard

these things, he was troubled, and all Jerusalem with him. And when he had gathered all the chief

priests and scribes of the people together, he demanded of them where Christ should be born. And

they said unto him, In Bethlehem of Judaea: [F]or thus it is written by the prophet, And thou Bethlehem,

in the land of Juda, art not the least among the princes of Juda: [F]or out of thee shall come a Governor,

that shall rule my people Israel. • And, behold, there was a man in Jerusalem, whose name *was* Simeon;

and the same man *was* just and devout, waiting for the consolation of Israel: and the Holy Ghost was

upon him. And it was revealed unto him by the Holy Ghost, that he should not see death, before he had

MATTHEW	MARK	LUKE	JOHN

seen the Lord's Christ. And he came by the Spirit into the temple: [A]nd when the parents brought in the child Jesus, to do for him after the custom of the law, [t]hen took he him up in his arms, and blessed God, and said, Lord, now lettest thou thy servant depart in peace, according to thy word: For mine eyes have seen thy salvation, [w]hich thou hast prepared before the face of all people; [a] light to lighten the Gentiles, and the glory of thy people Israel. And Joseph and his mother marvelled at those things which were spoken of him. And Simeon blessed them, and said unto Mary his mother, Behold this *child* is set for the fall and rising again of many in Israel; and for a sign which shall be spoken against; (Yea, a sword shall pierce through thine own soul also,) that the thoughts of many hearts may be revealed. And there was one Anna, a prophetess, the daughter of Phanuel, of the tribe of Aser: [S]he was of a great age, and had lived with an husband seven years from her virginity; [a]nd she *was* a widow of about four score and four years, which departed not from the temple, but served *God* with fastings and prayers night and day. And she coming in that instant gave thanks likewise unto the Lord, and spake of him to all them that looked for redemption in Jerusalem. • Then Herod, when he had privily called the wise men, inquired of them diligently what time the star appeared. And sent them to Bethlehem, and said, Go and search diligently for the young child; and when ye have found *him*, bring me word again, that I may come and worship him also. When they had heard the king, they departed; and, lo, the star, which they saw in the east, went before them, till it came and stood over where the young child was. When they saw the star, they rejoiced with exceeding great joy.

¶ And when they were come into the house, they saw the young child with Mary his mother, and fell down and worshipped him: [A]nd when they had opened their treasures, they presented unto him gifts; gold, and frankincense, and myrrh. And being warned of God in a dream that they should not return to Herod, they departed into their own country another way. And when they were departed, behold, the angel of he Lord appeareth to Joseph in a dream, saying, Arise, and take the young child and his mother, and flee into Egypt, and be thou there until I bring thee word: [F]or Herod will seek the young child to destroy him. When he arose, he took the young child and his mother by night, and

MATTHEW	MARK	LUKE	JOHN

departed into Egypt: And was there until the death of Herod: [T]hat it might be fulfilled which was spoken of the Lord by the prophet, saying, Out of Egypt have I called my son.

¶ Then Herod, when he saw that he was mocked of the wise men, was exceeding wroth, and sent forth, and slew all the children that were in Bethlehem, and in all the coasts thereof, from two years old and under, according to the time which he had diligently inquired of the wise men. Then was fulfilled that which was spoken by Jeremy the prophet, saying, In Rama was there a voice heard, lamentation, and weeping, and great mourning, Rachel weeping *for* her children, and would not be comforted, because they are not.

Ω

MATTHEW	MARK	LUKE	JOHN

- Strong in Spirit -

Matt 02:19-23 • Mark • Luke 02:39-52 • John

¶ But when Herod was dead, behold, an angel of the Lord appeareth in a dream to Joseph in Egypt, [s]aying, Arise, and take the young child and his mother, and go into the land of Israel: [F]or they are dead which sought the young child's life. And he arose, and took the young child and his mother, and came into the land of Israel. But when he heard that Archelaus did reign in Judæa in the room of his father Herod, he was afraid to go thither: [N]otwithstanding, • when they had performed all things according to the law of the Lord, • being warned of God in a dream, he turned aside • [a]nd they returned into • the parts of Galilee: And he came • to • and dwelt in • their own city • a city called Nazareth: [T]hat it might be fulfilled which was spoken by the prophets, He shall be called a Nazarene. • And the child grew, and waxed strong in spirit, filled with wisdom: [A]nd the grace of God was upon him. Now his parents went to Jerusalem every year at the feast of the passover. And when he was twelve years old, they went up to Jerusalem after the custom of the feast. And when they had fulfilled the days, as they returned, the child Jesus tarried behind in Jerusalem; and Joseph and his mother knew not of it. But they, supposing him to have been in the company, went a day's journey; and they sought him among their kinsfolk and acquaintance. And when they found him not, they turned back again to Jerusalem, seeking him. And it came to pass, that after three days they found him in the temple, sitting in the midst of the doctors, both hearing them, and asking them questions. And all that heard him were astonished at his understanding and answers. And when they saw him, they were amazed: [A]nd his mother said unto him, Son, why hast thou thus dealt with us? Behold, thy father and I have sought thee sorrowing. And he said unto them, How is it that ye sought me? [W]ist ye not that I must be about my Father's business? And they understood not the saying which he spake unto them. And he went down with them, and came to Nazareth, and was subject unto them: [B]ut his mother kept all these sayings in her heart. And Jesus increased in wisdom and stature, and in favor with God and man.

ΑΩ

Redaction: Call His Name Immanuel

MATTHEW	MARK	LUKE	JOHN

Chapter 2

To Restore and to Build

Daniel 9:24

Redaction: To Restore and to Build

MATTHEW	MARK	LUKE	JOHN

MATTHEW	MARK	LUKE	JOHN

- Prepare Ye the Way -

Matt 03:01-12 • Mark 01:01-08 • Luke 03:01-20 • John 01:06-28

¶ N[ow] in the fifteenth year of the reign of Tiberius Ceasar, Pontius Pilate being governor of Judea, and Herod being tetrarch of Galilee, and his brother Philip tetrarch of Ituræa and of the region of Trachonitis, and Lysanias the tetrarch of Abilene, • [in] those days • [t]here was a man sent from God, whose name *was* John. • Annas and Caiaphas being the high priests, the word of God came unto John the son of Zacharias in the wilderness. And • John the Baptist • came into all the country about Jordan, • preaching in the wilderness of Judæa, • the baptism of repentance for the remission of sins; • [a]nd saying, Repent ye: [F]or the kingdom of heaven is at hand. • The same came for a witness, to bear witness of the Light, that all *men* through him might believe. He was not that Light, but *was sent* to bear witness of that Light. • For this is he that was spoken of by the prophet Esaias, • [a]s it is written in the prophets, • in the book of the words of Esaias the prophet, saying, • Behold, I send my messenger before thy face, which shall prepare thy way before thee. The voice of one crying in the wilderness, Prepare ye the way of the Lord, make his paths straight. • Every valley shall be filled, every mountain and hill shall be brought low; and the crooked shall be made straight, and the rough ways *shall be* made smooth; [a]nd all flesh shall see the salvation of God. • *That* was the true Light, which lighteth every man that cometh into the world. He was in the world, and the world was made by him, and the world knew him not. He came unto his own, and his own received him not. But to as many as received him, to them gave he power to become the sons of God, *even* to them that believe on his name: Which were born, not of blood, nor of the will of the flesh, nor of the will of man, but of God. And the Word was made flesh, and dwelt among us, (and we beheld his glory, the glory as of the only begotten of the Father,) full of grace and truth. •

¶ John did baptize in the wilderness, and preach the baptism of repentance for the remission of sins. • And the same John had his raiment of camel's hair, and a leathern girdle about his loins; and his meat was locusts and wild honey. • John bare witness of him, and cried, saying, This was he of

MATTHEW	MARK	LUKE	JOHN

whom I spake, He that cometh after me is preferred before me: for he was before me. And of his fullness have all we received, and grace for grace. For the law was given by Moses, *but* grace and truth came by Jesus Christ. No man hath seen God at any time; the only begotten Son, which is in the bosom of the Father, he hath declared *him*. • Then • there went out unto him all • Jerusalem, and all • the land of Judæa, • and all the region round about Jordan, • and were all baptized of him in the river of Jordan, confessing their sins. And John was clothed with camel's hair, and with a girdle of a skin about his loins; and he did eat locusts and wild honey[.]

¶ But when he saw many of the Pharisees and Saducees come to his baptism, • [t]hen said he to the multitude that came forth to be baptized of him, • Oh generation of vipers, who hath warned you to flee from the wrath to come? • And this is the record of John, when the Jews sent priests and Levites from Jerusalem to ask him, Who art thou? • Bring forth therefore fruits {worthy / meet} for repentance: And {think / begin} not to say within yourselves, We have Abraham to *our* father: [F]or I say unto you, [t]hat God is able of these stones to raise up children unto Abraham. And now also the axe is laid unto the root of the trees: every tree therefore which bringeth not forth good fruit is hewn down, and cast into the fire. And the people asked him, saying, What shall we do then? He answereth and saith unto them, He that hath two coats, let him impart to him that hath none; and he that hath meat, let him do likewise. Then came also publicans to be baptized, and said unto him, Master, what shall we do? And he said unto them, Exact no more than that which is appointed you. And the soldiers likewise demanded of him, saying, And what shall we do? And he said unto them, Do violence to no man, neither accuse *any* falsely; and be content with your wages. And as the people were in expectation, and all men mused in their hearts of John, whether he were the Christ, or not; • he confessed, and denied not; but confessed, I am not the Christ. And they asked him, What then? Art thou Elias? And he saith, I am not. Art thou that prophet? [A]nd he answered, No. Then said they unto him, Who art thou? that we may give an answer to them that sent us. What sayest thou of thyself? He said, I *am* the voice of one crying in the wilderness, Make straight the way of the Lord, as said the prophet Esaias. And they

MATTHEW	MARK	LUKE	JOHN

which were sent were of the Pharisees. And they asked him, and said unto him, Why baptizest thou then, if thou be not that Christ, nor Elias, neither that prophet? John answered them, • [a]nd preached, • saying, • unto *them* all, • I indeed baptize you with water unto repentance: • [B]ut there standeth one among you, whom ye know not; • [t]here cometh one mightier • he that cometh after me is mightier than I, • [h]e it is, who coming after me is preferred before me, • the latchet of whose shoes I am not worthy to • stoop down and unloose • to bear: • I indeed have baptized you with water: but he shall baptize you with the Holy Ghost • and *with* fire: • Whose fan *is* in his hand, and he will thoroughly purge his floor, and will gather the wheat into his garner; • but he will burn up the chaff with unquenchable fire. • And many other things in his exhortation preached he unto the people. • These things were done in Bethabara beyond Jordan, where John was baptizing. • But Herod the tetrarch, being reproved by him for Herodias his brother Philip's wife, and for all the evils which Herod had done, [a]dded yet this above all, that he shut up John in prison.

Ω

MATTHEW	MARK	LUKE	JOHN

MATTHEW	MARK	LUKE	JOHN

- My Beloved Son -

Matt 03:13-03:17 • Mark 01:09-11 • Luke 03:21-03:38 • John 01:29-34

¶ Then • it came to pass in those days, that Jesus came from Nazareth of Galilee, • to Jordan unto John, to be baptized of him. • The next day John seeth Jesus coming unto him, and saith, Behold the Lamb of God, which taketh away the sin of the world. This is he of whom I said, After me cometh a man which is preferred before me: [F]or he was before me. And I knew him not: [B]ut that he should be made manifest to Israel, therefore am I come baptizing with water. • But John forbad him, saying, I have need to be baptized of thee, and comest thou to me? And Jesus answering said unto him, Suffer *it to be so* now: [F]or thus it becometh us to fulfill all righteousness. Then he suffered him. • Now when all the people were baptized, it came to pass, that Jesus • when he was baptized • of John in Jordan • went up straightway • coming up out of the water • and praying, the heaven was opened • unto him, and he saw the Spirit of God • the Holy Ghost descended in a bodily shape like a dove • lighting upon him: • And John bare record, saying, I saw the Spirit descending from heaven like a dove, and it abode upon him. And I knew him not: [B]ut he that sent me to baptize with water, the same said unto me, Upon whom thou shalt see the Spirit descending, and remaining on him, the same is he which baptizeth with the Holy Ghost. • And lo • there came a voice from heaven, *saying*, • This is my beloved Son, [t]hou art my beloved Son; in thee I am well pleased. And Jesus himself began to be about thirty years of age, being (as was supposed) the son of Joseph, which was *the son* of Heli, [w]hich was *the son* of Matthat, which was *the son* of Levi, which was *the son* of Melchi, which was *the son* of Janna, which was *the son* of Joseph, Which was *the son* of Mattathias, which was *the son* of Amos, which was *the son* of Naum, which was *the son* of Esli which was *the son* of Nagge, [w]hich was *the son* of Maath, which was *the son* of Mattathias, which was *the son* of Semei, which was *the son* of Joseph, which was *the son* of Juda, [w]hich was *the son* of Joanna, which was *the son* of Rhesa, which was *the son* of Zorobabel, which was *the son* of Salathiel, which was *the son* of Neri, w]hich was *the son* of Melchi, which was *the son* of Addi, [which was *the son* of Cosam, which was *the son* of Elmodam, which was *the son* of Er, [w]hich was *the son* of

MATTHEW	MARK	LUKE	JOHN

Jose, which was *the son* of Eliezer, which was *the son* of Jorim which was *the son* of Matthat, which was *the son* of Levi, Which was *the son* of Simeon, which was *the son* of Juda, which was *the son* of Joseph, which was *the son* of Jonan, which was *the son* of Eliakim, [w]hich was *the son* of Melea, which was *the son* of Menan, which was *the son* of Mattatha, which was *the son* of Nathan, which was *the son* of David, [w]hich was *the son* of Jesse, which was *the son* of Obed, which was *the son* of Booz, which was *the son* of Salmon, which was *the son* of Naasson, [w]hich was *the son* of Aminadab, which was *the son* of Aram, which was *the son* of Esrom, which was *the son* of Phares, which was *the son* of Juda, [w]hich was *the son* of Jacob, which was *the son* of Isaac, which was *the son* of Abraham, which was *the son* of Thara, which was *the son* of Nachor, [w]hich was *the son* of Saruch, which was *the son* of Ragau, which was *the son* of Phalec, which was *the son* of Heber, which was *the son* of Sala, [w]hich was *the son* of Cainan, which was *the son* of Arphaxad, which was *the son* of Sem, which was *the son* of Noe, which was *the son* of Lamech, [w]hich was *the son* of Methusala, which was *the son* of Enoch, which was *the son* of Jared, which was *the son* of Maleleel, which was *the son* of Cainan, [w]hich was *the son* of Enos, which was *the son* of Seth, which was *the son* of Adam, which was *the son* of God.

Ω

MATTHEW	MARK	LUKE	JOHN

- Beginning of Miracles -

Matt • Mark • Luke 04:1 • John 01:35-02:11

¶ A[nd] Jesus being full of the Holy Ghost returned from Jordan, • [a]gain the next day after John stood, and two of his disciples; [a]nd looking upon Jesus as he walked, he saith, Behold the Lamb of God! And the two disciples heard him speak, and they followed Jesus. Then Jesus turned, and saw them following, and saith unto them, What seek ye? They said unto him, Rabbi, (which is to say, being interpreted, Master,) where dwellest thou? He saith unto them, Come and see. They came and saw where he dwelt, and abode with him that day: for it was about the tenth hour. One of the two which heard John *speak*, and followed him, was Andrew, Simon Peter's brother. He first findeth his own brother Simon, and saith unto him, We have found the Messias, [W]hich is, being interpreted, the Christ. And he brought him to Jesus. And when Jesus beheld him, he said, Thou art Simon the son of Jona: Thou shalt be called Cephas, which is by interpretation, A stone.

¶ The day following Jesus would go forth into Galilee, and findeth Philip, and saith unto him, Follow me. Now Philip was of Bethsaida, the city of Andrew and Peter. Philip findeth Nathanael, and saith unto him, We have found him, of whom Moses in the law, and the prophets, did write, Jesus of Nazareth, the son of Joseph. And Nathanael said unto him, Can there any good thing come out of Nazareth? Philip saith unto him, Come and see. Jesus saw Nathanael coming to him, and saith of him, Behold an Israelite indeed, in whom is no guile! Nathanael saith unto him, Whence knowest thou me? Jesus answered and said unto him, Before that Philip called thee, when thou wast under the fig tree, I saw thee. Nathanael answered and saith unto him, Rabbi, thou art the Son of God; thou art the King of Israel. Jesus answered and said unto him, Because I said unto thee, I saw thee under the fig tree, believest thou? [T]hou shalt see greater things than these. And he saith unto him, Verily, verily, I say unto you, Hereafter ye shall see heaven open, and the angels of God ascending and descending upon the Son of man.

MATTHEW	MARK	LUKE	JOHN

¶ A[nd] the third day there was a marriage in Cana of Galilee; and the mother of Jesus was there: And both Jesus was called and his disciples, to the marriage. And when they wanted wine, the mother of Jesus saith unto him, They have no wine. Jesus saith unto her, Woman, what have I to do with thee? [M]ine hour is not yet come. His mother saith unto the servants, Whatsoever he saith unto you, do it. And there were set there six water pots of stone after the manner of the purifying of the Jews, containing two or three firkins apiece. Jesus saith unto them, Fill the waterpots with water. And they filled them up to the brim. And he saith unto them, Draw out now, and bear unto the governor of the feast. And they bare it. When the ruler of the feast had tasted the water that was made wine, and knew not whence it was: ([B]ut the servants which drew the water knew;) the governor of the feast called the bridegroom, [a]nd saith unto him, Every man at the beginning doth set forth good wine; and when men have well drunk, then that which is worse: but thou hast kept the good wine until now. This beginning of miracles did Jesus in Cana of Galilee, and manifested forth his glory; and his disciples believed on him.

Ω

MATTHEW	MARK	LUKE	JOHN

- Into the Wilderness -

Matt 04:01-11 • Mark 01:12-13 • Luke 04:1-13 • John

¶ T[hen] was Jesus led up of the Spirit • [a]nd immediately the Spirit driveth him into the wilderness • to be tempted of the devil. • And he was there in the wilderness • [b]eing forty days tempted • of Satan • the devil • and was with the wild beasts; • [a]nd in those days he did eat nothing: • And when he had fasted forty days and forty nights, • and when they were ended, • he was afterward an hungred. And when the tempter came to him, • the devil said unto him, If thou be the Son of God, • command that these stones be made bread. But • Jesus answered him, saying, It is written, That man shall not live by bread alone, • but by every word that proceedeth out of the mouth of God. • And the devil, taking him up into an high mountain, shewed unto him all the kingdoms of the world in a moment of time. And the devil said unto him, All this power will I give thee, and the glory of them: for that is delivered unto me; and to whomsoever I will I give it. If thou therefore wilt worship me, all shall be thine. And Jesus answered and said unto him, Get thee behind me, Satan: for it is written, Thou shalt worship the Lord thy God, and him only shalt thou serve. • Then the devil taketh him up into the holy city, • Jerusalem, and set him on a pinnacle of the temple, and said unto him, If thou be the Son of God, cast thy self down from hence: For it is written, He shall give his angels charge • concerning • over thee, to keep thee: And in *their* hands they shall bear thee up, lest at any time thou dash thy foot against a stone. And Jesus answering said unto him, • It is {written/said} • again, • Thou shalt not tempt the Lord thy God. • Again, the devil taketh him up into an exceeding high mountain, and sheweth him all the kingdoms of the world, and the glory of them; And saith unto him, All these things will I give thee, if thou wilt fall down and worship me. Then saith Jesus unto him, Get thee hence, Satan: [F]or it is written, Thou shalt worship the Lord thy God, and him only shalt thou serve. Then the devil leaveth him, • And when the devil had ended all the temptation, he departed from him for a season • and, behold, • the angels • came and ministered unto him. •

AΩ

Redaction: To Restore and to Build

MATTHEW	MARK	LUKE	JOHN

Chapter 3

THE ACCEPTABLE
YEAR OF THE LORD

Isaiah 61:01-04

Redaction: The Acceptable Year of the Lord

MATTHEW	MARK	LUKE	JOHN

MATTHEW	MARK	LUKE	JOHN

- The Zeal of Thine House -

Matt • Mark • Luke • John 02:12-03:36

¶ After this he went down to Capernaum, he, and his mother, and his bretheren, and his disciples: and they continued there not many days.

¶ And the Jews' passover was at hand, and Jesus went up to Jerusalem, [a]nd found in the temple those that sold oxen and sheep and doves, and the changers of money sitting: And when he had made a scourge of small cords, he drove them all out of the temple, and the sheep and the oxen; and poured out the changers' money, and overthrew the tables; [a]nd said unto them that sold doves, Take these things hence; make not my Father's house an house of merchandise. And his disciples remembered that it was written, The zeal of thine house hath eaten me up.

¶ Then answered the Jews and said unto him, What sign shewest thou unto us, seeing that thou doest these things? Jesus answered and said unto them, Destroy this temple, and in three days I will raise it up. Then said the Jews, Forty and six years was this temple in building, and wilt thou rear it up in three days? But he spake of the temple of his body. When therefore he was risen from the dead, his disciples remembered that he had said this unto them; and they believed the scripture, and the word which Jesus had said.

¶ Now when he was in Jerusalem at the passover, in the feast *day*, many believed in his name, when they saw the miracles which he did. But Jesus did not commit himself unto them, because he knew all *men*, And needed not that any should testify of man: [F]or he knew what was in man.

¶ T[here] was a man of the Pharisees, named Nicodemus, a ruler of the Jews: The same came to Jesus by night, and said unto him, Rabbi, we know that thou art a teacher come from God: [F]or no man can do these miracles that thou doest, except God be with him. Jesus answered and said unto him, Verily, verily I say unto thee, Except a man be born again, he cannot see the kingdom of God.

MATTHEW	MARK	LUKE	JOHN

Nicodemus saith unto him, How can a man be born when he is old? [C]an he enter the second time into his mother's womb, and be born? Jesus aswered, Verily, verily, I say unto thee, Except a man be born of water, and *of* the Spirit, he can not enter into the Kingdom of God. That which is born of the flesh is flesh; and that which is born of the Spirit is spirit. Marvel not that I said unto thee, Ye must be born again. The wind bloweth where it listeth, and thou hearest the sound thereof, but canst not tell whence it cometh, and whither it goeth: [S]o is every one that is born of the Spirit. Nicodemus answered and said unto him, How can these things be? Jesus answered and said unto him, Art thou a master of Israel, and knowest not these things? Verily, verily, I say unto thee, We speak that we do know, and testify that we have seen; and ye receive not our witness. If I have told you earthly things, and ye believe not, how shall ye believe, if I tell you *of* heavenly things? And no man hath ascended up to heaven, but he that came down from heaven, *even* the Son of man which is in heaven.

¶ And as Moses lifted up the serpent in the wilderness, even so must the Son of man be lifted up: That whosoever believeth in him should not perish, but have eternal life.

¶ For God so loved the world, that he gave his only begotten Son, that whosoever believeth in him should not perish, but have everlasting life. For God sent not his Son into the world to condemn the world; but that the world through him might be saved.

¶ He that believeth on him is not condemned: [B]ut he that believeth not is condemned already, because he hath not believed in the name of the only begotten Son of God. And this is the condemnation, that light is come into the world, and men loved darkness rather than light, because their deeds were evil. For every one that doeth evil hateth the light, neither cometh to the light, lest his deeds should be reproved. But he that doeth truth cometh to the light, that his deeds may be made manifest, that they are wrought in God.

¶ After these things came Jesus and his disciples into the land of Judæa; and there he tarried with them, and baptized.

MATTHEW	MARK	LUKE	JOHN

¶ And John also was baptizing in Ænon near to Salim, because there was much water there: [A]nd they came, and were baptized. For John was not yet cast into prison.

¶ Then there arose a question between *some* of John's disciples and the Jews about purifying. And they came unto John, and said unto him, Rabbi, he that was with thee beyond Jordan, to whom thou barest witness, behold, the same baptizeth, and all *men* come to him. John answered and said, A man can receive nothing, except it be given him from heaven. Ye yourselves bear me witness, that I said, I am not the Christ, but that I am sent before him. He that hath the bride is the bridegroom: but the friend of the bridegroom, which standeth and heareth him, rejoiceth greatly because of the bridegroom's voice: [T]his my joy therefore is fulfilled. He must increase, but I *must* decrease. He that cometh from above is above all: [H]e that is of the earth is earthly, and speaketh of the earth: [H]e that cometh from heaven is above all. And what he hath seen and heard, that he testifieth; and no man receiveth his testimony. He that hath received his testimony hath set to his seal that God is true. For he whom God hath sent speaketh the words of God: [F]or God giveth not the Spirit by measure *unto him*. The Father loveth the Son, and hath given all things into his hand. He that believeth on the Son hath everlasting life: [A]nd he that believeth not the Son shall not see life; but the wrath of God abideth on him.

Ω

Redaction: The Acceptable Year of the Lord

MATTHEW	MARK	LUKE	JOHN

MATTHEW	MARK	LUKE	JOHN

- A City of Samaria -

Matt • Mark • Luke • John 04:01-42

¶ Now after • when Jesus had heard that John was {cast into / put in} prison, • therefore the Lord knew how the Pharisees had heard that Jesus made and baptized more disciples than John, (Though Jesus himself baptized not, but his disciples,) He left Judea, and departed again into Galilee. And he must needs go through Samaria. Then cometh he to a city of Samaria, which is called Sychar, near to the parcel of ground that Jacob gave to his son Joseph. Now Jacob's well was there. Jesus therefore, being wearied with *his* journey, sat thus on the well: *and* it was about the sixth hour. There cometh a woman of Samaria to draw water: Jesus saith unto her, Give me to drink. (For his disciples were gone away into the city to buy meat.) Then saith the woman of Samaria unto him, How is it that thou, being a Jew, askest drink of me, which am a woman of Samaria? [F]or the Jews have no dealings with the Samaritans. Jesus answered and said unto her, If thou knewest the gift of God, and who it is that saith to thee, Give me to drink; thou wouldst have asked of him, and he would have given thee living water. The woman saith unto him, Sir, thou hast nothing to draw with, and the well is deep: from whence then hast thou that living water? Art thou greater than our father Jacob, which gave us the well, and drank thereof himself, and his children, and his cattle? Jesus answered and said unto her, Whosoever drinketh of this water shall thirst again: But whosoever drinketh of the water that I shall give him shall never thirst; but the water I shall give him shall be in him a well of water springing up into everlasting life. The woman saith unto him, Sir, give me this water, that I thirst not, neither come hither to draw. Jesus saith unto her, Go, call thy husband, and come hither. The woman answered and said, I have no husband. Jesus said unto her, Thou hast well said, I have no husband: For thou hast had five husbands; and he whom thou now hast is not thy husband: [I]n that saidst thou truly. The woman saith unto him, Sir, I perceive that thou art a prophet. Our fathers worshipped in this mountain; and ye say, that in Jerusalem is the place where men ought to worship. Jesus saith unto her, Woman, believe me, the hour cometh, when ye shall neither in this mountain, nor yet at Jerusalem, worship the Father. Ye worship ye

MATTHEW	MARK	LUKE	JOHN

know not what: We know what we worship: [F]or salvation is of the Jews. But the hour cometh, and now is, when the true worshippers shall worship the Father in spirit and in truth: [F]or the Father seeketh such to worship him. God *is* a Spirit: [A]nd they that worship him must worship *him* in spirit and in truth. The woman saith unto him, I know that Messias cometh, which is called Christ: [W]hen he is come, he will tell us all things. Jesus saith unto her, I that speak unto thee am *he*.

¶ And upon this came his disciples, and marvelled that he talked with the woman: [Y]et no man said, What seekest thou? or, Why talkest thou with her? The woman then left her waterpot, and went her way into the city, and saith to the men, Come, see a man which told me all things that ever I did: Is not this the Christ? Then they went out of the city, and came unto him.

¶ In the mean while his disciples prayed him, saying, Master, eat. But he said unto them, I have meat to eat that ye know not of. Therefore said the disciples one to another, Hath any man brought him *ought* to eat? Jesus saith unto them, My meat is to do the will of him that sent me, and to finish his work. Say not ye, There are yet four months, and *then* cometh harvest? [B]ehold, I say unto you, Lift up your eyes, and look on the fields; for they are white already to harvest. And he that reapeth receiveth wages, and gathereth fruit unto life eternal: [T]hat both he that soweth and he that reapeth may rejoice together. And herein is that saying true, One soweth, and another reapeth. I sent you to reap that whereon ye bestowed no labour: other men laboured, and ye are entered into their labours.

¶ And many of the Samaritans of that city believed on him for that saying of the woman, which testified, He told me all that ever I did. So when the Samaritans were come unto him, they besought him that he would tarry with them: And he abode there two days. And many more believed because of his own word; [a]nd said unto the woman, Now we believe, not because of thy saying: [F]or we have heard *him* ourselves, and know that this is indeed the Christ, the Saviour of the world.

Ω

MATTHEW	MARK	LUKE	JOHN

- Nazareth -

Matt 04:13 • Mark 01:14 • Luke 04:14-30 • John 4:43-54

¶ Now after two days he departed thence, • [a]nd Jesus returned in the power of the Spirit into Galilee: [A]nd there went out a fame of him through all the region round about. • For Jesus himself testified, that [A] prophet hath no honor in his own country. Then when he was come into Galilee, • preaching the gospel of the kingdom of God, • the Galilaeans received him, having seen all the things that he did at Jerusalem at the feast: [F]or they also went unto the feast. • And he taught in their synagogues, being glorified of all.

¶ And he came to Nazareth, where he had been brought up: [A]nd, as his custom was, he went into the synagogue on the sabbath day, and stood up for to read. And there was delivered unto him the book of the prophet Esaias. And when he had opened the book, he found the place where it was written, The Spirit of the Lord *is* upon me, because he hath anointed me to preach the gospel to the poor; he hath sent me to heal the broken hearted, to preach deliverance to the captives, and recovering of sight to the blind, to set at liberty them that are bruised, [t]o preach the acceptable year of the Lord. And he closed the book, and gave *it* again to the minister, and sat down. And the eyes of all them that were in the synagogue were fastened on him. And he began to say unto them, This day is this scripture fulfilled in your ears. And all bare him witness, and wondered at the gracious words which proceeded out of his mouth. And they said, Is not this Joseph's son? And he said unto them, Ye will surely say unto me this proverb, Physician, heal thyself: [W]hatsoever we have heard done in Capernaum, do also here in thy country. And he said, Verily I say unto you, No prophet is accepted in his own country. But I tell you of a truth, many widows were in Israel in the days of Elias, when the heaven was shut up three years and six months, when great famine was throughout all the land; [b]ut unto none of them was Elias sent, save unto Sarepta, *a city* of Sidon, unto a woman *that was* a widow. And many lepers were in Israel in the time of Eliseus the prophet; and none of them was cleansed, saving Naaman the Syrian. And all they in the synagogue, when they heard these things, were filled

MATTHEW	MARK	LUKE	JOHN

with wrath, [a]nd rose up, and thrust him out of the city, and led him unto the brow of the hill whereon their city was built, that they might cast him down headlong. But he passing through the midst of them went his way, • [a]nd leaving Nazareth, • [s]o Jesus came again into Cana of Galilee, where he made the water wine. And there was a certain nobleman, whose son was sick at Capernaum. When he heard that Jesus was come out of Judaea into Galilee, he went unto him, and besought him that he would come down, and heal his son: [F]or he was at the point of death. Then said Jesus unto him, Except ye see signs and wonders, ye will not believe. The nobleman saith unto him, Sir, come down ere my child die. Jesus saith unto him, Go thy way; thy son liveth. And the man believed the word that Jesus had spoken unto him, and he went his way. And as he was now going down, his servants met him, and told *him*, saying, Thy son liveth. Then inquired he of them the hour when he began to amend. And they said unto him, Yesterday at the seventh hour the fever left him. So the father knew that *it was* at the same hour, in thewhich Jesus said unto him, Thy son liveth: [A]nd himself believed, and his whole house. This *is* again the second miracle *that* Jesus did, when he was come out of Judaea into Galilee.

ΑΩ

Chapter 4

GALILEE OF THE NATIONS

Isaiah 9:01-07

Redaction: Galilee of the Nations

MATTHEW	MARK	LUKE	JOHN

MATTHEW	MARK	LUKE	JOHN

- Fishers of Men -

Matt 04:13-23 • Mark 01:15-39 • Luke 04:31-5:11 • John

¶ And • he came • down to Capernaum, a city of Galilee, • and dwelt in Capernaum, which is upon the sea coast, in the borders of Zabulon, and Nephthalim: That it might be fulfilled which was spoken by Esaias the prophet, saying, The land of Zabulon and the land of Nephthalim, *by* the way of the sea, beyond Jordan, Galilee of the Gentiles; The people which sat in darkness saw great light; and to them which sat in the region and shadow of death light is sprung up.

¶ From that time Jesus began to preach, • and taught them on the sabbath days • and to say, Repent: • The time is fulfilled, and the kingdom of God • of heaven • is at hand: [R]epent ye, and believe the gospel.

¶ Now as • Jesus • walked by the sea of Galilee, he saw • two brethren, Simon called Peter, and Andrew his brother, casting a net into the sea: [F]or they were fishers. • And Jesus said unto them, Come • [f]ollow • ye after me, and I will make you to become fishers of men. And straightway they {forsook / left} *their* nets, and followed him. • And when he had gone • on from thence, • a little further • he saw other two brethren, James *the son* of Zebedee, and John his brother, • who also were in the ship • with Zebedee their father, mending their nets; • [a]nd straightway he called them: • And they immediately left • their father Zebedee in the ship with the hired servants, and went after • and followed him. • And they went into Capernaum; and straightway on the sabbath day he entered into the synagogue, and taught. And they were astonished at his doctrine: [F]or he taught them as one that had authority, and not as the scribes. • [F]or his word was with power.

¶ And in the synagogue there was a man, which had a spirit of an unclean devil, and cried out with a loud voice, [s]aying, Let *us* alone; what have we to do with thee, *thou* Jesus of Nazareth? art thou come to destroy us? I know thee who thou art; the Holy One of God. And Jesus rebuked him, saying, Hold thy peace, and come out of him. And when the {devil / unclean spirit} had torn him, and • had

MATTHEW	MARK	LUKE	JOHN

thrown him in the midst, he • cried with a loud voice, • came out of him, and hurt him not. • And they were all amazed, insomuch that they questioned • and spake among themselves, saying, What a word *is* this! • What thing is this? [W}hat new doctrine *is* this? • [F]or with authority and power he commandeth • even the unclean spirits, and they do obey him • and they come out. • And immediately his fame spread abroad {throughout / into} every place of • all the {region / country} • round about Galilee.

¶ And he arose out of the synagogue, • forthwith, when they were come out of the synagogue, they entered into the house of Simon and Andrew, with James and John. But Simon's wife's mother lay sick • taken with a great fever; and they besought him for her • and anon they tell him of her. And he came and took her by the hand, and lifted her up; • [a]nd he stood over her, and rebuked the fever; • and immediately the fever left her, • and immediately she arose and ministered unto them.

¶ Now • at even, • when the sun was setting, all they that had any sick with divers diseases brought them unto him; • and them that were possessed with devils. And all the city was gathered together at the door. And he healed many that were sick of diverse diseases, • and he laid his hands on every one of them, and healed them. And devils also came out of many, crying out, and saying, Thou art Christ the Son of God. And he rebuking *them* • suffered not the devils to speak, because they knew him • that he was Christ. • And in the morning, rising up a great while before day, he went out, • [a]nd when it was day, he departed and went • into a {solitary / desert} place: • and there prayed. And Simon and • the people • that were with him followed after him • and came unto him, • [a]nd when they had found him, • stayed him, that he should not depart from them. •

¶ [T]hey said unto him, All *men* seek for thee. • And he said unto them, I must preach the kingdom of God to other cities also: for therefore am I sent. • Let us go into the next towns, that I may preach there also: for therefore came I forth. •

¶ And Jesus went about all Galilee, teaching in their synagogues, and preaching the gospel of

MATTHEW	MARK	LUKE	JOHN

the kingdom, and healing all manner of sickness and all manner of disease • and cast out devils •
among the people. •

¶ A[nd] it came to pass, that, as the people pressed upon him to hear the word of God, he
stood by the lake of Gennesaret, [a]nd saw two ships standing by the lake: [B]ut the fishermen were
gone out of them, and were washing *their* nets. And he entered into one of the ships, which was
Simon's, and prayed him that he would thrust out a little from the land. And he sat down, and taught the
people out of the ship. Now when he had left speaking, he said unto Simon, Launch out into the deep,
and let down your nets for a draught. And Simon answering said unto him, Master, we have toiled all
the night, and have taken nothing: nevertheless at thy word I will let down the net. And when they had
this done, they inclosed a great multitude of fishes: [A]nd their net brake. And they beckoned unto
their partners, which were in the other ship, that they should come and help them. And they came, and
filled both the ships, so that they began to sink. When Simon Peter saw *it,* he fell down at Jesus' knees,
saying, Depart from me; for I am a sinful man, O Lord. For he was astonished, and all that were with
him, at the draught of the fishes which they had taken: And so *was* also James, and John, the sons of
Zebedee, which were partners with Simon. And Jesus said unto Simon, Fear not; from hence forth thou
shalt catch men. And when they had brought their ships to land, they forsook all, and followed him.

Ω

Redaction: Galilee of the Nations

MATTHEW	MARK	LUKE	JOHN

MATTHEW	MARK	LUKE	JOHN

- His Disciples Came -

Matt 04:24-07:29 • Mark • Luke • John

¶ And his fame went throughout all Syria: [A]nd they brought unto him all sick people that were taken with divers diseases and torments, and those which were possessed with devils, and those which were lunatick, and those that had the palsy; and he healed them. And there followed him great multitudes of people from Galilee, and *from* Decapolis, and *from* Jerusalem, and *from* Judæa, and *from* beyond Jordan.

¶ A[nd] seeing the multitudes, he went up into a mountain: and when he was set, his disciples came unto him: And he opened his mouth, and taught them, saying, Blessed *are* the poor in spirit: [F]or theirs is the kingdom of heaven. Blessed *are* they that mourn: [F]or they shall be comforted. Blessed *are* the meek: [F]or they shall inherit the earth. Blessed *are* they which do hunger and thirst after righteousness: [F]or they shall be filled. Blessed *are* the merciful: [F]or they shall obtain mercy. Blessed *are* the pure in heart: [F]or they shall see God. Blessed *are* the peacemakers: [F]or they shall be called the children of God. Blessed *are* they which are persecuted for righteousness' sake: [F]or theirs is the kingdom of heaven. Blessed *are* ye, when *men* shall revile you, and persecute *you*, and shall say all manner of evil against you falsely, for my sake. Rejoice, and be exceeding glad: [F]or great *is* your reward in heaven: [F]or so persecuted they the prophets which were before you.

¶ Ye are the salt of the earth: [B]ut if the salt have lost his savour, wherewith shall it be salted? it is thenceforth good for nothing, but to be cast out, and to be trodden under foot of men. Ye are the light of the world. A city that is set on an hill cannot be hid. Neither do men light a candle, and put it under a bushel, but on a candlestick; and it giveth light unto all that are in the house. Let your light so shine before men, that they may see your good works, and glorify your Father which is in heaven.

¶ Think not that I am come to destroy the law, or the prophets: I am not come to destroy, but to fulfill. For verily I say unto you, Till heaven and earth pass, one jot or one tittle shall in no wise pass

MATTHEW	MARK	LUKE	JOHN

from the law, till all be fulfilled. Whosoever therefore shall break one of these least commandments, and shall teach men so, he shall be called the least in the kingdom of heaven: [B]ut whosoever shall do and teach *them*, the same shall be called great in the kingdom of heaven. For I say unto you, That except your righteousness shall exceed *the righteousness* of the scribes and Pharisees, ye shall in no case enter into the kingdom of heaven.

¶ Ye have heard that it was said by them of old time, Thou shalt not kill; and whosoever shall kill shall be in danger of the judgment: But I say unto you, That whosoever is angry with his brother without a cause shall be in danger of the judgment: [A]nd whosoever shall say to his brother, Raca, shall be in danger of the council: [B]ut whosoever shall say, Thou fool, shall be in danger of hell fire. Therefore if thou bring thy gift to the altar, and there rememberest that thy brother has ought against thee; [l]eave there thy gift before the altar, and go thy way; first be reconciled to thy brother, and then come and offer thy gift. Agree with thine adversary quickly, whiles thou art in the way with him; lest at anytime the adversary deliver thee to the judge, and the judge deliver thee to the officer, and thou be cast into prison. Verily I say unto thee, Thou shalt by no means come out thence, till thou hast paid the uttermost farthing.

¶ Ye have heard that it was said by them of old time, Thou shalt not commit adultery: But I say unto you, That whosoever looketh on a woman to lust after her hath committed adultery with her already in his heart. And if thy right eye offend thee, pluck it out, and cast *it* from thee: [F]or it is profitable for thee that one of thy members should perish, and not *that* thy whole body should be cast into hell. And if thy right hand offend thee, cut it off, and cast *it* from thee: [F]or it is profitable for thee that one of thy members should perish, and not *that* thy whole body should be cast into hell. It hath been said, Whosoever shall put away his wife, let him give her a writing of divorcement: But I say unto you, That whosoever shall put away his wife, saving for the cause of fornication, causeth her to commit adultery: [A]nd whosoever shall marry her that is divorced commiteth adultery.

MATTHEW	MARK	LUKE	JOHN

¶ Again ye have heard that it hath been said by them of old time, Thou shalt not forswear thyself, but shall perform unto the Lord thine oaths: But I say unto you, Swear not at all; neither by heaven; for it is God's throne: Nor by the earth; for it is his footstool: [N]either by Jerusalem; for it is the city of the great King. Neither shalt thou swear by thy head, because thou canst not make one hair white or black. But let your communication be, Yea, yea; Nay; nay: [F]or whatsoever is more than these cometh of evil.

¶ Ye have heard that it hath been said, An eye for an eye, and a tooth for a tooth: But I say unto you, That ye resist not evil: [B]ut whosoever shall smite thee on thy right cheek, turn to him the other also. And if any man will sue thee at the law, and take away thy coat, let him have *thy* cloke also. And whosoever shall compel thee to go a mile, go with him twain. Give to him that asketh thee, and from him that would borrow of thee turn thou not away.

¶ Ye have heard that it hath been said, Thou shalt love thy neighbor, and hate thine enemy. But I say unto you, Love your enemies, bless them that curse you, do good to them that hate you, and pray for them which despitefully use you, and persecute you; [t]hat ye may be the children of your Father which is in heaven: [F]or he maketh his sun to rise on the evil and on the good, and sendeth rain on the just and on the unjust. For if ye love them which love you, what reward have ye? [D]o not even the publicans the same? And if ye salute your brethren only, what do ye more *than others?* [D]o not even the publicans so? Be ye therefore perfect, even as your Father which is in heaven is perfect.

¶ T[ake] heed that ye do not your alms before men, to be seen of them: [O]therwise ye have no reward of your Father which is in heaven. Therefore when thou doest *thine* alms, do not sound a trumpet before thee, as the hypocrites do in the synagogues and in the streets, that they may have glory of men. Verily I say unto you, They have their reward. But when thou doest alms, let not thy left hand know what thy right hand doeth: That thine alms may be in secret: [A]nd thy Father which seeth in secret himself shall reward thee openly.

MATTHEW	MARK	LUKE	JOHN

¶ And when thou prayest, thou shalt not be as the hypocrites *are*: [F]or they love to pray standing in the synagogues and in the corners of the streets, that they may be seen of men. Verily I say unto you, They have their reward. But thou, when thou prayest, enter into thy closet, and when thou hast shut thy door, pray to thy Father, which is in secret; and thy Father which seeth in secret shall reward thee openly. But when ye pray, use not vain repetitions, as the heathen *do*: [F]or they think that they shall be heard for their much speaking. Be not ye therefore like unto them: [F]or your Father knoweth what things ye have need of, before ye ask him. After this manner therefore pray ye: Our Father which art in heaven, Hallowed be thy name. Thy kingdom come. Thy will be done in earth, as *it is* in heaven. Give us this day our daily bread. And forgive us our debts, as we forgive our debtors. And lead us not into temptation, but deliver us from evil: For thine is the kingdom, and the power, and the glory, forever. Amen. For if ye forgive men their trespasses, your heavenly Father will also forgive you: But if ye forgive not men their trespasses, neither will your Father forgive your trespasses.

¶ Moreover when ye fast, be not, as the hypocrites, of a sad countenance: [F]or they disfigure their faces, that they may appear unto men to fast. Verily I say unto you, They have their reward. But thou, when thou fastest, anoint thine head, and wash thy face; [t]hat thou appear not unto men to fast, but unto thy Father which is in secret: and thy Father, which seeth in secret, shall reward thee openly.

¶ Lay not up for yourselves treasures upon earth, where moth and rust doth corrupt, and where thieves break through and steal: But lay up for yourselves treasures in heaven, where neither moth nor rust doth corrupt, and where thieves do not break through nor steal: For where your treasure is, there will your heart be also. The light of the body is the eye: [I]f therefore thine eye be single, thy whole body shall be full of light. But if thine eye be evil, thy whole body shall be full of darkness. If therefore the light that is in thee be darkness, how great *is* that darkness!

¶ No man can serve two masters: [F]or either he will hate the one, and love the other; or else he will hold to the one, and despise the other. Ye can not serve God and mammon. Therefore I say unto

MATTHEW	MARK	LUKE	JOHN

you, Take no thought for your life, what ye shall eat, or what ye shall drink; nor yet for your body, what ye shall put on. Is not the life more than meat, and the body more than raiment? Behold the fowls of the air: [F]or they sow not, neither do they reap, nor gather into barns; yet your heavenly Father feedeth them. Are ye not much better than they? Which of you by taking thought can add one cubit unto his stature? And why take ye thought for raiment? Consider the lilies of the field, how they grow; they toil not, neither do they spin: And yet I say unto you, That even Solomon in all his glory was not arrayed like one of these. Wherefore, if God so clothe the grass of the field, which today is, and tomorrow is cast into the oven, *shall he* not much more *clothe* you, O ye of little faith? Therefore take no thought, saying, [W]hat shall we eat? [O]r, What shall we drink? [O]r, Wherewithal shall we be clothed? (For after all these things do the Gentiles seek:) [F]or your heavenly Father knoweth that ye have need of all these things. But seek ye first the kingdom of God, and his righteousness; and all these things shall be added unto you. Take therefore no thought for the morrow: [F]or the morrow shall take thought for the things of itself. Sufficient unto the day *is* the evil thereof.

¶ J[udge] not, that ye be not judged. For with what judgment ye judge, ye shall be judged: [A]nd with what measure ye mete, it shall be measured to you again. And why beholdest thou the mote that is in thy brother's eye, but considerest not the beam that is in thine own eye? Or how wilt thou say to thy brother, Let me pull out the mote out of thine eye; and, behold, a beam *is* in thine own eye? Thou hypocrite, first cast out the beam out of thine own eye; and then shalt thou see clearly to cast out the mote out of thy brother's eye.

¶ Give not that which is holy unto the dogs, neither cast ye your pearls before swine, lest they trample them under their feet, and turn again and rend you.

¶ Ask, and it shall be given you; seek, and ye shall find; knock, and it shall be opened unto you: For every one that asketh, receiveth; and he that seeketh findeth, and to him that knocketh it shall be opened. Or what man is there of you, whom if his son ask bread, will he give him a stone? Or if he

MATTHEW	MARK	LUKE	JOHN

ask a fish, will he give him a serpent? If ye then, being evil, know how to give good gifts unto your children, how much more shall your Father which is in heaven give good things to them that ask him? Therefore all things whatsoever ye would that men should do to you, do ye even so to them: [F]or this is the law and the prophets.

¶ Enter ye in at the strait gate: for wide *is* the gate, and broad *is* the way, that leadeth to destruction, and many there be which go in thereat: Because strait *is* the gate, and narrow *is* the way, which leadeth unto life, and few there be that find it.

¶ Beware of false prophets, which come to you in sheep's clothing, but inwardly they are ravening wolves. Ye shall know them by there fruits. Do men gather grapes of thorns, or figs of thistles? Even so every good tree bringeth forth good fruit; but a corrupt tree bringeth forth evil fruit. A good tree cannot bring forth evil fruit, neither *can* a corrupt tree bring forth good fruit. Every tree that bringeth forth not good fruit is hewn down, and cast into the fire. Wherefore by their fruits ye shall know them.

¶ Not everyone that saith unto me, Lord, Lord, shall enter into the kingdom of heaven; but he that doeth the will of my Father which is in heaven. Many will say to me in that day, Lord, Lord, have we not prophesied in thy name? [A]nd in thy name have cast out devils? [A]nd in thy name done many wonderful works? And then will I profess unto them, I never knew you: [D]epart from me, ye that work iniquity.

¶ Therefore whosoever heareth these sayings of mine, and doeth them, I will liken him unto a wise man, which built his house upon a rock: And the rain descended, and the floods came, and the winds blew, and beat upon that house; and it fell not: [F]or it was founded upon a rock. And every one that heareth these sayings of mine, and doeth them not, shall be likened unto a foolish man, which built his house upon the sand: And the rain descended, and the floods came, and the winds blew, and beat upon that house; and it fell: [A]nd great was the fall of it. And it came to pass, when Jesus had ended

MATTHEW	MARK	LUKE	JOHN

these sayings, the people were astonished at his doctrine: For he taught them as *one* having authority, and not as the scribes.

Ω

Redaction: Galilee of the Nations

MATTHEW	MARK	LUKE	JOHN

MATTHEW	MARK	LUKE	JOHN

- Country of the Gergesenes -

Matt 08:01-09:09 • Mark 01:40-02:14 • Luke 05:12-28 • John

¶ W[hen] he was come down from the mountain, great multitudes followed him. • And it came to pass, when he was in a certain city, • behold, there came • a man full of leprosy: who seeing Jesus • worshipped • beseeching him, and kneeling down to him, • fell on *his* face, and besought him, saying, • unto him, • Lord, if thou wilt, thou canst make me clean. • And Jesus, moved with compassion, put forth *his* hand, and touched him, and saith unto him, I will: be thou clean. And as soon as he had spoken, immediately the leprosy departed from him, and he was cleansed. And he straightly charged him, • to tell no man: • [A]nd forthwith sent him away; • [a]nd Jesus saith unto him, See thou {tell / say) nothing to any man: [B]ut go thy way, shew thyself to the priest, • and offer the gift • for thy cleansing • according • those things which Moses commanded, for a testimony unto them. But he went out, and began to publish *it* much, and to blaze abroad the matter, insomuch that Jesus could no more openly enter the city, but was without in desert places: • But so much the more went there a fame abroad of him: [A]nd great multitudes came together to hear • him from every quarter • and to be healed by him of their infirmities. •

¶ And when Jesus was entered into Capernaum, there came unto him a centurion, beseeching him, And saying, Lord, my servant lieth at home sick of the palsy, grievously tormented. And Jesus saith unto him, I will come and heal him. The centurion answered and said, Lord, I am not worthy that thou shouldst come under my roof: [B]ut speak the word only, and my servant shall be healed. For I am a man under authority, having soldiers under me: [A]nd I say to this *man*, Go, and he goeth; and to another, Come, and he cometh; and to my servant, Do this, and he doeth *it*. When Jesus heard *it*, he marvelled, and said to them that followed, Verily I say unto you, I have not found so great faith, no, not in Israel. And I say unto you, That many shall come from the east and west, and shall sit down with Abraham, and Isaac, and Jacob, in the kingdom of heaven. But the children of the kingdom shall be cast out into outer darkness: [T]there shall be weeping and gnashing of teeth. And Jesus said unto the

MATTHEW	MARK	LUKE	JOHN

centurion, Go thy way; and as thou hast believed, *so* be it done unto thee. And his servant was healed in the selfsame hour.

¶ And when Jesus was come into Peter's house, he saw his wife's mother laid, and sick of a fever. And he touched her hand, and the fever left her: [A]nd she arose, and ministered unto them.

¶ When the even was come, they brought unto him many that were possessed with devils: [A]nd he cast out the spirits with *his* word, and healed all that were sick: That it might be fulfilled which was spoken by Esaias the prophet, saying, Himself took our infirmities, and bare *our* sicknesses.

¶ Now when Jesus saw great multitudes about him, he gave commandment to depart unto the other side. And a certain scribe came, and said unto him, Master, I will follow thee whithersoever thou goest. And Jesus saith unto him, The foxes have holes, and the birds of the air *have* nests; but the Son of man hath not where to lay *his* head. And another of his disciples said unto him, Lord, suffer me first to go and bury my father. But Jesus said unto him, Follow me; and let the dead bury their dead.

¶ And when he was entered into a ship, his disciples followed him. And, behold, there arose a great tempest in the sea, insomuch that the ship was covered with the waves: [B]ut he was asleep. And his disciples came to *him*, and awoke him, saying, Lord, save us: we perish. And he saith unto them, Why are ye fearful, O ye of little faith? Then he arose, and rebuked the winds and the sea; and there was a great calm. But the men marvelled, saying, What manner of man is this, that even the winds and the sea obey him!

¶ And when he was come to the other side into the country of the Gergesenes, there met him two possessed with devils, coming out of the tombs, exceeding fierce, so that no man might pass by that way. And, behold, they cried out, saying, What have we to do with thee, Jesus, thou Son of God? [A]rt thou come hither to torment us before the time? And there was a good way off from them an herd of many swine feeding. So the devils besought him, saying, If thou cast us out, suffer us to go away into

MATTHEW	MARK	LUKE	JOHN

the herd of swine. And he said unto them, Go. And when they were come out, they went into the herd of swine: [A]nd, behold, the whole herd of swine ran violently down a steep place into the sea, and perished in the waters. And they that kept them fled, and went there ways into the city, and told every thing, and what was befallen to the possessed of the devils. And, behold, the whole city came out to meet Jesus: [A]nd when they saw him, they besought *him* that he would depart out of their coasts.

Ω

Redaction: Galilee of the Nations

MATTHEW	MARK	LUKE	JOHN

MATTHEW	MARK	LUKE	JOHN

- Power on Earth -

Matt 09:01-08 • Mark 02:01-02:13 • Luke 05:16-26 • John

¶ A[nd] he entered into a ship, and passed over, • [a]nd he withdrew himself into the wilderness, and prayed. • A[nd] again he {entered / came} into his own city • Capernaum, after *some* days; and it was noised that he was in the house. And straightway many were gathered together, insomuch that there was no room to receive *them*, no, not so much as about the door: [A]nd he preached the word unto them. • And it came to pass on a certain day, as he was teaching, that there were Pharisees and doctors of the law sitting by, which were come out of every town of Galilee, and Judaea, and Jerusalem: [A]nd the power of the Lord was *present* to heal them.

¶ And, behold, men • come unto him, {bringing / brought} in a bed a man which was taken • sick {of the / with a} palsy: • Lying on a bed • which was borne of four • and they sought *means* to bring him in, and to lay *him* before him. And when they could not find by what *way* they might bring him in • nigh unto him {for / because} the press, • of the multitude, they went upon the housetop, • uncovered the roof where he was: [A]nd when they had broken *it* up, • let him down through the tiling with *his* {couch / bed} wherein the sick of the palsy lay • into the midst before Jesus. • When Jesus saw their faith, he said unto the sick of the palsy, • Son, be of good cheer; thy sins be forgiven thee. • But there were certain of the scribes • and the Pharisees • sitting there, and • began to reason, • in their hearts, • within themselves, • saying, • This *man* blasphemeth. • Who is this which speaketh blasphemies? • Why doth this *man* thus speak blasphemies? who can forgive sins but God {only? / alone?} • And immediately when Jesus perceived in his spirit • knowing their thoughts • answering said unto them, {What / Wherefore / Why} {reason / think} ye evil in your hearts? For whether • is it easier to say to the sick of the palsy, *Thy* sins be forgiven thee; or to say, Arise and take up thy bed, and walk? But that ye may know that the Son of man hath power on earth to forgive sins, (he saith to the sick of the palsy,) I say unto thee, Arise and take up thy bed, and go thine way into thine house. • And immediately he rose up before them, • and took up the bed, • whereon he lay, • and went forth before them all; • and

Redaction: Galilee of the Nations

MATTHEW	MARK	LUKE	JOHN

departed to his own house, glorifying God. • But when the multitudes saw *it*, • insomuch that they were all amazed, • marvelled, and glorified God, which had given such power unto men. • And and were filled with fear, saying, We have seen strange things today. • We never saw it on this fashion. And he went forth again by the seaside; and all the multitude resorted unto him, and he taught them. •

AΩ

Chapter 5

The Feast
of Weeks

Exodus 34:22

Redaction: The Feast of Weeks

MATTHEW	MARK	LUKE	JOHN

MATTHEW	MARK	LUKE	JOHN

- The Lord of the Harvest -

Matt 09:09-38 • Mark 02:14-03:12 • Luke 05:27-06:11 • John

¶ And after these things he went forth, • [a]nd as Jesus passed forth from thence, he saw a man, named Matthew, • Levi the *son* of Alphaeus sitting at the receipt of custom, • and he said unto him, Follow me. And he left all, rose up, and followed him.

¶ And Levi made him a great feast in his own house: • And it came to pass, that, as Jesus sat at meat in his house, • behold, {many / there was a great company} of publicans • and sinners • and of others that • also came and sat down • together with Jesus and his disciples: For there were many, and they followed him. But • when • their scribes and Pharisees • saw him eat with publicans and sinners, they • murmured against his disciples, saying, Why do ye eat and drink with publicans and sinners? • {Why / How} is it that • your Master eateth and drinketh with publicans and sinners? • But when Jesus heard *that*, • Jesus answering said unto them, • They that are whole have no need of the physician, but they that are sick: • But go ye and learn what *that* meaneth, I will have mercy, and not sacrifice: for I am not come to call the righteous, but sinners to repentance. •

¶ And the disciples of John and the Pharisees used to fast: • Then came to him the disciples of John, • [a]nd they said unto him, Why do the disciples of John fast often, and make prayers, and likewise *the disciples* of the Pharisees; • but thy disciples fast not? • [B]ut thine eat and drink? • And Jesus said unto them, Can the children of the bridechamber mourn, • [c]an ye make the children of the bridechamber fast, while the bridegroom is with them? • [A]as long as they have the bridegroom with them, they cannot fast. But the days will come, when the bridegroom shall be taken away from them, and then shall they fast in those days. •

¶ And he spake also a parable unto them; • No man also {seweth / putteth} a piece of new {garment / cloth} on an old garment: {else / for / if otherwise}, then both • {the new piece / that} which is put in to fill it up • maketh a rent, and the piece that was *taken* out of the new {agreeth not with /

MATTHEW	MARK	LUKE	JOHN

taketh away from} the old • garment, and the rent is made worse. {Neither do men / And no man} putteth new wine into old bottles: [E]lse the new wine {doth / will} {burst the bottles, / the bottles break}, and the wine runneth out, • and be spilled, • and the bottles will be marred: • and the bottles shall perish. But new wine must be put into new bottles; • and both are preserved. • No man also having drunk old *wine* straightway desireth new: [f]or he saith, The old is better. •

¶ While he spake these things unto them, behold, there came a certain ruler, and worshiped him, saying, My daughter is even now dead: but come and lay thy hand upon her, and she shall live. And Jesus arose, and followed him, and *so did* his disciples.

¶ And, behold, a woman, which was diseased with an issue of blood twelve years, came behind *him*, and touched the hem of his garment: For she said within herself, If I may but touch his garment, I shall be whole. But Jesus turned him about, and when he saw her, he said, Daughter, be of good comfort; thy faith hath made thee whole. And the woman was made whole from that hour. And when Jesus came into the ruler's house, he saw the minstrels and the people making a noise, And when Jesus came into the ruler's house, he saw the minstrels and the people making a noise, He said unto them, Give place: for the maid is not dead, but sleepeth. And they laughed him to scorn. But when the people were put forth, he went in, and took her by the hand, and the maid arose. And the fame hereof went abroad into all that land.

¶ And when Jesus departed thence, two blind men followed him, crying, and saying, *Thou* Son of David, have mercy on us. And when he was come into the house, the blind men came to him: [A]nd Jesus saith unto them, Believe ye that I am able to do this? They said unto him, Yea, Lord. Then touched he their eyes, saying, According to your faith be it unto you. And there eyes were opened; and Jesus straitly charged them, saying, See *that* no man know *it*. But they, when they were departed, spread abroad his fame in all that country.

¶ As they went out, behold, they brought to him a dumb man possessed with a devil. And

MATTHEW	MARK	LUKE	JOHN

when the devil was cast out, the dumb spake: [A]nd the multitudes marvelled, saying, It was never so seen in Israel. But the Pharisees said, He casteth out devils through the prince of the devils. •

¶ A[nd] it came to pass on the second sabbath after the first, that he went through the cornfields • on the sabbath day; and his disciples began, as they went, to pluck the ears of corn • and did eat, rubbing *them* in *their* hands. And certain of the Pharisees said unto them, • Behold, why do they • do ye that which is not lawful to do on the sabbath days? And Jesus answering them said, • unto them, Have ye never read what David did, when he had need, and was an hungered, he, and they that were with him? How he went into the house of God in the days of Abiathar the high priest, • and did take and eat the shewbread, and gave also to them that were with him; which it is not lawful to eat but for the priests alone? • And he said unto them, The sabbath was made for man, and not man for the sabbath: Therefore the Son of man is Lord also of the sabbath. •

¶ And it came to pass also on another sabbath, that he entered • again into the synagogue; and there was a man there • whose right hand was withered. And the scribes and the Pharisees watched him, whether he would heal • him on the sabbath day; • that they might find an accusation against him. But he knew there thoughts, and said to the man which had the withered hand, Rise up, and stand forth in the midst. And he arose and stood forth. Then said Jesus unto them, I will ask you one thing; Is it lawful on the sabbath days to do good, or to do evil? [T]o save life, or to {destroy *it*? / kill?} But they held their peace. And when he had looked • round about upon them all • with anger, being grieved for the hardness of there hearts, he saith unto the man, Stretch forth thine hand. And he stretched *it* out: and his hand was restored whole as the other. And the Pharisees • were filled with madness; and communed one with another what they might do to Jesus. • And the Pharisees went forth, and straightway took counsel with the Herodians against him, how they might destroy him. • And Jesus went about all the cities and villages, teaching in their synagogues, and preaching the gospel of the kingdom, and healing every sickness and every disease among the people. • But Jesus withdrew himself with his disciples to the sea: [A]nd a great multitude from Galilee followed him, and from

MATTHEW	MARK	LUKE	JOHN

Judea, [a]nd from Jerusalem, and from Idumea, and *from* beyond Jordan; and they about Tyre and Sidon, a great multitude, when they had heard what great things he did, came unto him. And he spake to his disciples, that a small ship should wait on him because of the multitude, lest they should throng him.

¶ But when he saw the multitudes, he was moved with compassion on them, because they fainted, and were scattered abroad, as sheep having no shepherd. • For he had healed many; insomuch that they pressed upon him for to touch him, as many as had plagues. And unclean spirits, when they saw him, fell down before him, and cried, saying, Thou art the Son of God. And he straitly charged them that they should not make him known. • Then saith he unto his disciples, The harvest truly *is* plenteous, but the labourers *are* few; Pray ye therefore the Lord of the harvest, that he will send forth labourers into his harvest.

Ω

MATTHEW	MARK	LUKE	JOHN

- The Twelve Apostles -

Matt 10:01-42 • Mark 03:13-19 • Luke 06:12-16 • John

¶ And it came to pass in those days, that he went out • [a]nd he goeth up into a mountain, • to pray, and continued all night in prayer to God.

¶ And when it was day, he called *unto him* his disciples: • who he would: and they came unto him. • [A]nd of them he chose • [a]nd he ordained twelve, that they should be with him, and that he might send them forth to preach, • [and] when he had called unto *him* his twelve disciples, • whom als ohe named apostles; • he gave them power *against* unclean spirits, to cast them out, and • to have power to heal • all manner of sickness and all manner of disease. Now the names of the twelve apostles are these; The first, Simon, • whom he also {named / called / surnamed} Peter; • and Andrew his brother; • [a]nd James the *son* of Zebedee, and John the brother of James; and he surnamed them Boanerges, which is, The sons of thunder: And • Philip, and Bartholomew; Thomas, and Matthew the publican; James *the son* of Alphaeus, • and Simon the Canaanite, • called Zelotes, And Judas • Lebbaeus, whose surname was Thaddaeus • *the brother* of James, and Judas Iscariot, which also was the traitor • who also betrayed him. These twelve Jesus sent forth, and commanded them, saying, Go not into the way of the Gentiles, and into *any* city of the Samaritans enter ye not: But go rather to the lost sheep of the house of Israel. And as ye go, preach, saying, The kingdom of heaven is at hand. Heal the sick, cleanse the lepers, raise the dead, cast out devils: freely you have received, freely give. Provide neither gold, nor silver, nor brass in your purses, Nor scrip for *your* journey, neither two coats, neither shoes, nor yet staves: for the workman is worthy of his meat. And into whatsoever city or town ye shall enter, inquire who in it is worthy; and there abide till ye go thence. And when ye come into an house, salute it. And if the house be worthy, let your peace come upon it: but if it be not worthy, let your peace return to you. And whosoever shall not receive you, nor hear your words, when ye depart out of that house or city, shake off the dust of your feet. Verily I say unto you, It shall be more tolerable for the land of Sodom and Gomorrha in the day of judgment, than for that city.

MATTHEW	MARK	LUKE	JOHN

¶ Behold, I send you forth as sheep in the midst of wolves: [B]e ye therefore wise as serpents, and harmless as doves. But beware of men: [F]or they will deliver you up to the councils, and they will scourge you in their synagogues; [a]nd ye shall be brought before governors and kings for my sake, for a testimony against them and the Gentiles. But when they deliver you up, take no thought how or what ye shall speak: [F]or it shall be given you in that same hour what ye shall speak. For it is not ye that speak, but the Spirit of your Father which speaketh in you. And the brother shall deliver up the brother to death, and the father the child: [A]nd the children shall rise up against *their* parents, and cause them to be put to death. And ye shall be hated of all *men* for my name's sake: [B]ut he that endureth to the end shall be saved. But when they persecute you in this city, flee ye into another: [F]or verily I say unto you, Ye shall not have gone over the cities of Israel, till the Son of man be come. The disciple is not above *his* master, nor the servant above his lord. It is enough for the disciple that he be as his master, and the servant as his lord. If they have called the master of the house Beelzebub, how much more *shall they call* them of his household? Fear them not therefore: for there is nothing covered, that shall not be revealed; and hid, that shall not be known. What I tell you in darkness, *that* speak ye in light: and what ye hear in the ear, *that* preach ye upon the housetops. And fear not them which kill the body, but are not able to kill the soul: [B]ut rather fear him which is able to destroy both soul and body in hell. Are not two sparrows sold for a farthing? and one of them shall not fall on the ground without your Father.

¶ But the very hairs of your head are all numbered. Fear ye not therefore, ye are of more value than many sparrows. Whosoever then shall confess me before men, him will I confess also before my Father which is in heaven. But whosoever shall deny me before men, him will I also deny before my Father which is in heaven. Think not that I am come to send peace on earth: I came not to send peace, but a sword. For I am come to set a man at variance against his father, and the daughter against her mother, and the daughter in law against her mother in law. And a man's foes *shall be* they of his own household. He that loveth father or mother more than me is not worthy of me: [A]nd he that loveth son

MATTHEW	MARK	LUKE	JOHN

or daughter more than me is not worthy of me. And he that taketh not his cross, and followeth after me, is not worthy of me. He that findeth his life shall lose it: and he that loseth his life for my sake shall find it.

¶ He that receiveth you receiveth me, and he that receiveth me receiveth him that sent me. He that receiveth a prophet in the name of a prophet shall receive a prophet's reward; and he that receiveth a righteous man in the name of a righteous man shall receive a righteous man's reward. And whosoever shall give to drink unto one of these little ones a cup of cold *water* only in the name of a disciple, verily I say unto you, he shall in know wise lose his reward.

Ω

Redaction: The Feast of Weeks

MATTHEW	MARK	LUKE	JOHN

MATTHEW	MARK	LUKE	JOHN

- God Hath Visited -

Matt 11:01 • Mark • Luke 06:17-07:18 • John

¶ A[nd] it came to pass, when Jesus had made an end of commanding his twelve disciples, he departed thence to teach and to preach in their cities. • And he came down with them, and stood in the plain, and the company of his disciples, and a great multitude of people out of all Judæa and Jerusalem, and from the sea coast of Tyre and Sidon, which came to hear him, and to be healed of their diseases; [a]nd they that were vexed with unclean spirits: and they were healed. And the whole multitude sought to touch him: for there went virtue out of him, and healed *them* all.

¶ And he lifted up his eyes on his disciples, and said, Blessed *be ye* poor: [F]or yours is the kingdom of God. Blessed *are ye* that hunger now: [F]or ye shall be filled. Blessed *are ye* that weep now: for ye shall laugh. Blessed are ye, when men shall hate you, and when they shall separate you *from their company*, and shall reproach *you*, and cast out your name as evil, for the Son of man's sake. Rejoice ye in that day, and leap for joy: [F]or, behold, your reward *is* great in heaven: [F]or in the like manner did their fathers unto the prophets. But woe unto you that are rich! [F]or ye have received your consolation. Woe unto you that are full! [F]or ye shall hunger. Woe unto you that laugh now! [F]or ye shall mourn and weep. Woe unto you, when all men shall speak well of you! [F]or so did their fathers to the false prophets.

¶ But I say unto you which hear, Love your enemies, do good to them which hate you, [b]less them that curse you, and pray for them which despitefully use you. And unto him that smiteth thee on the *one* cheek offer also the other; and him that taketh away thy cloke forbid not *to take thy* coat also. Give to every man that asketh of thee; and of him that taketh away thy goods ask *them* not again. And as ye would that men should do to you, do ye also to them likewise. For if ye love them which love you, what thank have ye? [F]or sinners also love those that love them. And if ye do good to them which do good to you, what thank have ye? [F]or sinners also do even the same. And if ye lend *to them* of whom

MATTHEW	MARK	LUKE	JOHN

ye hope to receive, what thank have ye? [F]or sinners also lend to sinners, to receive as much again. But love ye your enemies, and do good, and lend, hoping for nothing again; and your reward shall be great, and ye shall be the children of the Highest: [F]or he is kind unto the unthankful and *to* the evil. Be ye therefore merciful, as your Father also is merciful. Judge not, and ye shall not be judged: [C]ondemn not, and ye shall not be condemned: forgive, and ye shall be forgiven: Give, and it shall be given unto you; good measure, pressed down, and shaken together, and running over, shall men give into your bosom. For with the same measure ye mete withal it shall be measured to you again. And he spake a parable unto them, Can the blind lead the blind? [S]hall they not both fall into the ditch? The disciple is not above his master: but everyone that is perfect shall be as his master. And why beholdest thou the mote that is in thy brother's eye, but perceivest not the beam that is in thine own eye? Either how canst thou say to thy brother, Brother, let me pull out the mote that is in thine eye, when thou thyself beholdest not the beam that is in thine own eye? Thou hypocrite, cast out first the beam out of thine own eye, and then shalt thou see clearly to pull out the mote that is in thy brother's eye. For a good tree bringeth not forth corrupt fruit; neither doth a corrupt tree bring forth good fruit. For every tree is known by his own fruit. For of thorns men do not gather figs, nor of a bramble bush gather they grapes. A good man out of the good treasure of his heart bringeth forth that which is good; and an evil man out of the evil treasure of his heart bringeth forth that which is evil: for of the abundance of the heart his mouth speaketh.

¶ And why call ye me, Lord, Lord, and do not the things which I say? Whosoever cometh to me, and heareth my sayings, and doeth them, I will shew you to whom he is like: He is like a man which built an house, and digged deep, and laid the foundation on a rock: and when the flood arose, the stream beat vehemently upon that house, and could not shake it: [F]or it was founded upon a rock. But he that heareth, and doeth not, is like a man that without a foundation built an house upon the earth; against which the stream did beat vehemently, and immediately it fell; and the ruin of the house was great.

MATTHEW	MARK	LUKE	JOHN

¶ N[ow] when he had ended all his sayings in the audience of the people, he entered into Capernaum. And a certain centurion's servant, who was dear unto him, was sick, and ready to die. And when he heard of Jesus, he sent unto him the elders of the Jews, beseeching him that he would come and heal his servant. And when they came to Jesus, they besought him instantly, saying, That he was worthy for whom he should do this: For he loveth our nation, and hath built us a synagogue. Then Jesus went with them. And when he was now not far from the house, the centurion sent friends to him, saying unto him, Lord, trouble not thyself: [F]or I am not worthy that thou shouldst enter under my roof: Wherefore neither thought I myself worthy to come unto thee: [B]ut say in a word and my servant shall be healed. For I also am a man set under authority, having under me soldiers, and I say unto one, Go, and he goeth; and to another, Come, and he cometh; and to my servant, Do this, and he doeth *it*. When Jesus heard these things, he marvelled at him, and turned him about, and said unto the people that followed him, I say unto you, I have not found so great faith, no, not in Israel. And they that were sent, returning to the house, found the servant whole that had been sick.

¶ And it came to pass the day after, that he went into a city called Nain; and many of his disciples went with him, and much people. Now when he came nigh to the gate of the city, behold, there was a dead man carried out, the only son of his mother, and she was a widow: [A]nd much people of the city was with her. And when the Lord saw her, he had compassion on her, and said unto her, Weep not. And he came and touched the bier: and they that bare *him* stood still. And he said, Young man, I say unto thee, Arise. And he that was dead sat up, and began to speak. And he delivered him to his mother. And there came a fear on all: [A]nd they glorified God, saying, That [A] great prophet is risen up among us; and, That God hath visited his people. And this rumor of him went forth throughout all Judæa, and throughout all the region round about. And the disciples of John shewed him of all these things.•

Ω

Redaction: The Feast of Weeks

MATTHEW	MARK	LUKE	JOHN

MATTHEW	MARK	LUKE	JOHN

- Equal with God -

Matt • Mark • Luke • John 05:01-31

¶ A[fter] this there was a feast of the Jews; and Jesus went up to Jerusalem. Now there is at Jerusalem by the sheep *market* a pool, which is called in the Hebrew tongue Bethesda, having five porches. In these lay a great multitude of impotent folk, of blind, halt, withered, waiting for the moving of the water. For an angel went down at a certain season into the pool, and troubled the water: [W]hosoever then first after the troubling of the water stepped in was made whole of whatsoever disease he had. And a certain man was there, which had an infirmity thirty and eight years. When Jesus saw him lie, and knew that he had been now a long time *in that case*, he saith unto him, Wilt thou be made whole? The impotent man answered him, Sir, I have no man, when the water is troubled, to put me into the pool: [B]ut while I am coming, another steppeth down before me. Jesus saith unto him, Rise, take up thy bed, and walk. And immediately the man was made whole, and took up his bed, and walked: and on the same day was the sabbath.

¶ The Jews therefore said unto him that was cured, It is the sabbath day: [I]t is not lawful for thee to carry *thy* bed. He answered them, He that made me whole, the same said unto me, Take up thy bed, and walk. Then asked they him, What man is that which said unto thee, Take up thy bed, and walk? And he that was healed wist not who it was: [F]or Jesus had conveyed himself away, a multitude being in *that* place. Afterward Jesus findeth him in the temple, and said unto him, Behold, thou art made whole: [S]in no more, lest a worse thing come unto thee. The man departed, and told the Jews that it was Jesus, which had made him whole. And therefore did the Jews persecute Jesus, and sought to slay him, because he had done these things on the sabbath day.

¶ But Jesus answered them, My Father worketh hitherto, and I work. Therefore the Jews sought the more to kill him, because he not only had broken the sabbath, but said also that God was his Father, making himself equal with God. Then answered Jesus and said unto them, Verily, verily, I say

MATTHEW	MARK	LUKE	JOHN

unto you, The Son can do nothing of himself, but what he seeth the Father do: [F]or what things soever he doeth, these also doeth the Son likewise. For the Father loveth the Son, and sheweth him all things that himself doeth: [A]nd he will shew him greater works than these, that ye may marvel. For as the Father raiseth up the dead, and quickeneth *them*; even so the Son quickeneth whom he will. For the Father judgeth no man, but hath committed all judgment unto the Son: That all *men* should honor the Son, even as they honor the Father. He that honoreth not the Son honoreth not the Father which hath sent him. Verily, verily, I say unto you, He that heareth my word, and believeth on him that sent me, hath everlasting life, and shall not come into condemnation; but is passed from death unto life. Verily, verily, I say unto you, The hour is coming, and now is, when the dead shall hear the voice of the Son of God: [A]nd they that hear shall live. For as the Father hath life in himself; so hath he given to the Son to have life in himself; [a]nd hath given him authority to execute judgment also, because he is the Son of man. Marvel not at this: [F]or the hour is coming, in the which all that are in the graves shall hear his voice, [a]nd shall come forth; they that have done good, unto the resurrection of life; and they that have done evil, unto the resurrection of damnation. I can of my own self do nothing: [A]s I hear, I judge: [A]nd my judgment is just; because I seek not my own will, but the will of the Father which hath sent me. If I bear witness of myself, my witness is not true.

AΩ

Chapter 6

ELIJAH
THE PROPHET

Malachi 4:05-06

Redaction: Elijah the Prophet

MATTHEW	MARK	LUKE	JOHN

MATTHEW	MARK	LUKE	JOHN

- This is Elias -

Matt 11:02-19 • Mark • Luke 07:19-35 • John 05:32-47

¶ Now when John had heard in the prison the works of Christ, he • calling *unto him* two of his disciples sent • sent two of his disciples, • to Jesus, saying, Art thou he that should come? [O]r look we for another? When the men were come unto him, they said, John Baptist hath sent us unto thee, saying, Art thou he that should come? or • do we look for another? • And in that same hour he cured many of *their* infirmities and plagues, and of evil spirits; and unto many *that were* blind he gave sight. Then Jesus answering said unto them, Go your way, • shew • and tell John • again those things which ye do hear and see: The blind receive their sight, and the lame walk, the lepers are cleansed, and the deaf hear, the dead are raised up, and the poor have the gospel preached to them. And blessed is *he*, whosoever shall not be offended in me. •

¶ And when the messengers of John were departed, he began to speak unto the {people / multitudes} concerning John, • There is another that beareth witness of me; and I know that the witness which he witnesseth of me is true. • What went ye out into the wilderness for to see? A reed shaken with the wind? But what went ye out for to see? A man clothed in soft raiment? Behold, they which are gorgeously apparelled, • that wear soft *clothing* • and live delicately, are in kings' courts / houses. • Ye sent unto John, and he bare witness unto the truth. But I receive not testimony from man: but these things I say, that ye might be saved. He was a burning and a shining light: and ye were willing for a season to rejoice in his light. • For this is *he*, of whom it is written, Behold, I send my messenger before thy face, which shall prepare thy way before thee. • For • [v]erily I say unto you, Among them that are born of women there hath not risen a greater • prophet than John the Baptist: • than John the Baptist: notwithstanding he that is least in the kingdom of heaven is greater than he. And from the days of John the Baptist until now the kingdom of heaven suffereth violence, and the violent take it by force. For all the prophets and the law prophesied until John. And if ye will receive *it*, this is Elias, which was for to come. He that hath ears to hear, let him hear. • And all the people that heard *him*, and the publicans,

MATTHEW	MARK	LUKE	JOHN

justified God, being baptized with the baptism of John. But the Pharisees and lawyers rejected the counsel of God against themselves, being not baptized of him.

¶ And the Lord said, Whereunto then shall I liken the men of this generation? [A]nd to what are they like? They are like unto children sitting in the marketplace, and calling one to another, • unto their fellows, And saying, We have piped unto you, and ye have not danced; we have mourned unto you, and ye have not {lamented / wept.} For John the Baptist came neither eating bread nor drinking wine; and ye say, He hath a devil. The Son of man is come eating and drinking; and ye say, Behold a gluttonous man, and a winebibber, a friend of publicans and sinners! But wisdom is justified of all her children. •

¶ But I have greater witness than *that* of John: for the works which the Father hath given me to finish, the same works that I do, bear witness of me, that the Father hath sent me. And the Father himself, which hath sent me, hath borne witness of me. Ye have neither heard his voice at any time, nor seen his shape. And ye have not his word abiding in you: for whom he hath sent, him ye believe not.

¶ Search the scriptures; for in them ye think ye have eternal life: and they are they which testify of me. And ye will not come to me, that ye might have life. I receive not honor from men. But I know you, that ye have not the love of God in you. I am come in my Father's name, and ye receive me not: if another shall come in his own name, him ye will receive. How can ye believe, which receive honor one of another, and seek not the honor that *cometh* from God only? Do not think that I will accuse you to the Father: there is *one* that accuseth you, *even* Moses, in whom ye trust. For had ye believed Moses, ye would have believed me: for he wrote of me. But if ye believe not his writings, how shall ye believe my words?

Ω

MATTHEW	MARK	LUKE	JOHN

- The Pharisee's House -

Matt 11:20-30 • Mark • Luke 07:36-08:03 • John

¶ And one of the Pharisees desired him that he would eat with him. And he went into the Pharisees's house, and sat down to meat. And, behold, a woman in the city, which was a sinner, when she knew that *Jesus* sat at meat in the Pharisees's house, brought an alabaster box of ointment, [a]nd stood at his feet behind *him* weeping, and began to wash his feet with tears, and did wipe *them* with the hairs of her head, and kissed his feet and anointed *them* with the ointment. Now when the Pharisee which had bidden him saw *it*, he spake within himself, saying, This man, if he were a prophet, would have known who and what manner of woman *this is* that toucheth him: for she is a sinner. And Jesus answering said unto him, Simon, I have somewhat to say unto thee. And he saith, Master, say on. There was a certain creditor which had two debtors: [T]he one owed five hundred pence, and the other fifty. And when they had nothing to pay, he frankly forgave them both. Tell me therefore, which of them will love him most? Simon answered and said, I suppose that *he*, to whom he forgave most. And he said unto him, Thou hast rightly judged. And he turned to the woman, and said unto Simon, Seest thou this woman? I entered into thine house, thou gavest me no water for my feet: [B]ut she hath washed my feet with tears, and wiped *them* with the hairs of her head. Thou gavest me no kiss: [B]ut this woman since the time I came in hath not ceased to kiss my feet. My head with oil thou didst not anoint: [B]ut this woman hath anointed my feet with ointment. Wherefore I say unto thee, Her sins, which are many, are forgiven; for she loved much: [B]ut to whom little is forgiven, *the same* loveth little. And he said unto her, Thy sins are forgiven. And they that sat at meat with him began to say within themselves, Who is this that forgiveth sins also? And he said to the woman, [T]hy faith hath saved thee; go in peace.

¶ A[nd] it came to pass afterward, that he went throughout every city and village, preaching and shewing the glad tidings of the kingdom of God: [A]nd the twelve *were* with him. And certain women, which had been healed of evil spirits and infirmities, Mary called Magdalene, out of whom

MATTHEW	MARK	LUKE	JOHN

went seven devils, And Joanna the wife of Chuza Herod's steward, and Susanna, and many others, which ministered unto him of their substance. •

¶ Then began he to upbraid the cities wherein most of his mighty works were done, because they repented not: Woe unto thee, Chorazin! [W]oe unto thee, Bethsaida! [F]or if the mighty works, which were done in you, had been done in Tyre and in Sidon, they would have repented long ago in sackcloth and ashes. But I say unto you, It shall be more tolerable for Tyre and Sidon at the day of judgment, than for you. And thou, Capernaum, which art exalted unto heaven, shalt be brought down to hell: [F]or if the mighty works, which have been done in thee, had been done in Sodom, it would have remained until this day. But I say unto you, That it shall be more tolerable for the land of Sodom in the day of judgment, than for thee.

¶ At that time Jesus answered and said, I thank thee, O Father, Lord of heaven and earth, because thou hast hid these things from the wise and prudent, and hast revealed them unto babes. Even so, Father: [F]or so it seemed good in thy sight. All things are delivered unto me of my Father: [A]nd no man knoweth the Son, but the Father; neither knoweth any man the Father, save the Son, and *he* to whomsoever the Son will reveal *him*.

¶ Come unto me, all *ye* that labour and are heavy laden, and I will give you rest. Take my yoke upon you, and learn of me; for I am meek and lowly in heart: [A]nd ye shall find rest unto your souls. For my yoke *is* easy, and my burden is light.

Ω

MATTHEW	MARK	LUKE	JOHN

- Behold My Servant -

Matt 12:01-50 • Mark 03:19-35 • Luke • John

¶ A[t] that time Jesus went on the Sabbath day through the corn; and his disciples were an hungered, and began to pluck the ears of corn, and to eat. But when the Pharisees saw it, they said unto him, Behold thy disciples do that which is not lawful to do upon the sabbath day. But he said unto them, Have ye not read what David did, when he was an hungered, and they that were with him; [h]ow he entered into the house of God, and did eat the shew bread, which was not lawful for him to eat, neither for them which were with him, but only for the priests? Or have you not read in the law, how that on the sabbath days the priests in the temple profane the sabbath, and are blameless? But I say unto you, That in this place is one greater than the temple. But if ye had known what this meaneth, I will have mercy, and not sacrifice, ye would not have condemned the guiltless. For the Son of man is Lord even of the sabbath day. And when he was departed thence, he went into their synagogue:

¶ And, behold, there was a man which had his hand withered. And they asked him, saying, Is it lawful to heal on the sabbath days? that they might accuse him. And he said unto them, What man shall there be among you, that shall have one sheep, and if it fall into a pit on the sabbath day, will he not lay hold on it, and lift it out? How much then is a man better than a sheep? Wherefore it is lawful to do well on the sabbath days. Then saith he to the man, Stretch forth thine hand. And he stretched it forth; and it was restored whole, like as the other.

¶ Then the Pharisees went out, and held a council against him, how they might destroy him. But when Jesus knew it, he withdrew himself from thence: [A]nd great multitudes followed him, and he healed them all; [a]nd charged them that they should not make him known: That it might be fulfilled which was spoken by Esaias the prophet, saying, Behold my servant, whom I have chosen; my beloved, in whom my soul is well pleased: I will put my spirit upon him, and he shall shew judgment to the Gentiles. He shall not strive, nor cry; neither shall any man hear his voice in the streets. A bruised

MATTHEW	MARK	LUKE	JOHN

reed shall he not break, and smoking flax shall he not quench, till he send forth judgment unto victory. And in his name shall the Gentiles trust.

¶ Then was brought unto him one possessed with a devil, blind and dumb: [A]nd he healed him, insomuch that the blind and dumb both spake and saw. And all the people were amazed, and said, Is not this the Son of David? • [A]nd they went into an house. And the multitude cometh together again, so that they could not so much as eat bread. And when his friends heard *of it*, they went out to lay hold on him: [F]or they said, He is beside himself. •

¶ But when the Pharisees • [a]nd the scribes which came down from Jerusalem heard *it*, they said, This *fellow* doth not cast out devils, • [h]e hath Beelzebub, and by the prince of the devils casteth he out devils. • And Jesus knew their thoughts, • [a]nd he called them *unto him*, and said unto them in parables, How can Satan cast out Satan? • Every kingdom divided against itself is brought to desolation; • [a]nd if a kingdom be divided against itself, that kingdom can not stand. • [A]nd every city or • if a house be divided against itself, that house • shall not stand: • And if Satan rise up against himself, • [a]nd if Satan cast out Satan, he is divided against himself; how shall then his kingdom stand? • [H]e can not stand, but hath an end. • And if I by Beelzebub cast out devils, by whom do your children cast *them* out? [T]herefore they shall be your judges. But if I cast out devils by the Spirit of God, then the kingdom of God is come unto you. Or else how can one enter into a strong man's house [?] • No man can enter into a strong man's house, and spoil his goods, except he will first bind the strong man; and then he will spoil his house. • He that is not with me is against me; and he that gathereth not with me scattereth abroad.

¶ Wherefore • [v]erily I say unto you, • All manner of • sins shall be forgiven unto the sons of men, and blasphemies where with soever they shall blaspheme: • [B]ut the blasphemy *against* the *Holy Ghost* shall not be forgiven unto men. And whosoever speaketh a word against the Son of man, it shall be forgiven him: [B]ut whosoever speaketh against the Holy Ghost, • hath never forgiveness, • it shall

MATTHEW	MARK	LUKE	JOHN

not be forgiven him, neither in this world, neither in the *world* to come • but is in danger of eternal damnation: • Either make the tree good, and the fruit good; or else make the tree corrupt, and his fruit corrupt: [F]or the tree is known by *his* fruit. O generation of vipers, how can ye being evil, speak good things? [F]or out of the abundance of the heart the mouth speaketh. A good man out of the good treasure of the heart bringeth forth good things: [A]nd an evil man out of the evil treasure bringeth forth evil things. But I say unto you, That every idle word that men shall speak, they shall give account thereof in the day of judgment. For by thy words thou shalt be justified, and by thy words thou shalt be condemned. • Because they said, He hath an unclean spirit. •

¶ Then certain of the scribes and Pharisees answered, saying, Master, we would see a sign from thee. But he answered and said unto them, An evil and adulterous generation seeketh after a sign; and there shall no sign be given to it, but the sign of the prophet Jonas: For as Jonas was three days and three nights in the whale's belly; so shall the Son of man be three days and three nights in the heart of the earth. The men of Nineveh shall rise in judgment with this generation, and shall condemn it: [B]ecause they repented at the preaching of Jonas; and, behold, a greater than Jonas *is* here. The Queen of the south shall rise up in the judgment with this generation, and shall condemn it: [F]or she came from the uttermost parts of the earth to hear the wisdom of Solomon; and behold, a greater than Solomon *is* here. When the unclean spirit is gone out of a man, he walketh through dry places, seeking rest, and findeth none. Then he saith, I will return into my house from whence I came out; and when he is come, he findeth *it* empty, swept, and garnished. Then goeth he, and taketh with himself seven other spirits more wicked than himself; and they enter in and dwell there: [A]nd the last *state* of that man is worse than the first. Even so shall it be also unto this wicked generation.

¶ While he yet talked to the people, behold, • [t]here came then his brethren and his mother, and standing without, • desiring to speak with him • sent unto him, calling him. And the multitude sat about him, and • [t]hen one said unto him, Behold, thy mother and thy brethren stand without, • seek for thee • desiring to speak with thee. But he anwered • them, • and said unto him that told him, Who is my

Redaction: Elijah the Prophet

MATTHEW	MARK	LUKE	JOHN

mother? and who are my brethren? • And he looked round about on them which sat about him, • [a]nd

he stretched forth his hand toward his disciples, and said, Behold my mother and my brethren! For

whosoever shall do the will of • God, • my Father which is in heaven, the same is my brother, and sister,

and mother.

AΩ

Chapter 7

Open My Mouth in a Parable

Psalms 78:01-08

Redaction: Open My Mouth in a Parable

MATTHEW	MARK	LUKE	JOHN

MATTHEW	MARK	LUKE	JOHN

- Many Such Parables -

Matt 13:01-52 • Mark 04:01-34 • Luke 08:04-21 • John

¶ T[he] same day went Jesus out of the house, and sat • [and] he began again to teach by the sea side: • And when much people were gathered together, • there was • come to him out of every city, • a great multitude • so that he {went / entered} into a ship, and sat in the sea; and the whole multitude stood • by the sea on the {land / shore.} And he taught them • [a]nd he spake many things unto them in parables, • and said unto them in his doctrine, Hearken; Behold, there went {out / forth} • a sower to sow • his seed: • And it came to pass, {as / when} he sowed, some *seeds* fell by the way side, • and it was trodden down, • and the fowls of the air came and devoured {it / them} up: Some fell upon {stony places, / stony ground, / a rock;} • where {they / it} had not much earth; and {immediately / forthwith} {they sprung / it sprang} up because {it / they} had no {deepness / depth} of earth: But when the sun was up, • and as soon as it was sprung up, • they were scorched; • because it lacked moisture • and because {they / it} had no root, {it / they} withered away. And some fell among thorns; and the thorns {sprung / grew} up, • with it, and choked {it / them:} and it yielded no fruit. • But other fell into / on good ground, and did yield / bare / brought forth fruit, • that sprang up and increased; and brought forth, • some an hundred fold, some sixtyfold, some thirtyfold. • And when he had said these things, he cried, He {that / [w]ho} hath ears to hear, let him hear. • And when he was alone, they that were about him with the twelve • disciples came, and asked of him the parable • saying, What might this parable be? • Why speakest thou unto them in parables? He answered and said unto them, Because it is given unto you to know the mysteries of the kingdom of heaven, • of God: [B]ut unto {them / others} • that are without, all *these* things are done in parables: • [T]o them it is not given. For whosoever hath, to him shall be given, and he shall have more abundance: [B]ut whosoever hath not, from him shall be taken away even that he hath. Therefore speak I to them in parables: [B]ecause they seeing see not; and hearing they hear not, neither do they understand. And in them is fulfilled the prophecy of Esaias, which saith, By hearing ye shall hear, and shall not understand; and seeing ye shall see, and shall not

MATTHEW	MARK	LUKE	JOHN

perceive: For this people's heart is waxed gross, and *their* ears are dull of hearing, and their eyes they have closed; lest at any time they should see with *their* eyes, and hear with *their* ears, and should understand with *their* heart, and should be converted, and I should heal them • and *their* sins should be forgiven them.• But blessed *are* your eyes, for they see: [A]nd your ears, for they hear. For verily I say unto you, That many prophets and righteous *men* have desired to see *those things* which ye see, and have not seen *them*; and to hear *those things* which ye hear, and have not heard *them*. • And he said unto them, Know ye not this parable? [A]nd how then will ye know all parables? •

¶ Hear ye therefore the parable of the sower. • Now the parable is this: The seed is the word of God. • The sower soweth the word. • {Those / [T]hese} • by the way side are they that hear; • where the word is sown; but when {they / anyone} • {have heard, / heareth} the word of the kingdom, and understandeth *it* not, • then cometh the devil, • Satan • the wicked *one*, • immediately, and {taketh / catcheth} away • the word {that / which} was sown in {his / their} hearts • out of their hearts, lest they should believe and be saved. • This is he which received seed by the way side. • And these are they likewise • that received the seed • which are sown {on / into} {stony places, / stony ground; / the rock} • the same • {*are they,* which, / is he that / who,} when they {have heard / hear, / heareth} the word, and {anon / immediately} • with {joy / gladness}; • receiveth {it / the word}[.] Yet • these • {hath / have} {no root in themselves / he not root in himself,} {but dureth for a while: / and so endure but for a time:} • [W]hich for a while believe, and in time of temptation fall away. [F]or • afterward, • when tribulation or • afflicttion or persecution ariseth {for / because} of the • word's sake, {immediately / by and by} {he is / they are} offended. • And that which fell among thorns • these are {they / [h]e} also that received seed • which are sown among thorns; such as • that heareth the word; • which, when they have heard, go forth, • [a]nd the cares of this world, and the deceitfulness of riches, and the lusts of other {things / pleasures} of *this* life, • entering in, choke the word, and it becometh unfruitful • and bring no fruit to perfection. But {that / these} • on the good ground are {they / he} that received seed, • which are sown {on / into} the good ground is {he / such} as hear the word, and receive *it*, • and understandeth *it*; •

MATTHEW	MARK	LUKE	JOHN

which in an honest and good heart, having heard the word, keep *it*, • also beareth fruit, • and bring forth fruit with patience • some thirtyfold, some sixty, and some an hundred.

¶ And he said unto them, Is a candle brought to be put under a bushel or under a bed? [A]nd not to be set on a candlestick? • No man, when he hath lighted a candle, covereth it with a vessel, or putteth it under a bed; but setteth *it* on a candlestick, that they which enter in may see the light. • For there is nothing {hid, / secret,} {that / which} shall not be {manisfested; / made manifest;} • neither was anything kept {secret, / hid,} {that shall not / but that it should} • be known and come abroad. • If any man hath ears to hear, let him hear. And he said unto them, Take heed • therefore {how / what} ye hear: [W]ith what measure ye mete, it shall be measured to you: [A]nd unto you that hear shall more be given. For he • whosoever • that hath, to him shall be given: [A]nd he • whosoever • that hath not, • from him shall be taken even that which he seemeth to have.

¶ Then came to him *his* mother and his brethren, and could not come at him for the press. And it was told him *by certain* which said, Thy mother and thy brethren stand without, desiring to see thee. And he answered and said unto them, My mother and my brethren are these which hear the word of God, and do it. •

¶ Another parable put he forth unto them, saying, The kingdom of heaven is likened unto a man which sowed good seed in his field: But while men slept, his enemy came and sowed tares among the wheat, and went his way. But when the blade was sprung up, and brought forth fruit, then appeared the tares also. So the servants of the householder came and said unto him, Sir, didst not thou sow good seed in thy field? [F]rom whence then hath it tares? He said unto them, An enemy hath done this. The servants said unto him, Wilt thou then that we go and gather them up? But he said, Nay; lest while ye gather up the tares, ye root up also the wheat with them. Let both grow together until the harvest: [A]nd in the time of harvest I will say to the reapers, Gather ye together first the tares, and bind them in bundles to burn them: [B]ut gather the wheat into my barn.•

MATTHEW	MARK	LUKE	JOHN

¶ And he said, So is the kingdom of God, as if a man should cast seed into the ground; [a]nd should sleep, and rise night and day, and the seed should spring and grow up, he knoweth not how. For the earth bringeth forth fruit of herself; first the blade, then the ear, after that the full corn in the ear. But when the fruit is brought forth, immediately he putteth in the sickle, because the harvest is come.•

¶ Another parable put he forth unto them, saying, • Whereunto shall we liken the kingdom of God? [O]r with what comparison shall we compare it? • The kingdom of heaven is like to a grain of mustard seed, which a man took, and sowed in his field: • [W]hich, when it is sown in the earth, • indeed is the {least of / less than} all the seeds that be in the earth: But when it is sown, it growth up, • when it is grown, it • becometh • the greatest among • all herbs, • and becometh a tree, • and shooteth out great branches; so that the {fowls / birds} of the air • may • come and lodge in the branches thereof • under the shadow of it. •

¶ Another parable spake he unto them; The kingdom of heaven is like unto leaven, which a woman took, and hid in three measures of meal, till the whole was leavened. All these things spake Jesus unto the multitude in parables; • [a]nd with many such parables spake he the word unto them, as they were able to hear *it*. But without a parable spake he not unto them: • That it might be fulfilled which was spoken by the prophet, saying, I will open my mouth in parables; I will utter things which have been kept secret from the foundation of the world. Then Jesus sent the multitude away, and went into the house: [A]nd his disciples came unto him, saying, Declare unto us the parable of the tares of the field. • [A]nd when they were alone, he expounded all things to his disciples. • He answered and said unto them, He that soweth the good seed is the Son of man; [t]he field is the world; the good seed are the children of the kingdom; but the tares are the children of the wicked *one*; [t]he enemy that sowed them is the devil; the harvest is the end of the world; and the reapers are the angels. As therefore the tares are gathered and burned in the fire; so shall it be in the end of this world. The Son of man shall send forth his angels, and they shall gather out of his kingdom all things that offend, and

MATTHEW	MARK	LUKE	JOHN

them which do iniquity; [a]nd shall cast them into a furnace of fire: [T]here shall be wailing and gnashing of teeth. Then shall the righteous shine forth as the sun in the kingdom of their Father. Who hath ears to hear let him hear.

¶ Again, the kingdom of heaven is like unto treasure hid in a field; the which when a man hath found, he hideth, and for joy thereof goeth and selleth all that he hath, and buyeth that field.

¶ Again, the kingdom of heaven is like unto a merchant man, seeking goodly pearls: Who, when he had found one pearl of great price, went and sold all that he had, and bought it.

¶ Again, the kingdom of heaven is like unto a net, that was cast into the sea, and gathered of every kind: Which, when it was full, they drew to shore, and sat down, and gathered the good into vessels, but cast the bad away. So shall it be at the end of the world: [T]he angels shall come forth, and sever the wicked from among the just, [a]nd shall cast them into the furnace of fire: [T]here shall be wailing and gnashing of teeth. Jesus saith unto them, Have ye understood all these things? They say unto him, Yea, Lord. Then said he unto them, Therefore every scribe *which is* instructed unto the kingdom of heaven is like unto a man *that is* an householder, which bringeth forth out of his treasure *things* new and old.•

Ω

Redaction: Open My Mouth in a Parable

MATTHEW	MARK	LUKE	JOHN

MATTHEW	MARK	LUKE	JOHN

- Country of the Gadarenes -

Matt 13:53 • Mark 04:35-05:21 • Luke 08:22-40 • John

¶ Now it came to pass • that when Jesus had finished these parables, • on {a certain / the same} day, when the even was come, • that he went into a ship with his disciples: and he said unto them, • Let us {pass / go} over unto the other side of the lake. • And when they had sent away the multitude, • he departed thence • [a]nd they launched forth. • [T]hey took him even as he was in the ship. And there were also with him other little ships. • But as they sailed he fell asleep: and there {came down / arose} a great storm of wind, • on the lake; • and the waves beat into the ship, • they were filled *with water*, • that it was now full • and were in jeopardy. • And he was in the hinder part of the ship, asleep on a pillow: • And they came to him, and {awoke / awake} him, and they and say unto him, Master, carest thou not that we perish? • Then he arose, and rebuked the wind and the raging of the water: • [A]nd said unto the sea, Peace, be still. And the wind ceased, and there was a great calm. • And he said unto them, Where is your faith? • Why are ye so fearful? [H]ow is it that ye have no faith? • And they being afraid • feared exceedingly, and • wondered, saying one to another, What manner of man is this! [F]or he commandeth even the winds and water, and they obey him. •

¶ A[nd] they came over unto the other side of the sea, • [a]nd they arrived at the country of the Gadarenes, which is over against Galilee. • And when he was come out of the ship, • he went forth to land, • immediately there met him out of the tombs • of the city a certain man, • with an unclean spirit, • which had devils long time, and ware no clothes, neither abode in *any* house, • [w]ho had *his* dwelling among the tombs; and no man could bind him, no, not with chains: Because that he had been often bound with fetters and chains, and the chains had been plucked asunder by him, and the fetters broken in pieces: [N]either could any *man* tame him. And always, night and day, he was in the mountains, and in the tombs, crying, and cutting himself with stones. But when he saw Jesus afar off, • he cried out, • he ran • and fell down before him, • and worshipped him, [a]nd cried with a loud voice, and said, What have I to do with thee, Jesus, *thou* Son of the most high God? • I {beseech / adjure} thee

MATTHEW	MARK	LUKE	JOHN

by God, that thou torment me not. For he said unto him, Come out of the man, *thou* unclean spirit. • For oftentimes it had caught him: and he was kept bound with chains and in fetters; and he brake the bands and was driven of the devil into the wilderness. And Jesus asked him, saying, What is thy name? And he answered, saying, My name *is* Legion: for we are many. • [B]ecause many devils were entered into him. And they besought him much that he would not {send / command} • them away out of the country • out into the deep. • Now there was there nigh unto the mountains a great • herd of many swine feeding on the mountain: • And all the devils besought him, • that he would suffer them to enter into them • saying, Send us into the swine, that we may enter into them. • And he suffered them. • And forthwith Jesus gave them leave. Then went the • {unclean spirits / devils} out of the man, and entered into the swine: [A]nd the herd ran violently down a steep place into the {lake, / sea,} (they were about two thousand;) and were choked in the sea. • When they that fed *them* saw what was done, they fled, and went and told *it* in the city and in the country. • And they went out to see what it was that was done. And they come to Jesus, • and found the man, • that was possessed with the devil, and had the legion, • out of whom the devils were departed, sitting at the feet of Jesus, clothed, and in his right mind: [A]nd they were afraid. They also which saw *it* told them {by what means / how} it befell to {him / he} that was possessed of the devils was healed • and *also* concerning the swine.•

¶ Then the whole multitude of the country of the Gadarenes round about besought • And they began to pray him • to depart from them; • out of their coasts • for they were taken with great fear: [A]nd he went up into the ship, • [a]nd when he was come into the ship, • and returned back again. Now the man out of whom the devils were departed {besought / prayed} • him that he might be with him: • Howbeit Jesus suffered him not, • but Jesus sent him away, saying • unto him, Go home to thy friends, • [r]eturn to thine own house, • and tell them • and show how great things • the Lord • God hath done {unto / for} thee, and hath had compassion on thee. • And he went his way, • [a]nd he departed, and began to publish • throughout the whole city • in Decapolis how great things Jesus had done {for / unto} him • and all *men* did marvel. • And it came to pass, that, when Jesus was {returned / passed over}

MATTHEW	MARK	LUKE	JOHN

again by ship unto the other side, much people gathered unto him: [A]nd he was nigh unto the sea. •

[T]he people *gladly* received him: [F]or they were all waiting for him.

Ω

Redaction: Open My Mouth in a Parable

MATTHEW	MARK	LUKE	JOHN

MATTHEW	MARK	LUKE	JOHN

- A Man Named Jairus -

Matt 13:54-58 • Mark 05:22-06:1-13 • Luke 08:41- 09:01-06 • John

¶ And, behold, there came a man named Jairus, and he was • one of the rulers • of the synagogue: • [A]nd when he saw him, • he fell down at Jesus' feet, and besought him • greatly • that he would come into his house: • And saying, My little daughter lieth at the point of death: *I pray thee*, come and lay thy hands on her, that she may be healed; and she shall live. • For he had one only daughter, about twelve years of age, and she lay a dying. • And *Jesus* went with him; and much people followed him, • [b]ut as he went the people thronged him.

¶ And a certain woman, which had an issue of blood twelve years, And had suffered many things of many physicians, and had spent all • her living • that she had,• upon physicians, • and was nothing bettered, • neither could be healed of any, • but rather grew worse, [w]hen she had heard of Jesus, came in the press behind • *him*, and touched the border of his garment: For she said, If I may touch but his clothes, I shall be whole. And {straightway / immediately} her {issue / fountain} of her blood was {dried up / stanched.} • [A]nd she felt in *her* body that she was healed of that plague. And Jesus, immediately knowing in himself that virtue had gone out of him, turned him about in the press, and said, Who touched my clothes? • Who touched me? When all denied, Peter and {they / his disciples} • that were with him said, Master, • Thou seest the multitude thronging thee, • and press *thee*, and sayest thou, Who touched me? And Jesus said, Somebody hath touched me: [F]or I perceive that virtue is gone out of me. • And he looked round about to see her that had done this thing. • And when the woman saw that she was not hid, she came • fearing and trembling, knowing what was done in her, • and falling down before him, she declared unto him before all the people • the truth • for what cause she had touched him, and how she was healed immediately. And he said unto her, Daughter, be of good comfort: [T]hy faith hath made thee whole; go in peace • and be whole of thy plague. •

MATTHEW	MARK	LUKE	JOHN

¶ While he yet spake, there cometh one from the ruler of the synagogue's *house*, • which said, Thy daughter is dead: [W]hy troublest thou the Master any further? As soon as Jesus heard the word that was spoken, • he answered him, saying, • unto the ruler of the synagogue, • Fear not: • Be not afraid, • believe only, and she shall be made whole. • And he suffered no man to follow him, save Peter, and James, and John the brother of James. And he cometh to the house of the ruler of the synagogue, and seeth the tumult, and them that wept and wailed greatly. • And when he came into the house, he suffered no man to go in, save Peter, and James, and John, and the father and the mother of the maiden. And all wept, and bewailed her: [B]ut he said, • unto them, Why make ye this ado, and weep? • Weep not; • the damsel is not dead, but sleepeth. • And they laughed him to scorn, knowing that she was dead. And he put them all out, • But when he had put them all out, he taketh the father and the mother of the damsel, and them that were with him, and entereth in where the damsel was lying. And he took the damsel by the hand, and said unto her, Talitha cumi; which is, being interpreted, {Damsel, / Maid,} • I say unto thee, arise. • And her spirit came again, and • straightway the damsel arose, and walked; for she was *of the age* of twelve years. • [A]nd he commanded to give her meat. And her parents were astonished: • [W]ith a great astonishment. And he charged them straitly that no man should know it; • that they should tell know man what was done • and commanded that something should be given her to eat. •

¶ A[nd] he went out from thence, and came into his own country; • [a]nd when he was come into his own country, • his disciples follow him. And when the sabbath day was come, he began to teach in the synagogue: [I]nsomuch that • many hearing *him* were astonished, saying, From whence hath this *man* these things? • Whence hath this *man* this wisdom, • [A]nd [W]hat wisdom *is* this which is given unto him, that even such mighty works are wrought by his hands? • Is not this the carpenter's son? [I]s not his mother called Mary? • Is not this the carpenter, the son of Mary, the brother of James, and Joses, and of • Simon, and Judas? And his sisters, are they not all • here with us? • Whence then hath this *man* all these things? • And they were offended {at / in} him. • But Jesus said unto them, A prophet is

MATTHEW	MARK	LUKE	JOHN

not without honor, but in his own country, and among his own kin, and in his own house. • And he did not many mighty works there because of their unbelief • save that he laid his hands upon a few sick folk, and healed *them*. And he marvelled because of there unbelief. And he went round about the villages, teaching. •

¶ T[hen] he called his twelve disciples together, • and began to send them forth by two and two; • and gave them power and authority over all {devils / unclean spirits;} • and to cure diseases. And he sent them to preach the kingdom of God, and to heal the sick. • And commanded them that they should take nothing for *their* journey, • [a]nd he said unto them, Take nothing for *your* journey, neither staves, nor scrip, neither bread, neither money; • save a staff only; [b]ut *be* shod with sandals; • neither have two coats apeice. • And he said unto them, In what place soever ye enter into an house, there abide till ye depart from that place • and thence depart. • And whosoever shall not receive you, nor hear you, when ye {depart thence, / go out} of that city • shake off the dust under your feet for a testimony against them. Verily I say unto you, It shall be more tolerable for Sodom and Gomorrah in the day of judgment, than for that city. • And they departed, and went through the towns, preaching the gospel, • that men should repent. And they cast out many devils, and anointed with oil many that were sick, and healed *them* • healing everywhere.

Ω

Redaction: Open My Mouth in a Parable

MATTHEW	MARK	LUKE	JOHN

MATTHEW	MARK	LUKE	JOHN

- Herod the Tetrarch -

Matt 14:01-12 • Mark 06:14-29 • Luke 09:07-09 • John

¶ Now [at] that time Herod the tetrarch heard of the fame of Jesus, • all that was done by him: • ([F]or his name was spread abroad:) • [A]nd he was perplexed, because that it was said of some, that John was risen from the dead; • [a]nd said unto his servants, This is John the Baptist; he is risen from the dead; and therefore mighty works do shew forth themselves in him. • Others said, [t]hat [I]t is Elias. • [T]hat Elias had appeared • [a]nd others said, [t]hat [I]t is a prophet, or as one of the prophets. • [T]hat [O]ne of the old prophets was risen again. • But when Herod heard *thereof*, he said, It is John, whom I have beheaded: [H]e is risen from the dead.

¶ For Herod himself had sent forth and laid hold upon John, and bound him • and put *him* in prison for Herodias' sake, his brother Philip's wife • for he had married her. For John had said unto Herod, It is not lawful for thee to have thy brother's wife. Therefore Herodias had a quarrel against him, and would have killed him; but she could not: For Herod feared John, knowing that he was a just man and an holy, and observed him; and when he heard him, he did many things, and heard him gladly. • And when he would have put him to death, he feared the multitude, because they counted him as a prophet. But when Herod's birthday was kept, • a convenient day was come, that Herod on his birthday made a supper to his lords, high captains, and chief *estates* of Galilee; [a]nd when the daughter of the said Herodias came in, and danced, and pleased Herod and them that sat with him, • [w]hereupon • the king • promised with an oath • unto the damsel, Ask of me whatsoever thou wilt, and I will give *it* thee. And he sware unto her, Whatsoever thou shalt ask of me, I will give *it* thee, unto the half of my kingdom. And she went forth, and said unto her mother, What shall I ask? And she said, The head of John the Baptist. And she came in straightway with haste unto the king, [a]nd she, being before instructed, of her mother, • asked, saying, I will that thou give me by and by in a charger the head of John the Baptist. And the king was exceeding sorry; *yet* • nevertheless • for his oath's sake, and for their sakes which sat with him • at meat, • he would not reject her. • [H]e commanded *it* to be given *her*. • And

MATTHEW	MARK	LUKE	JOHN

immediately the king sent an executioner, and commanded his head to be brought: [A]nd he went and beheaded him in the prison, [a]nd brought his head in a charger, and gave it to the damsel: • [A]nd she brought *it* to her mother • and the damsel gave it to her mother. And when his disciples heard *of it*, they came and took up his {corpse / the body} • and laid it in a tomb • and buried it, and went and told Jesus. • And Herod said, John have I beheaded: [B]ut who is this, of whom I hear such things? And he desired to see him.

AΩ

Chapter 8

BREAD FROM HEAVEN

Nehemiah 9:13-15

Redaction: Bread from Heaven

MATTHEW	MARK	LUKE	JOHN

MATTHEW	MARK	LUKE	JOHN

- A Desert Place -

Matt 14:13-21 • Mark 06:30-44 • Luke 09:10-17 • John 06:1-14

¶ A[fter] these things • the apostles, when they were returned, • gathered themselves together unto Jesus, and told him all things, both what they had done, and what they had taught. • W[hen] Jesus heard *of it*, • he said unto them, Come ye yourselves apart into a desert place, and rest a while: [F]or there were many coming and going, and they had no leisure so much as to eat. • And {he / Jesus} • took them, • [a]nd they departed • thence by ship • over the sea of Galilee, which is *the sea* of Tiberias • and went aside privately • into a desert place apart: • [B]elonging to the city called Bethsaida. • And the people saw them departing, and many knew him, • [a]nd the people, when they {knew *it*, / had heard *thereof*,} they followed him • and ran afoot thither out of all • the cities • and outwent them, and came together unto him. • And a great multitude followed him, because they saw his miracles which he did on them that were diseased. And Jesus went up into a mountain, and there he sat with his disciples. And the passover, a feast of the Jews, was nigh.

¶ W[hen] Jesus lifted up *his* eyes, and saw a great company come unto him, • [a]nd Jesus, when he came out, • went forth, and saw {a great multitude, / much people,} and was moved with compassion toward them, because they were as sheep not having a shepherd: • [A]nd he received them, and spake unto them of the kingdom of God, • and he began to teach them many things • and healed them that had need of healing.

¶ A[nd] when {it was evening, / the day was now far spent, / the day began to wear away,} then • his • twelve • disciples came to him, saying • unto him, • This is a desert place, and now the time *is* far passed: • Send the multitude away, that they may go into the {towns / villages,} • and country round about, and lodge, • and buy themselves {victuals / bread:} [F]or they have nothing to eat. • But Jesus said unto them, They need not depart; give ye them to eat. • And they say unto him, Shall we go and buy two hundred pennyworth of bread, and give them to eat? • [H]e saith unto Philip, Whence shall

MATTHEW	MARK	LUKE	JOHN

we buy bread, that these may eat? And this he said to prove him: [F]or he himself knew what he would do. Philip answerd him, Two hundred pennyworth of bread is not sufficient for them, that every one of them may take a little. • He saith unto them, How many loaves have ye? [G]o and see. And when they knew, • [o]ne of his disciples, Andrew, Simon Peter's brother, saith unto him, There is a lad here, which hath • no more than • five barley loaves, and two small fishes: [B]ut what are they among so many? • [E]xcept we should go and by meat for all this people. For they were about five thousand men. • He said, Bring them hither to me. And he commanded the multitude to sit down on the grass, • [a]nd Jesus said • to his disciples, Make them sit down by fifties in a company • upon the green grass. • And they did so, and made them all sit down. • Now there was much grass in the place. So the men sat down, • in ranks, by hundreds, and by fifties • in number about five thousand. • Then {he / Jesus} took • the five loaves and two fishes, • [a]nd when he had taken the five loaves and the two fishes, he looked up to heaven, and blessed, and break the loaves, • and when he had given thanks, he {distributed / gave} them to his disciples • and the disciples to • set before {them / the multitude} • that were set down; and likewise of the • the two fishes divided he amongst them all • as much as they would. • And they did eat, and were all filled: • When they were filled, he said unto his disciples, Gather up the fragments that remain, that nothing be lost. Therefore they gathered *them* together, and filled twelve baskets • and there was taken up • twelve baskets full of the fragments • with the fragments of the five barley loaves, • and of the fishes • which remained over and above unto them that had eaten. • And they that had eaten • of the loaves • were about five thousand men, beside women and children. • Then those men, when they had seen the miracle that Jesus did, said, This is of a truth that prophet that should come into the world.

Ω

MATTHEW	MARK	LUKE	JOHN

- Walking on the Sea -

Matt 14:22-36 • Mark 06:45-56 • Luke • John 06:15-21

¶ W[hen] Jesus therefore perceived that they would come and take him by force, to make him a king, Jesus constrained his disciples • to get into the ship, • and go before him unto the other side, • unto Bethsaida, while he sent {away the people / the multitudes away.} And when he had sent the multitudes away, he {went up / departed} again into a mountain himself • apart to pray: [H]e was there alone • [a]nd when • the evening • was *now* come, his disciples went down unto the sea, [a]nd entered into a ship, and went over the sea toward Capernaum. And it was now dark, and Jesus was not come to them. • But the ship was now in the midst of the sea, • and he alone on the land. • And the sea arose by reason of a great wind that blew. • And he saw them toiling in rowing; • tossed with waves: • [F]or the wind was contrary unto them: • So when they had rowed about five and twenty or thirty furlongs, • in • about • the fourth watch of the night Jesus {went / cometh} unto them, walking upon the sea, and would have passed by them. • [T]hey see Jesus walking on the sea, and drawing nigh unto the ship: • But when • the disciples saw him walking on the sea, they were troubled, • they supposed it had been a spirit, • saying, It is a spirit; [A]nd they {cried out for fear. / were afraid.} For they all saw him, and were troubled. • But {straightway / immediately} Jesus {spake unto / talked with} them, and said unto them, Be of good cheer: [I]t is I; be not afraid. • And Peter answered him and said, Lord, if it be thou, bid me come unto thee on the water. And he said, Come. And when Peter was come down out of the ship, he walked on the water, to go to Jesus. But when he saw the wind boisterous, he was afraid; and beginning to sink, he cried, saying, Lord, save me. And immediately Jesus stretched forth *his* hand, and caught him, and said unto him, O thou of little faith, wherefore didst thou doubt? • Then they willingly received him into the ship: • And he went up unto them into the ship; • [a]nd when they were come into the ship, the wind ceased • and they were sore amazed in themselves beyond measure, and wondered. For they considered not *the miracle* of the loaves: [F]or their heart was hardened. • Then they that were in the ship came and worshipped him, saying, Of a truth thou art the Son of God.

Redaction: Bread from Heaven

MATTHEW	MARK	LUKE	JOHN

¶ A[nd] when they were {gone / passed} over, • immediately • they came into the land of Gennesaret, • and the ship was at the land whither they went • and drew to the shore. And when they were come out of the ship, straightway • when the men of that place had knowledge of him, they sent out into • [a]nd ran through • all • that whole {region / country} round about, • and began to carry about in beds those that were sick, • and brought unto him all that were diseased; • where they heard he was. And whithersoever he entered, into villages, or cities, or country, they laid the sick in the streets, and besought him that they might • only touch • if it were but the {border / hem} of his garment: • and as many as touched him were made • perfectly whole.

Ω

MATTHEW	MARK	LUKE	JOHN

- The Bread of God -

Matt • Mark • Luke • John 06:22-71

¶ T[he] day following, when the people which stood on the other side of the sea saw that there was none other boat there, save that one whereinto his disciples were entered, and that Jesus went not with his disciples into the boat, but *that* his disciples were gone away alone; ([h]owbeit there came other boats from Tiberias nigh unto the place where they did eat bread, after that the Lord had given thanks:) When the people therefore saw that Jesus was not there, neither his disciples, they also took shipping, and came to Capernaum, seeking for Jesus. And when they had found him on the other side of the sea, they said unto him, Rabbi, when camest thou hither? Jesus answered them and said, Verily, verily, I say unto you, Ye seek me, not because ye saw the miracles, but because ye did eat of the loaves and were filled. Labor not for the meat which perisheth, but for that meat which endureth unto everlasting life, which the Son of man shall give unto you: [F]or him hath God the Father sealed. Then said they unto him, What shall we do, that we might work the works of God? Jesus answered and said unto them, This is the work of God, that ye believe on him whom he hath sent. They said therefore unto him, What sign shewest thou then, that we may see, and believe thee? [W]hat dost thou work? Our fathers did eat manna in the desert; as it is written, He gave them bread from heaven to eat. Then Jesus said unto them, Verily, verily, I say unto you, Moses gave you not that bread from heaven; but my Father giveth you the true bread from heaven. For the bread of God is he which cometh down from heaven, and giveth life unto the world. Then said they unto him, Lord, evermore give us this bread. And Jesus said unto them, I am the bread of life: [H]e that cometh to me shall never hunger; and he that believeth on me shall never thirst. But I said unto you, That ye also have seen me, and believe not. All that the Father giveth me shall come to me; and him that cometh to me I will in no wise cast out. For I came down from heaven, not to do mine own will, but the will of him that sent me. And this is the Father's will which hath sent me, that of all which he hath given me I should lose nothing, but should raise it up again at the last day. And this is the will of him that sent me, that everyone which seeth the

MATTHEW	MARK	LUKE	JOHN

Son, and believeth on him, may have everlasting life: [A]nd I will raise him up at the last day. The Jews then murmured at him, because he said, I am the bread which came down from heaven. And they said, Is not this Jesus, the son of Joseph, whose father and mother we know? [H]ow is it then that he saith, I came down from heaven? Jesus therefore answered and said unto them, Murmur not among yourselves. No man can come to me, except the Father which hath sent me draw him: [A]nd I will raise him up at the last day. It is written in the prophets, And they shall be all taught of God. Every man therefore that hath heard, and hath learned of the Father, cometh unto me. Not that any man hath seen the Father, save he which is of God, he hath seen the Father. Verily, verily, I say unto you, He that believeth on me hath everlasting life. I am that bread of life. Your fathers did eat manna in the wilderness, and are dead. This is the bread which cometh down from heaven, that a man may eat thereof, and not die. I am the living bread which came down from heaven: [I]f any man eat of this bread, he shall live forevever: [A]nd the bread that I will give is my flesh, which I will give for the life of the world. The Jews therefore strove among themselves, saying, How can this man give us *his* flesh to eat? Then Jesus said unto them, Verily, verily, I say unto you, Except ye eat the flesh of the Son of man, and drink his blood, ye have no life in you, [w]hoso eateth my flesh, and drinketh my blood, hath eternal life; and I will raise him up at the last day. For my flesh is meat indeed, and my blood is drink indeed. He that eateth my flesh, and drinketh my blood, dwelleth in me, and I in him. As the living Father hath sent me, and I live by the Father: [S]o he that eateth me, even he shall live by me. This is the bread which came down from heaven: [N]ot as your fathers did eat manna, and are dead: [H]e that eateth of this bread shall live for ever. These things said he in the synagogue, as he taught in Capernaum. Many therefore of his disciples, when they had heard *this*, said, This is an hard saying; who can hear it? When Jesus knew in himself that his disciples murmured at it, he said unto them, Doth this offend you? *What* and if ye shall see the Son of man ascend up where he was before? It is the spirit that quickeneth; the flesh profiteth nothing: [T]he words that I speak unto you, *they* are spirit and *they* are life. But there are some of you that believe not. For Jesus knew from the beginning who they were

MATTHEW	MARK	LUKE	JOHN

that believed not, and who should betray him. And he said, Therefore said I unto you, that no man can come unto me, except it were given unto him of my Father.

¶ F[rom] that *time* many of his disciples went back, and walked no more with him. Then said Jesus unto the twelve, Will ye also go away? Then Simon Peter answered him, Lord, to whom shall we go? [T]hou hast the words of eternal life. And we believe and art sure that thou are that Christ, the Son of the living God. Jesus answered them, Have not I chosen you twelve, and one of you is a devil? He spake of Judas Iscariot *the son* of Simon: [F]or he it was that should betray him, being one of the twelve.

Ω

Redaction: Bread from Heaven

MATTHEW	MARK	LUKE	JOHN

MATTHEW	MARK	LUKE	JOHN

- Tradition of Men -

Matt 15:01-28 • Mark 07:01-30 • Luke • John

¶ T[hen] came together unto • Jesus • the Pharisees, and certain of the scribes, which came from Jerusalem. And when they saw some of his disciples eat bread with defiled, that is to say, with unwashen, hands, they found fault. For the Pharisees and all the Jews, except they wash *their* hands oft, eat not, holding the tradition of the elders. And *when they come* from the market, except they wash, they eat not. And many other things there be, which they have received to hold, *as* the washng of cups, and pots, brasen vessels, and of tables. Then the Pharisees and scribes asked him, • saying, Why do thy disciples transgress the tradition of the elders? • Why walk not thy disciples according to the tradition of the elders, • for they wash not their hands when they eat bread • but eat bread with unwashen hands? • But he answered and said unto them, Why do ye also transgress the commandment of God by your tradition? • He answered and said unto them, Well hath Esaias prophesied of you hypocrites, as it is written, This people honoureth me with *their* lips, but their heart is far from me. Howbeit in vain do they worship me, teaching *for* doctrines the commandments of men. For laying aside the commandment of God, ye hold the tradition of men, *as* the washing of pots and cups: [A]nd many other such like things ye do. And he said unto them, Full well ye reject the commandment of God, that ye may keep your own tradition. For Moses said, • God commanded, saying, • Honour thy father and thy mother; and, {Whoso / He that} curseth father or mother, let him die the death. • But ye say, {If a man / Whosoever} shall say to *his* father or *his* mother, • *It is* Corban, that is to say, • *It is* a gift, by whatsoever thou mightest be profited by me; [a]nd honor not his father or his mother, *he shall be free.* • And ye suffer him no more to do ought for his father or his mother; • [t]hus have ye made the commandment of • the word of God of none effect through your tradition, which ye have delivered: [A]nd many such like things do ye. • *Ye* hypocrites, well did Esaias prophesy of you, saying, This people draweth nigh unto me with their mouth, and honoureth me with *their* lips; but their heart is far from me. But in vain they do worship me, teaching *for* doctrines the commandments of men. •

MATTHEW	MARK	LUKE	JOHN

¶ A[nd] when he had called all the {people / multitude} • *unto him*, he said unto them, • {Hear, / Hearken} unto me every one *of you*, and understand: There is nothing from without a man, that entering into him can defile him: • Not that which goeth into the mouth defileth a man; but that which cometh out of the mouth, • the things which come out of him, those are they that defile the man. If any man hath ears to hear, let him hear. • Then came his disciples, and said unto him, Knowest thou that the Pharisees were offended, after they heard this saying? But he answered and said, Every plant, which my heavenly Father hath not planted, shall be rooted up. Let them alone: [T]hey be blind leaders of the blind. And if the blind lead the blind, both shall fall into the ditch. • And when he was entered into the house from the people, his disciples asked him concerning the parable. • Then answered Peter and said unto him, Declare unto us this parable. And Jesus said, • unto them, Are ye so without understanding also? • Do not ye yet understand, • [d]o ye not perceive, that whatsoever thing from without entereth into the man, *it* can not defile him; [b]ecause it entereth not into his heart, • that whatsoever entereth in at the mouth goeth into the belly, and is cast out into the draught • purging all meats? • But those things which proceed out of the mouth come forth from the heart; • [t]hat which cometh out of the man, that defileth the man. For from within, out of the heart of men, proceed evil thoughts, adulteries, fornications, murders, • thefts, false witness, • coveteousness, wickedness, deceit, lasciviousness, an evil eye, blasphemy, pride, foolishness: All these evil things come from within, • which defile a man: [B]ut to eat with unwashen hands defileth not a man.

Ω

MATTHEW	MARK	LUKE	JOHN

- Bread in the Wilderness -

Matt 15:29-16:12 • Mark 07:31-08: 26 • Luke • John

¶ Then Jesus • arose, • went • from • thence, and departed into the {coasts / borders} of Tyre and Sidon, and entered into an house, and would have no man know *it:* [B]ut he could not be hid. • And, behold, • [f]or a *certain* woman, • of Canaan came out of the same coasts, • whose young daughter had an unclean spirit, heard of him, and came and fell at his feet: The woman was a Greek, a Syrophenician by nation; and she besought him • and cried unto him, saying, Have mercy on me, O Lord, *thou* Son of David; my daughter is greviously vexed with a devil. • [T]hat he would cast forth the devil out of her daughter. But he answered her not a word. And his disciples came and besought him, saying, Send her away; for she crieth after us. But he answered and said, I am not sent but unto the lost sheep of the house of Israel. Then came she and worshipped him, saying, Lord, help me. • But Jesus • answered and said • unto her, Let the children first be filled: • It is not meet to take the children's bread, and to cast *it* • unto the dogs. And she answered and said unto him, • Truth, • [y]es, Lord: [Y]et the dogs under the table eat of the children's crumbs • which fall from their masters' table. Then Jesus answered and said unto her, O woman, great *is* thy faith: [B]e it unto thee even as thou wilt. • For this saying go thy way; the devil is gone out of thy daughter. And when she was come to her house, she found the devil gone out, and her daughter laid upon the bed. • And her daughter was made whole from that very hour.

¶ And Jesus departed from thence, • [a]nd again, departing from the coasts of Tyre and Sidon, he came • nigh unto the sea of Galilee; • through the midst of the coasts of Decapolis • and went up into a mountain, and sat down there. And great multitudes came unto him, having with them *those that were* lame, blind, dumb, maimed, and many others, and cast them down at Jesus' feet; and he healed them: Insomuch that the multitude wondered, when they saw the dumb to speak, the maimed to be whole, the lame to walk, and the blind to see: • And they bring unto him one that was deaf, and had an impediment in his speech; and they beseech him to put his hand upon him. And he took him aside from the multitude, and put his fingers into his ears, and he spit, and touched his tongue; [a]nd looking up to

MATTHEW	MARK	LUKE	JOHN

heaven, he sighed, and saith unto him, E[phphatha], that is, Be opened. And straightway his ears were opened, and the string of his tongue was loosed, and he spake plain. And he charged them that they should tell no man: [B]ut the more he charged them, so much the more a great deal they published *it*; • and they glorified the God of Israel. • And were beyond measure astonished, saying, He hath done all things well: [H]e maketh both the deaf to hear and the dumb to speak.

¶ I[n] those days the multitude being very great, and having nothing to eat, • [t]hen Jesus called his disciples *unto him*, • and saith unto them, I have compassion on the multitude, because they {have now been with me / continue with me now} three days, and have nothing to eat: • And if I send them away fasting to their own houses, they will faint by the way: • I will not send them away fasting, lest they faint in the way • for diverse of them came from far. And his disciples answered • unto him, • From whence can a man satisfy these *men* with bread here in the wilderness? • Whence should we have so much bread in the wilderness, to fill so great a multitude? And Jesus saith unto them, How many loaves have ye? And they said, Seven, and a few little fishes. And he commanded the {multitude / people} to sit down on the ground: [A]nd he took the seven loaves, and gave thanks, and brake, and gave to his disciples to set before *them*; and they did set *them* before the people. And they had a few small fishes: [A]nd he blessed, and commanded to set them also before *them*. • And they did all eat, and were filled: [A]nd they took up of the broken *meat* that was left seven baskets full.

¶ And they that had eaten were about four thousand • men, beside women and children • and he sent • the multitude • away.

¶ And straightway he entered into a ship with his disciples, and came into the parts of Dalmanutha • into the coasts of Magdala. • And the Pharisees • also with the Sadducees • came forth, and began to question with him, • {desired / seeking} of him • that he would shew them a sign from • heaven, tempting him. And he sighed deeply in his spirit, and • He answered and said unto them, When it is evening, ye say, *It will be* fair weather: [F]or the sky is red. And in the morning, *It will be* foul

MATTHEW	MARK	LUKE	JOHN

weather to day: [F]or the sky is red and lowring. O *ye* hypocrites, ye can discern the face of the sky;

but can ye not *discern* the signs of the times? • Why doth this generation seek after a sign? • A wicked

and adulterous generation seeketh after a sign; and there shall no sign be given unto {it, / this

generation} • but the sign of the prophet Jonas. • And he left them, and entering into the ship again

departed to the other side.

¶ Now • when his disciples were come to the other side, they had forgotten to take bread •

neither had they in the ship with them more than one loaf. • Then {Jesus / he} charged them, saying, •

Take heed and beware of the leaven of the Pharisees, and of the Sadducees • and *of* the leaven of Herod. •

And they reasoned among themselves, saying, *It is* because we have taken no bread. *Which* when Jesus

{perceived / knew *it,*} • he said unto them, O ye of little faith, why reason ye among yourselves, because

ye have brought no bread? • [P]erceive ye not yet, neither understand? [H]ave ye your heart yet

hardened? Having eyes, see ye not? [A]nd having ears, hear ye not? [A]nd do ye not remember? When I

break the five loaves among five thousand, how many baskets full of fragments took ye up? They say unto

him, Twelve. And when the seven among four thousand, how many baskets full of fragments took ye up?

And they said, Seven. • How is it that ye do not understand that I spake *it* not to you concerning bread, that

ye should beware of the leaven of the Pharisees and of the Saducees? Then understood they how that he

bade *them* not beware of the leaven of bread, but of the doctrine of the Pharisees and of the Saducees. •

¶ And he cometh to Bethsaida; and they bring a blind man unto him, and besought him to

touch him. And he took the blind man by the hand, and led him out of the town; and when he had spit

on his eyes, and put his hands upon him, he asked him if he saw ought. And he looked up, and said, I

see men as trees, walking. After that he put *his* hands again upon his eyes, and made him look up:

[A]nd he was restored, and saw every man clearly. And he sent him away to his house, saying, Neither

go into the town, nor tell *it* to any in the town.

ΑΩ

Redaction: Bread from Heaven

MATTHEW	MARK	LUKE	JOHN

Chapter 9

THE DAY OF ATONEMENT

Leviticus 26:27-28

Redaction: The Day of Atonement

MATTHEW	MARK	LUKE	JOHN

MATTHEW	MARK	LUKE	JOHN

- Whom Say Ye That I Am -

Matt 16:13-28 • Mark 08:27-09:01 • Luke 09:18-27 • John

¶ When Jesus {came / went} out, and his disciples, • into the coasts of • the towns of Caesarea Philippi: • [I]t came to pass, • by the way • as he was alone praying, his disciples were with him: [A]nd he asked {them / his disciples,} saying, Whom • {say the people / do men say} that I the Son of man am? • They answering said, • Some *say that thou art* John the Baptist: • [B]ut some *say*, Elias; and others *say*, • Jeremias, or • that one of the old prophets is risen again. • And he saith unto them, But whom say ye that I am? • And Simon Peter answered and said, Thou art the Christ, the Son of the living God. And Jesus answered and said unto him, Blessed art thou, Simon Barjona: [F]or flesh and blood hath not revealed *it* unto thee, but my Father which is in heaven. And I say also unto thee, That thou art Peter, and upon this rock I will build my church; and the gates of hell shall not prevail against it. And I will give unto thee the keys of the kingdom of heaven: [A]nd whatsoever thou shalt bind on earth shall be bound in heaven: [A]nd whatsoever thou shalt loose on earth shall be loosed in heaven. Then • he straitly charged • his disciples • and commanded *them* to tell no man that thing • of him • that he was Jesus the Christ.

¶ From that time forth began Jesus to {shew / teach} • unto his disciples, how that he must go unto Jerusalem, • [s]aying, The Son of man must suffer many things, and be rejected of the elders and chief priests and scribes, • and be killed, and • after three days • be raised again the third day. • And he spake that saying openly. • Then Peter took him, and began to rebuke him, saying, Be it far from thee, Lord: [T]his shall not be unto thee. • But when he had turned about and looked on his disciples, he rebuked Peter, saying, Get thee behind me, Satan: • [T]hou art an offence unto me: [F]or thou savourest not the things that be of God, • but the things that be of men.

¶ And when he had called the people *unto him* with his disciples also • [t]hen said Jesus unto • *them* all, {If any *man* / Whomsoever} will come after me, let him deny himself, • and take up his cross

MATTHEW	MARK	LUKE	JOHN

daily, and follow me. For whosoever will save his life shall lose it: [B]ut whosoever will lose his life for

my sake, • and the gospel's, the same shall {save / find} it. For what is a man {profited / advantaged}, if

he gain the whole world, and lose {himself / his own soul • or be cast away? • Or what shall a man give

in exhange for his soul? Whosoever therefore shall be ashamed of me and of my words, in this

adulterous and sinful generation; of him also shall the Son of man be ashamed, • when he shall come in

his own glory, and *in his* Father's, • with the holy angels. • For the Son of man shall come in the glory of

his Father with his angels; and then he shall reward every man according to his works.

¶ A[nd] he said unto them, • {I tell you of a truth / Verily I say unto you}, That there be some of

them that stand here, • which shall not taste of death, till they see the Son of man coming in his

kingdom. • [T]he kingdom of God come with power.

Ω

MATTHEW	MARK	LUKE	JOHN

- Transfigured Before Them -

Matt 17:01-13: • Mark 09:02-13 • Luke 09:28-36 • John

¶ And after six days Jesus taketh *with him* Peter, and James, and John, • his brother, • [a]nd it came to pass about an eight days after these sayings, he took Peter and John and James, • and {bringeth / leadeth} them up into an high mountain apart by themselves: • [T]o pray. And as he prayed, the fashion of his countenance was altered, • and he was transfigured before them. • And his face did shine as the sun, • and his raiment • became shining exceeding white as snow; • white *and* glistering • as the light • so as no fuller on earth can white them. • And, behold, there appeared unto them • two men, which were Moses and Elias • and they were talking with Jesus. • Who appeared in glory, and spake of his decease which he should accomplish at Jerusalem. But Peter and they that were with him were heavy with sleep: [A]nd when they were awake, they saw his glory, and the two men that stood with him. And it came to pass, as they departed from him, Peter said unto Jesus, • Lord, it is good for us to be here: [I]f thou wilt, let us make here three tabernacles; • one for thee, and one for Moses, and one for Elias: [N]ot knowing what he said. • For he wist not what to say; for they were sore afraid. • While he thus spake, • behold, • there came a • bright cloud • and overshadowed them: [A]nd they feared as they entered into the cloud. And • behold • there came a voice out of the cloud, • which said, This is my beloved Son, in whom I am well pleased; hear ye him. And when the disciples heard *it*, they fell on their face, and were sore afraid. And Jesus came and touched them, and said, Arise, and be not afraid. • And suddenly, • when the voice was past, • when they had lifted up their eyes, • looked round about, • Jesus was found alone. • [T]hey saw no man, • any more, save Jesus only with themselves. • And as they came down from the mountain, Jesus charged them, • that they should tell no man what things they had seen, • saying, Tell the vision to no man, until the Son of man be risen again from the dead. • And they kept that saying • close • with themselves, • and told no man in those days any of those things which they had seen. • Questioning one with another what the rising from the dead should mean. •

MATTHEW	MARK	LUKE	JOHN

¶ And his disciples asked him, saying, Why then say the scribes that Elias must first come? And Jesus answered • and told them, Elias verily cometh first, and restoreth all things; and how it is written of the Son of man, that he must suffer many things, and be set at nought. • But I say unto you, That Elias is • indeed come • already, and they knew him not, • and they have done unto him whatsoever they listed, as it is written of him. Likewise shall also the Son of man suffer of them. Then the disciples understood that he spake unto them of John the Baptist.

Ω

MATTHEW	MARK	LUKE	JOHN

- Help Thou Mine Unbelief -

Matt 17:14-21: • Mark 09:14-29 • Luke 09:37-42 • John

¶ And it came to pass, that on the next day, when they were come down from the hill, • when he came to *his* disciples, he saw a great multitude about them, and the scribes questioning with them. And straightway all the people, when they beheld him, were greatly amazed, and running to *him* saluted him. And he asked the scribes, What question ye with them? • And, behold, • there came to him a *certain* man, • of the company • kneeling down to him, • cried out, saying, Master, I beseech thee, • have mercy on my son: [F]or he is lunatic, and sore vexed: • I have brought unto thee my son, which hath a dumb spirit; • look upon my son: [F]or he is mine only child. And, lo, a spirit taketh him, and he suddenly crieth out; • [a]nd wheresoever he taketh him, he teareth him • that he foameth again, • and nasheth with his teeth, and pineth away: • [F]or oft times he falleth into the fire, and oft into the water • and bruising him hardly departeth from him. • And I brought him to thy disciples, • And I besought • and I spake to thy disciples that they should cast him out; and they could not • cure him. Then Jesus answered and said, O faithless and perverse generation, how long shall I be with you? [H]ow long shall I suffer you? • Bring thy son hither • unto me. And they brought him unto him: [A]nd when he saw him, • as he was yet a coming, • straightway the {spirit / the devil} threw him down, and tare *him* • and he fell on the ground, and wallowed foaming. And he asked his father, How long is it ago since this came unto him? And he said, Of a child. And ofttimes it hath cast him into the fire, and into the waters, to destroy him: [B]ut if thou canst do anything, have compassion on us, and help us. Jesus said unto him, If thou canst believe, all things *are* possible to him that believeth. And straightway the father of the child cried out, and said with tears, Lord, I believe; help thou mine unbelief. When Jesus saw that the people came running together, • Jesus rebuked the {devil / unclean spirit / foul spirit}, saying unto him, *Thou* dumb and deaf spirit, I charge thee, come out of him, and enter no more into him. And *the spirit* cried, and rent him sore, • and he departed out of him: • [A]nd he was as one dead; insomuch that many said, He is dead. But Jesus took him by the hand, • and healed the child, • and lifted him up; and he arose • and

MATTHEW	MARK	LUKE	JOHN

delivered him again to his father. • [A]nd the child was cured from that very hour. Then came the disciples to Jesus apart, • [a]nd when he was come into the house, his disciples asked him privately, • and said, Why could not we cast him out? And Jesus said unto them, Because of your unbelief: [F]or verily I say unto you, If ye have faith as a grain of mustard seed, ye shall say unto this mountain, Remove hence to yonder place; and it shall remove; and nothing shall be impossible unto you. Howbeit this kind {goeth not out / come forth} by nothing, but by prayer and fasting.

Ω

MATTHEW	MARK	LUKE	JOHN

- Who Should Be Greatest -

Matt 17:22-18:14 • Mark 09:30-50 • Luke 09:43-50 • John

¶ And they departed thence, and passed through Galilee; and he would not that any man should know *it.* • And while they abode in Galilee, • he taught his disciples, • [a]nd they were all amazed at the mighty power of God. But while they wondered everyone at all things which Jesus did, • Jeus said • unto his disciples, Let these sayings sink down into your ears: [F]or the Son of man shall be {delivered / betrayed} into the hands of men: And they shall kill him, and the third day he shall be raised again. And they were exceeding sorry. • But they understood not this saying, and it was hid from them, that they perceived it not: [A]nd they feared to ask him of that saying.

¶ Then there arose a reasoning among them, which of them should be greatest. • And when they were come to Capernaum, they that received tribute *money* came to Peter, and said, Doth not your master pay tribute? He saith, Yes. And when he was come into the house, Jesus prevented him, saying, What thinkest thou, Simon? [O]f whom do the kings of the earth take custom or tribute? [O]f their own children, or of strangers? Peter saith unto him, Of strangers. Jesus saith unto him, Then are the children free. Notwithstanding, lest we should offend them, go thou to the sea, and cast an hook, and take up the fish that first cometh up; and when thou hast opened his mouth, thou shalt find a piece of money: [T]hat take, and give unto them for me and thee. • [A]nd being in the house he asked them, What was it that ye disputed among yourselves by the way? But they held their peace: [F]or by the way they had disputed among themselves, who *should* be the greatest. And he sat down, and • Jesus, perceiveing the thought of their heart, • called the twelve, and saith unto them, If any man desire to be first, *the same* shall be last of all, and servant of all. •

¶ A[t] the same time came the disciples unto Jesus, saying, Who is the greatest in the kingdom of heaven? And Jesus called a little child unto him, • and set him by him • in the midst of them, • and when he had taken him in his arms, he said unto them, • Verily I say unto you, Except ye be converted,

MATTHEW	MARK	LUKE	JOHN

and become as little children, ye shall not enter into the kingdom of heaven. Whosoever therefore shall humble himself as this little child, the same is greatest in the kingdom of heaven. • Whosoever shall receive one of such • little • children in my name, receiveth me: [A]nd whosoever shall receive me, receiveth not me, but • receiveth him that sent me: [F]or he that is least among you all, the same shall be great. •

¶ And John answered him, saying, Master, we saw one casting out devils in thy name, and he followeth not us: [A]nd we forbad him, because he followeth • not with us. • But Jesus said • unto him, • Forbid him not: [F]or there is no man that shall do a miracle in my name, that can lightly speak evil of me. For he that is not against us is {on our part / for us}. • For whosoever shall give you a cup of water to drink in my name, because ye belong to Christ, verily I say unto you, he shall not lose his reward. • But whoso shall offend one of these little ones which believe in me, • it is better for him that a millstone were hanged about his neck, and he were cast into the sea • and that he were drowned in the depth of the sea.

¶ Woe uno the world because of offences! [F]or it must needs be that offences come; but woe to that man by whom the offence cometh! • And if thy hand offend thee, cut it off: [I]t is better for thee to enter into life maimed, than having two hands to go into hell, into the fire that never shall be quenched: Where their worm dieth not, and the fire is not quenched. And if thy foot offend thee, cut it off: [I]t is better for thee to enter halt into life, than having two feet to be cast into hell, into the fire that never shall be quenched: Where their worm dieth not, and the fire is not quenched. • Wherefore if thy hand or thy foot offend thee, cut them off, and cast them from thee: [I]t is better for thee to enter into life halt or maimed, rather than having two hands or two feet to be cast into everlasting fire. And if thine eye offend thee, pluck it out, and cast it from thee: [I]t is better for thee to enter into life • into the kingdom of God with one eye, • rather than having two eyes • to be cast into hell fire: Where their worm dieth not, and the fire is not quenched. For every one shall be salted with fire, and every sacrifice shall be salted with salt. Salt is good: [B]ut if the salt have lost his saltness, wherewith will ye season it? Have salt

MATTHEW	MARK	LUKE	JOHN

in yourselves, and have peace one with another. • Take heed that ye despise not one of these little ones; for I say unto you, That in heaven their angels do always behold the face of my Father which is in heaven. For the Son of man is come to save that which was lost. How think ye? If a man have an hundred sheep, and one of them be gone astray, doth he not leave the ninety and nine, and goeth into the mountains, and seeketh that which is gone astray? And if so be that he find it, verily I say unto you, he rejoiceth more of that *sheep*, than of the ninety and nine which went not astray. Even so it is not the will of your Father which is in heaven, that one of these little ones should perish.

ΑΩ

Redaction: The Day of Atonement

MATTHEW	MARK	LUKE	JOHN

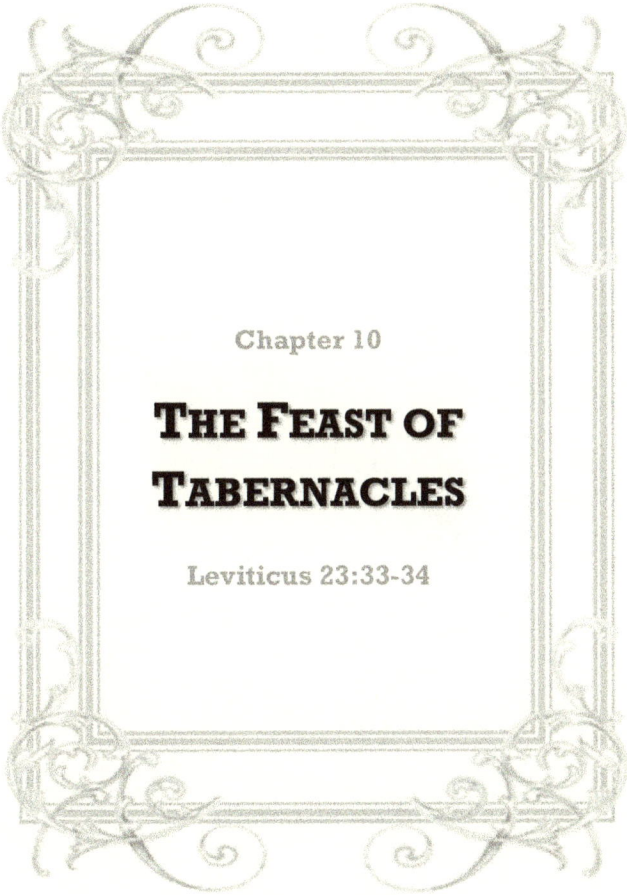

Chapter 10

THE FEAST OF TABERNACLES

Leviticus 23:33-34

Redaction: The Feast of Tabernacles

MATTHEW	MARK	LUKE	JOHN

MATTHEW	MARK	LUKE	JOHN

- My Time is Not Yet -

Matt • Mark • Luke • John 07:01-53

¶ A[fter] these things Jesus walked in Gaslilee: [F]or he would not walk in Jewry, because the Jews sought to kill him. Now the Jews' feast of tabernacles was at hand. His brethren therefore said unto him, Depart thence, and go into Judaea, that thy disciples may also see the works that thou doest. For *there is* no man *that* doeth anything in secret, and he himself seeketh to be known openly. If thou do these things, shew thyself to the world. For neither did his brethren believe in him. Then Jesus said unto them, My time is not yet come: [B]ut your time is alway ready. The world cannot hate you; but me it hateth, because I testify of it, that the works thereof are evil. Go ye up unto this feast: I go not up yet unto this feast; for my time is not yet full come. When he said these words unto them, he abode *still* in Galilee.

¶ B[ut] when his brethren were gone up, then went he also up unto the feast, not openly, but as it were in secret. Then the Jews sought him at the feast, and said, Where is he? And there was much murmuring among the people concerning him: [F]or some said, He is a good man: [O]thers said, Nay; but he decieveth the people. Howbeit no man spake openly of him for fear of the Jews.

¶ N[ow] about the midst of the feast Jesus went up into the temple, and taught. And the Jews marveled, saying, How knoweth this man letters, having never learned? Jesus answered them, and said, My doctrine is not mine, but his that sent me. If any man will do his will, he shall know of the doctrine, whether it be of God, or *whether* I speak of myself. He that speaketh of himself seeketh his own glory: [B]ut he that seeketh his glory that sent him, the same is true, and no unrighteousness is in him. Did not Moses give you the law, and *yet* none of you keepeth the law? Why go ye about to kill me? The people answered and said, Thou hast a devil: [W]ho goeth about to kill thee? Jesus answered and said unto them, I have done one work, and ye all marvel. Moses therefore gave unto you circumcision; (not because it is of Moses, but of the fathers;) and ye on the sabbath day circumcise a man. If a man on the sabbath day receive circumcision, that the law of Moses should not be broken; are ye angry at me,

MATTHEW	MARK	LUKE	JOHN

because I have made a man every whit whole on the sabbath day? Judge not according to the appearance, but judge righteous judgment. Then said some of them of Jerusalem, Is not this he, whom they seek to kill? But, lo, he speaketh boldly, and they say nothing unto him. Do the rulers know indeed that this is the very Christ? Howbeit we know this man whence he is: [B]ut when Christ cometh, no man knoweth whence he is. Then cried Jesus in the temple as he taught, saying, Ye both know me, and ye know whence I am: [A]nd I am not come of myself, but he that sent me is true, whom ye know not. But I know him: [F]or I am from him, and he hath sent me. Then they sought to take him: [B]ut no man laid hands on him, because his hour was not yet come. And many of the people believed on him, and said, When Christ cometh, will he do more miracles than these which this *man* hath done?

¶ T[he] Pharisees heard that the people murmured such things concerning him; and the Pharisees and chief priests sent officers to take him. Then said Jesus unto them, Yet a little while am I with you, and *then* I go unto him that sent me. Ye shall seek me, and shall not find *me:* [A]nd where I am, *thither* ye can not come. Then said the Jews among themselves, Whither will he go, that we shall not find him? [W]ill he go unto the dispersed among the Gentiles, and teach the Gentiles? What *manner of* saying is this that he said, Ye shall seek me, and shall not find *me:* [A]nd where I am, *thither* ye cannot come? In the last day, that great *day* of the feast, Jesus stood and cried, saying, If any man thirst, let him come unto me, and drink. He that believeth on me, as the scripture hath said, out of his belly shall flow rivers of living water. (But this spake he of the Spirit, which which they that believe on him should receive: [F]or the Holy Ghost was not yet *given:* [B]ecause that Jesus was not yet glorified.)

¶ M[any] of the people therefore, when they heard this saying, said, Of a truth this is the Prophet. Others said, This is the Christ. But some said, Shall Chirst come out of Galilee? Hath not the scripture said, That Christ cometh of the seed of David, and out of the town of Bethlehem, where David was? So there was a division among the people because of him. And some of them would have taken him; but no man laid hands on him.

MATTHEW	MARK	LUKE	JOHN

¶ T[hen] came the officers to the chief priests and Pharisees; and they said unto them, Why have ye not brought him? The officers answered, Never man spake like this man. Then answered them the Pharisees, Are ye also deceived? Have any of the rulers of the Pharisees believed on him? But this people who knoweth not the law are cursed. Nicodemus saith unto them, (he that came to Jesus by night, being one of them,) Doth our law judge *any* man, before it hear him, and know what he doeth? They answered and said unto him, Art thou also of Galiee? Search, and look: [F]or out of Galilee ariseth no prophet. And every man went unto his own house.

Ω

Redaction: The Feast of Tabernacles

MATTHEW	MARK	LUKE	JOHN

MATTHEW	MARK	LUKE	JOHN

- Not of This World -

Matt • Mark • Luke • John 08:01-59

¶ J[esus] went unto the mount of Olives. And early in the morning he came again into the temple, and all the people came unto him; and he sat down, and taught them. And the scribes and Pharisees brought unto him a woman taken in adultery; and when they had set her in the midst, [t]hey say unto him, Master, this woman was taken in adultery; in the very act. Now Moses in the law commanded us, that such should be stoned: [B]ut what sayest thou? This they said, tempting him, that they might have to accuse him. But Jesus stooped down, and with *his* finger wrote on the ground, *as though he heard them not.* So when they continued asking him, he lifted up himself, and said unto them, He that is without sin among you, let him first cast a stone at her. And again he stooped down, and wrote on the ground. And they which heard *it,* being convicted by *their own* conscience, went out one by one, beginning at the eldest, *even* unto the last: [A]nd Jesus was left alone, and the woman standing in the midst. When Jesus had lifted up himself, and saw none but the woman, he said unto her, Woman, where are those thine accusers? [H]ath no man condemned thee? She said, No man, Lord. And Jesus said unto her, Neither do I condemn thee: [G]o, and sin no more.

¶ T[hen] spake Jesus again unto them, saying, I am the light of the world: He that followeth me shall not walk in darkness, but shall have the light of life. The Pharisees therefore said unto him, Thou bearest record of thyself; thy record is not true. Jesus answered and said unto them, Though I bear record of myself, *yet* my record is true: [F]or I know whence I came, and whither I go; but ye can not tell whence I come, and whither I go. Ye judge after the flesh; I judge no man. And yet if I judge, my judgment is true: [F]or I am not alone, but I and the Father that sent me. It is also written in your law, that the testimony of two men is true. I am one that beareth witness of myself, and the Father that sent me beareth witness of me. Then said they unto him, Where is thy Father? Jesus answered, Ye neither know me, nor my Father: [I]f ye had known me, ye should have known my Father also. These words spake Jesus in the treasury, as he taught in the temple: [A]nd no man laid hands on him; for his hour

MATTHEW	MARK	LUKE	JOHN

was not yet come. Then said Jesus again unto them, I go my way, and ye shall seek me, and shall die in your sins: [W]hither I go, ye cannot come. Then said the Jews, Will he kill himself? [B]ecause he saith, Whither I go, ye cannot come. And he said unto them, Ye are from beneath: I am from above: [Y]e are of this world; I am not of this world. I said therefore unto you, that ye shall die in your sins: [F]or if ye believe not that I am *he*, ye shall die in your sins. Then said they unto him, Who art thou? And Jesus saith unto them, Even *the same* that I said unto you from the beginning. I have many things to say and to judge of you: [B]ut he that sent me is true; and I speak to the world those things which I have heard of him. They understood not that he spake to them of the Father. Then said Jesus unto them, When ye have lifted up the Son of man, then shall ye know that I am *he*, and *that* I do nothing of myself; but as my Father hath taught me, I speak these things. And he that sent me is with me: [T]he Father hath not left me alone; for I do always those things that please him. As he spake these words, many believed on him. Then said Jesus to those Jews which believed on him, If ye continue in my word, *then* are ye my disciples indeed; [a]nd ye shall know the truth, and the truth shall make you free.

¶ T[hey] answered him, We be Abraham's seed, and were never in bondage to any man: [H]ow sayest thou, Ye shall be made free? Jesus answered them, Verily, verily, I say unto you, Whosoever committeth sin is the servant of sin. And the servant abideth not in the house forever: *[B]ut the Son abideth ever.* If the Son therefore shall make you free, ye shall be free indeed. I know that ye are Abraham's seed; but ye seek to kill me, because my word hath no place in you. I speak that which I have seen with my Father: [A]nd ye do that which ye have seen with your father. They answered and said unto him, Abraham is our father. Jesus saith unto them, If ye were Abraham's children, ye would do the works of Abraham. But now ye seek to kill me, a man that hath told you the truth, which I have heard of God: [T]his did not Abraham. Ye do the deeds of your father. Then said they unto him, We be not born of fornication; we have one Father, *even* God. Jesus said unto them, If God were your Father, ye would love me: [F]or I proceeded forth and came from God; neither came I of myself, but he sent me. Why do ye not understand my speech? *[E]ven* because ye can not hear my word. Ye are of *your*

MATTHEW	MARK	LUKE	JOHN

father the devil, and the lusts of your father ye will do. He was a murderer from the beginning, and abode not in the truth, because there is no truth in him. When he speaketh a lie, he speaketh of his own: [F]or he is a liar and the father of it. And because I tell *you* the truth, ye believe me not. Which of you convinceth me of sin? And if I say the truth, why do ye not believe me? He that is of God heareth God's words: [Y]e therefore hear *them* not, because ye are not of God. Then answered the Jews, and said unto him, Say we not well that thou art a Samaritan, and hast a devil? Jesus answered, I have not a devil; but I honor my Father, and ye do dishonour me. And I seek not my own glory: [T]here is one that seeketh and judgeth. Verily, verily, I say unto you, If a man keep my saying, he shall never see death. Then said the Jews unto him, Now we know that thou hast a devil. Abraham is dead, and the prophets; and thou sayest, If a man keep my saying, he shall never taste of death. Art thou greater than our father Abraham, which is dead? And the prophets are dead: [W]hom makest thou thyself? Jesus answered, If I honour myself, my honour is nothing: [I]t is my Father that honoureth me; of whom ye say, that he is your God: Yet ye have not known him; but I know him: [A]nd if I should say, I know him not, I shall be a liar like unto you: [B]ut I know him, and keep his saying. Your father Abraham rejoiced to see my day: [A]nd he saw *it,* and was glad. Then said the Jews unto him, Thou art not yet fifty years old, and hast thou seen Abraham? Jesus said unto them, Verily, verily, I say unto you, Before Abraham was, I am. Then took they up stones to cast at him: [B]ut Jesus hid himself, and went out of the temple, going through the midst of them, and so passed by.

Ω

Redaction: The Feast of Tabernacles

MATTHEW	MARK	LUKE	JOHN

MATTHEW	MARK	LUKE	JOHN

- A Marvellous Thing -

Matt • Mark • Luke • John 09:01-41

¶ A[nd] as *Jesus* passed by, he saw a man which was blind from *his* birth. And his disciples asked him, saying, Master, who did sin, this man, or his parents, that he was born blind? Jesus answered, Neither hath this man sinned, nor his parents: [B]ut that the works of God should be made manifest in him. I must work the works of him that sent me, while it is day: [T]he night cometh, when no man can work. As long as I am in the world, I am the light of the world. When he had thus spoken, he spat on the ground, and made clay of the spittle, and he anointed the eyes of the blind man with the clay, [a]nd he said unto him, Go, wash in the pool of Siloam, (which is by interpretation, Sent.) He went his way therefore, and washed, and came seeing.

¶ T[he] neighbors therefore, and they which before had seen him that he was blind, said, Is not this he that sat and begged? Some said, This is he: [O]thers *said*, He is like him: *[B]ut* he said, I am *he*. Therefore said they unto him, How were thine eyes opened? He answered and said, A man that is called Jesus made clay, and anointed mine eyes, and said unto me, Go to the pool of Siloam, and wash: [A]nd I went and washed, and I received sight. Then said they unto him, Where is he? He said, I know not.

¶ T[hey] brought to the Pharisees him that aforetime was blind. And it was the sabbath day when Jesus made the clay, and opened his eyes. Then again the Pharisees also asked him how he had received his sight. He said unto them, He put clay upon my eyes, and I washed, and do see. Therefore said some of the Pharisees, This man is not of God, because he keepeth not the sabbath day. Others said, How can a man that is a sinner do such miracles? And there was a division among them. They say unto the blind man again, What sayest thou of him, that he hath opened thine eyes? He said, He is a prophet. But the Jews did not believe concerning him, that he had been blind, and received his sight, until they called the parents of him that had received his sight. And they asked them, saying, Is this your son, who ye say was born blind? [H]ow then doth he now see? His parents answered them and said, We know that this is our son,

MATTHEW	MARK	LUKE	JOHN

and that he was born blind: But by what means he now seeth, we know not; or who hath opened his eyes, we know not: [H]e is of age; ask him: [H]e shall speak for himself. These *words* spake his parents, because they feared the Jews: [F]or the Jews had agreed already, that if any man did confess that he was Christ, he should be put out of the synagogue. Therefore said his parents, He is of age; ask him. Then again called they the man that was blind, and said unto him, Give God the praise: [W]e know that this man is a sinner. He answered and said, Whether he be a sinner *or no*, I know not: [O]ne thing I know, that, whereas I was blind, now I see. Then said they to him again, What did he to thee? [H]ow opened he thine eyes? He answered them, I have told you already, and ye did not hear: [W]herefore would ye hear *it* again? will ye also be his disciples? Then they reviled him, and said, Thou art his disciple; but we are Moses' disciples. We know that God spake unto Moses: *[A]s for* this *fellow*, we know not from whence he is. The man answered and said unto them, Why herein is a marvellous thing, that ye know not from whence he is, and *yet* he hath opened mine eyes. Now we know that God heareth not sinners: [B]ut if any man be a worshipper of God, and doeth his will, him he heareth. Since the world began was it not heard that any man opened the eyes of one that was born blind. If this man were not of God, he could do nothing. They answered and said unto him, Thou wast altogether born in sins, and dost thou teach us? And they cast him out. Jesus heard that they had cast him out; and when he had found him, he said unto him, Dost thou believe on the Son of God? He answered and said, Who is he, Lord, that I might believe on him? And Jesus said unto him, Thou hast both seen him, and it is he that talketh with thee. And he said, Lord, I believe. And he worshipped him.

¶ A[nd] Jesus said, For judgment I am come into this world, that they which see not might see; and that they which see might be made blind. And *some* of the Pharisees which were with him heard these words, and said unto him, Are we blind also? Jesus said unto them, If ye were blind, ye should have no sin: [B]ut now ye say, We see; therefore your sin remaineth.

Ω

MATTHEW	MARK	LUKE	JOHN

- The Good Shepherd -

Matt • Mark • Luke • John 10:1-21

¶ V[erily], verily, I say unto you, He that entereth not by the door into the sheepfold, but climbeth up some other way, the same is a thief and a robber. But he that entereth in by the door is the shepherd of the sheep. To him the porter openeth; and the sheep hear his voice: [A]nd he calleth his own sheep by name, and leadeth them out. And when he puteth forth his own sheep, he goeth before them, and the sheep follow him: [F]or they know his voice. And a stranger will they not follow, but will flee from him: [F]or they know not the voice of strangers. This parable spake Jesus unto them: [B]ut they understood not what things they were which he spake unto them. Then said Jesus unto them again, Verily, verily, I say unto you, I am the door of the sheep. All that ever came before me are thieves and robbers: [B]ut the sheep did not hear them. I am the door: [B]y me if any man enter in, he shall be saved, and shall go in and out, and find pasture. The thief commeth not, but for to steal, and to kill, and to destroy: I am come that they might have life, and that they might have *it* more abundantly. I am the good shepherd: [T]he good shepherd giveth his life for the sheep. But he that is an hireling, and not the shepherd, whose own the sheep are not, seeth the wolf coming, and leaveth the sheep, and fleeth: [A]nd the wolf catcheth them, and scattereth the sheep. The hireling fleeth, because he is an hireling, and careth not for the sheep. I am the good shepherd, and know my *sheep*, and am known of mine. As the Father knoweth me, even so know I the Father: [A]nd I lay down my life for the sheep. And other sheep I have, which are not of this fold: [T]hem also I must bring, and they shall hear my voice; and there shall be one fold, *and* one shepherd. Therefore doth my Father love me, because I lay down my life, that I might take it again. No man taketh it from me, but I lay it down of myself. I have power to lay it down, and I have power to take it again. This commandment have I received of my Father.

Redaction: The Feast of Tabernacles

MATTHEW	MARK	LUKE	JOHN

¶ T[here] was a division therefore again among the Jews for these sayings. And many of them said, He hath a devil, and is mad; why hear ye him. Others said, These are not the words of him that hath a devil. Can a devil open the eyes of the blind?

ΑΩ

Chapter 11

AT THE DEDICATION

Nehemiah 12:27

Redaction: At the Dedication

MATTHEW	MARK	LUKE	JOHN

MATTHEW	MARK	LUKE	JOHN

- The Seventy -

Matt • Mark • Luke 09:51-10:24 • John 10:22-39

¶ And it came to pass, when the time was come that he should be received up, he steadfastly set his face to go to Jerusalem, [a]nd sent messengers before his face: [A]nd they went, and entered into a village of the Samaritans, to make ready for him. And they did not receive him, because his face was as though he would go to Jerusalem. And when his disciples James and John saw *this*, they said, Lord, wilt thou that we command fire to come down from heaven, and consume them, even as Elias did? But he turned, and rebuked them, and said, Ye know not what manner of spirit ye are of. For the Son of man is not come to destroy men's lives, but to save *them*. And they went to another village.

¶ And it came to pass, that, as they went in the way, a certain man said unto him, Lord, I will follow thee whithersoever thou goest. And Jesus said unto him, Foxes have holes, and birds of the air *have* nests; but the Son of man hath not where to lay *his* head. And he said unto another, Follow me. But he said, Lord, suffer me to first go and bury my father. Jesus said unto him, Let the dead bury their dead: [B]ut go thou and preach the kingdom of God. And another also said, Lord, I will follow thee; but let me first go bid them farewell, which are at home at my house. And Jesus said unto him, No man, having put his hand to the plough, and looking back, is fit for the kingdom of God.

¶ A[fter] these things the Lord appointed other seventy also, and sent them two and two before his face into every city and place, whither he himself would come. Therefore said he unto them, The harvest truly *is* great, but the labourers *are* few: [P]ray ye therefore the Lord of the harvest, that he would send forth labourers into his harvest. Go your ways: [B]ehold, I send you forth as lambs among wolves. Carry neither purse nor scrip, nor shoes: [A]nd salute no man by the way. And into whatsoever house ye enter, first say, Peace *be* to this house. And if the son of peace be there, your peace shall rest upon it: [I]f not, it shall turn to you again. And in the same house remain, eating and drinking such things as they give: [F]or the labourer is worthy of his hire. Go not from house to house. And into

MATTHEW	MARK	LUKE	JOHN

whatsoever city ye enter, and they receive you, eat such things as are set before you: [A]nd heal the sick that are therein, and say unto them, The kingdom of God is come nigh unto you. But into whatsoever city ye enter, and they receive you not, go your ways out into the streets of the same, and say, Even the very dust of your city, which cleaveth on us, we do wipe off against you: [N]otwithstanding be ye sure of this, that the kingdom of God is come nigh unto you. But I say unto you, that it shall be more tolerable in that day for Sodom, than for that city. Woe unto thee, Chorazin! Woe unto thee, Bethsaida! [F]or if the mighty works had been done in Tyre, and Sidon, which have been done in you, they had a great while ago repented, sitting in sackcloth and ashes. But it shall be more tolerable for Tyre and Sidon at the judgement, than for you. And thou, Capernaum, which art exalted to heaven, shalt be thrust down to hell. He that heareth you heareth me; and he that despiseth you despiseth me; and he that despiseth me despiseth him that sent me.

¶ And it was at Jerusalem the feast of the dedication, and it was winter. And Jesus walked in the temple in Solomon's porch. Then came the Jews round about him, and said unto him, How long dost thou make us to doubt? If thou be the Christ, tell us plainly. Jesus answered them, I told you, and ye believed not: [T]he works that I do in my Father's name, they bear witness of me. But ye believe not, because ye are not of my sheep, as I said unto you. My sheep hear my voice, and I know them, and they follow me: And I give unto them eternal life; and they shall never perish, neither shall any *man* pluck them out of my hand. My Father, which gave *them* me, is greater than all; and no *man* is able to pluck *them* out of my Father's hand. I and *my* Father are one. Then the Jews took up stones again to stone him. Jesus answered them, Many good works have I shewed you from my Father; for which of those works do ye stone me? The Jews answered him, saying, For a good work we stone thee not; but for blasphemy; and because that thou, being a man, makest thyself God. Jesus answered them, Is it not written in your law, I said, Ye are gods? If he called them gods, unto whom the word of God came, and the scripture can not be broken; [s]ay ye of him, whom the Father hath sanctified, and sent into the world, Thou blasphemest; [B]ecause I said, I am the Son of God? If I do not the works of my Father,

MATTHEW	MARK	LUKE	JOHN

believe me not. But if I do, though ye believe not me, believe the works: [T]hat ye may know, and believe, that the Father *is* in me, and I in him. Therefore they sought again to take him: [B]ut he escaped out of their hand, [a]nd went away again beyond Jordan into the place where John at first baptized; and there he abode. And many resorted unto him, and said, John did no miracle: [B]ut all things that John spake of this man were true. And many believed on him there. •

¶ And the seventy returned again with joy, saying, Lord, even the devils are subject unto us through thy name. And he said unto them, I beheld Satan as lightning fall from heaven. Behold, I give unto you power to tread on serpents and scorpions, and over all the power of the enemy: [A]nd nothing shall by any means hurt you. Notwithstanding in this rejoice not, that the spirits are subject unto you; but rather rejoice, because your names are written in heaven.

¶ In that hour Jesus rejoiced in spirit, and said, I thank thee, O Father, Lord of heaven and earth, that thou hast hid these things from the wise and the prudent, and hast revealed them unto babes: [E]ven so, Father; for so it seemed good in thy sight. All things are delivered to me of my Father: [A]nd no man knoweth who the Son is, but the Father; and who the Father is, but the Son, and *he* to whom the Son will reveal *him*.

¶ And he turned him unto *his* disciples, and said privately, Blessed *are* the eyes which see the things that ye see: For I tell you, that many prophets and kings have desired to see those things which ye see, and have not seen *them*; and to hear those things which ye hear, and have not heard *them*.

Ω

Redaction: At the Dedication

MATTHEW	MARK	LUKE	JOHN

MATTHEW	MARK	LUKE	JOHN

- Who is My Neighbor -

Matt • Mark • Luke 10:25-11:38 • John

¶ And, behold, a certain lawyer stood up, and tempted him, saying, Master, what shall I do to inherit eternal life? He said unto him, What is written in the law? [H]ow readest thou? And he answering said, Thou shalt love the Lord thy God with all thy heart, and with all thy soul, and with all thy strength, and with all thy mind; and thy neighbor as thyself. And he said unto him, Thou hast answered right: [T]his do, and thou shalt live. But he, willing to justify himself, said unto Jesus, And who is my neighbor? And Jesus answering said, A certain *man* went down from Jerusalem to Jericho, and fell among thieves, which stripped him of his raiment, and wounded *him*, and departed, leaving *him* half dead. And by chance there came down a certain priest that way: [A]nd when he saw him, he passed by on the other side. And likewise a Levite, when he was at the place, came and looked *on him*, and passed by on the other side. But a certain Samaritan, as he journeyed, came where he was: [A]nd when he saw him, he had compassion *on him*, [a]nd went to *him*, and bound up his wounds, pouring in oil and wine, and set him on his own beast, and brought him to an inn, and took care of him. And on the morrow when he departed, he took out two pence, and gave *them* to the host, and said unto him, Take care of him; and whatsoever thou spendest more, when I come again, I will repay thee. Which now of these three, thinkest thou, was neighbor unto him that fell among the thieves? And he said, He that shewed mercy on him. Then said Jesus unto him, Go, and do thou likewise.

¶ Now it came to pass, as they went, that he entered into a certain village: [A]nd a certain woman named Martha received him into her house. And she had a sister called Mary, which also sat at Jesus's feet and heard his word. But Martha was cumbered about much serving, and came to him, and said, Lord, dost thou not care that my sister hath left me to serve alone? [B]id her therefore that she help me. And Jesus answered and said unto her, Martha, Martha, thou art careful and troubled about many things: But one thing is needful: [A]nd Mary hath chosen that good part, which shall not be taken away from her.

MATTHEW	MARK	LUKE	JOHN

¶ A[nd] it came to pass, that, as he was praying in a certain place, when he ceased, one of his disciples said unto him, Lord, teach us to pray, as John also taught his disciples. And he said unto them, When ye pray, say, Our Father which art in heaven, Hallowed be thy name. Thy kingdom come. Thy will be done, as in heaven, so in earth. Give us day by day our daily bread. And forgive us our sins; for we also forgive everyone that is indebted to us. And lead us not into temptation; but deliver us from evil. And he said unto them, Which of you shall have a friend, and shall go unto him at midnight, and say unto him, Friend, lend me three loaves; [f]or a friend of mine in his journey is come to me, and I have nothing to set before him? And he from within shall answer and say, Trouble me not: [T]he door is now shut, and my children are with me in bed; I can not rise and give thee. And I say unto you, Ask, and it shall be given unto you; seek, and ye shall find; knock, and it shall be opened unto you. For everyone that asketh receiveth; and he that seeketh findeth; and to him that knocketh, it shall be opened. If a son shall ask bread of any of you that is a father, will he give him a stone? [O]r if *he ask* a fish, will he for a fish give him a serpent? Or if he ask an egg, will he offer him a scorpion? If ye then, being evil, know how to give good gifts unto your children: [H]ow much more shall *your* heavenly Father give the Holy Spirit to them that ask him?

¶ And he was casting out a devil, and it was dumb. And it came to pass, when the devil was gone out, the dumb spake; and the people wondered. But some of them said, He casteth out devils through Beelzebub the chief of the devils. And others, tempting *him*, sought of him a sign of heaven. But he, knowing their thoughts, said unto them, Every kingdom divided amongst itself is brought to desolation; and a house *divided* against a house falleth. If Satan also be divided against himself, how shall his kingdom stand? Because ye say that I cast out devils through Beelzebub. And if I by Beelzebub cast out devils, by whom do your sons cast *them* out? Therefore shall they be your judges. But if I with the finger of God cast out devils, no doubt the kingdom of God is come upon you. When a strong man armed keepeth his palace, his goods are in peace: But when a stronger than he shall come upon him, and overcome him, he taketh from him all his armour wherein he trusted, and divideth his spoils. He

MATTHEW	MARK	LUKE	JOHN

that is not with me is against me: [A]nd he that gathereth not with me scattereth. When the unclean

spirit is gone out of a man, he walketh through dry places, seeking rest; and finding none, he saith, I

will return unto my house whence I came out. And when he cometh he findeth *it* swept and garnished.

Then goeth he, and taketh *to him* seven other spirits more wicked than himself; and they enter in, and

dwell there: [A]nd the last *state* of that man is worse than the first.

¶ And it came to pass, as he spake these things, a certain woman of the company lifted up her

voice, and said unto him, Blessed *is* the womb that bare thee, and the paps which thou hast sucked. But

he said, Yea rather, [B]lessed *are* they that hear the word of God, and keep it.

Ω

Redaction: At the Dedication

MATTHEW	MARK	LUKE	JOHN

MATTHEW	MARK	LUKE	JOHN

- An Evil Generation -

Matt • Mark • Luke 11:29-12:12 • John

¶ And when the people were gathered thick together, he began to say, This is an evil generation: [T]hey seek a sign; and there shall no sign be given it, but the sign of Jonas the prophet. For as Jonas was a sign unto the Ninevites, so shall also the Son of man be to this generation. The queen of the south shall rise up in the judgment with the men of this generation, and condemn them: [F]or she came from the utmost parts of the earth to hear the wisdom of Solomon; and, behold, a greater than Solomon *is* here. The men of Nineve shall rise up in the judgment with this generation, and shall condemn it: [F]or they repented at the preaching of Jonas; and, behold, a greater than Jonas *is* here. No man, when he hath lighted a candle, putteth *it* in a secret place, neither under a bushel, but on a candlestick, that they which come in may see the light. The light of the body is the eye: [T]herefore when thine eye is single, thy whole body is also full of light; but when *thine eye* is evil, thy body also *is* full of darkness. Take heed therefore that the light which is in thee be not darkness. If thy whole body therefore *be* full of light, having no part dark, the whole shall be full of light, as when the bright shining of a candle doth give thee light.

¶ And as he spake, a certain Pharisee besought him to dine with him: [A]nd he went in, and sat down to meat. And when the Pharisee saw *it*, he marvelled that he had not first washed before dinner. And the Lord said unto him, Now do ye Pharisees make clean the outside of the cup and the platter; but your inward part is full of ravening and wickedness. *Ye* fools, did not he that made that which is without make that which is within also? But rather give alms of such things as ye have; and, behold, all things are clean unto you. But woe unto you, Pharisees! for ye tithe mint and rue and all manner of herbs, and pass over judgment and the love of God: [T]hese ought ye to have done, and not to leave the other undone. Woe unto you, Pharisees! [F]or ye love the uppermost seats in the synagogues, and greetings in the markets. Woe unto you, scribes and Pharisees, hypocrites! for ye are as graves which appear not, and the men that walk over *them* are not aware of *them*.

MATTHEW	MARK	LUKE	JOHN

¶ Then answered one of the lawyers, and said unto him, Master, thus saying thou reproachest us also. And he said, Woe unto you also, ye lawyers! [F]or ye lade men with burdens grievous to be borne, and ye yourselves touch not the burdens with one of your fingers. Woe unto you! [F]or ye build the selpulchres of the prophets, and your fathers killed them. Truly ye bear witness that ye allow the deeds of your fathers: [F]or they indeed killed them, and ye build their sepulchres. Therefore also said the wisdom of God, I will send them prophets and apostles, and *some* of them they shall slay and persecute: That the blood of all the prophets, which was shed from the foundation of the world, may be required of this generation; [f]rom the blood of Abel unto the blood of Zacharias, which perished between the altar and the temple: verily I say unto you, It shall be required of this generation. Woe unto you, lawyers! [F]or ye have taken away the key of knowledge: [Y]e entered not in yourselves, and them that were entering in ye hindered. And as he said these things unto them, the scribes and the Pharisees began to urge *him* vehemently, and to provoke him to speak of many things: Laying wait for him, and seeking to catch something out of his mouth, that they might accuse him.

¶ I[n] the mean time, when there were gathered together an innumerable multitude of people, insomuch that they trode one upon another, he began to say unto his disciples first of all, Beware ye of the leaven of the Pharisees, which is hypocrisy. For there is nothing covered, that shall not be revealed; neither which ye have hid, that shall not be known. Therefore whatsoever ye have spoken in darkness shall be heard in the light; and that spoken in the ear in closets shall be proclaimed upon the housetops. And I say unto you my friends, Be not afraid of them that kill the body, and after that have no more that they can do. But I will forewarn you whom ye shall fear: Fear him, which after he hath killed hath power to cast into hell; yea, I say unto you, Fear him. Are not five sparrows sold for two farthings, and not one of them is forgotten before God? But even the very hairs of your head are all numbered. Fear not therefore: [Y]e are of more value than many sparrows. Also I say unto you, Whosoever shall confess me before men, him shall the Son of man also confess before the angels of God: But he that denieth me before men shall be denied before the angels of God. And whosoever shall speak a word

MATTHEW	MARK	LUKE	JOHN

against the Son of man, it shall be forgiven him: [B]ut unto him that blasphemeth against the Holy Ghost it shall not be forgiven. And when they bring you unto the synagogues, and *unto* magistrates, and powers, take ye no thought how or what thing ye shall answer, or what ye shall say: For the Holy Ghost shall teach you in the same hour what ye ought to say.

Ω

Redaction: At the Dedication

MATTHEW	MARK	LUKE	JOHN

MATTHEW	MARK	LUKE	JOHN

- Seek Ye the Kingdom of God -

Matt 18:15-35 • Mark • Luke 12:13-59 • John

¶ And one of the company said unto him, Master, speak to my brother, that he divide the inheritance with me. And he said unto him, Man, who made me a judge or a divider over you? And he said unto them, Take heed, and beware of covetousness: [F]or a man's life consists not in the abundance of the things which he possesseth. And he spake a parable unto them, saying, The ground of a certain rich man brought forth plentifully: And he thought within himself, saying, What shall I do, because I have no room where to bestow my fruits? And he said, This will I do: I will pull down my barns, and build greater; and there will I bestow all my fruits and my goods. And I will say to my soul, Soul, thou hast much goods laid up for many years; take thine ease, eat, drink, *and* be merry. But God said unto him, *Thou* fool, this night thy soul shall be required of thee: [T]hen whose shall those things be, which thou hast provided? So is he that layeth up treasure for himself, and is not rich toward God. •

¶ Moreover if thy brother shall trespass against thee, go and tell him his fault between thee and him alone: [I]f he shall hear thee, thou hast gained thy brother. But if he will not hear *thee, then* take with thee one or two more, that in the mouth of two or three witnesses every word may be established. And if he shall neglect to hear them, tell *it* unto the church: [B]ut if he neglect to hear the church, let him be unto thee as an heathen man and a publican. Verily I say unto you, Whatsoever ye shall bind on earth shall be bound in heaven: [A]nd whatsoever ye shall loose on earth shall be loosed in heaven. Again I say unto you, That if two of you shall agree on earth as touching any thing that they shall ask, it shall be done for them of my Father which is in heaven. For where two or three are gathered together in my name, there am I in the midst of them.

¶ Then came Peter to him, and said, Lord, how oft shall my brother sin against me, and I forgive him? till seven times? Jesus saith unto him, I say not unto thee, Until seven times: [B]ut, Until seventy times seven.

MATTHEW	MARK	LUKE	JOHN

¶ Therefore is the kingdom of heaven likened unto a certain king, which would take account of his servants. And when he had begun to reckon, one was brought unto him, which owed him ten thousand talents. But forasmuch as he had not to pay, his lord commanded him to be sold, and his wife, and children, and all that he had, and payment to be made. The servant therefore fell down, and worshipped him, saying, Lord, have patience with me, and I will pay thee all. Then the lord of that servant was moved with compassion, and loosed him, and forgave him the debt. But the same servant went out, and found one of his fellowservants, which owed him an hundred pence: [A]nd he laid hands on him, and took *him* by the throat, saying, Pay me that thou owest. And his fellow servant fell down at his feet, and besought him, saying, Have patience with me, and I will pay thee all. And he would not: [B]ut went and cast him into prison, till he should pay the debt. So when his fellowservants saw what was done, they were very sorry, and came and told unto their lord all that was done. Then his lord, after that he had called him, said unto him, O thou wicked servant, I forgave thee all that debt, because thou desiredst me: Shouldest not thou also have had compassion on thy fellowservant, even as I had pity on thee? And his lord was wroth and delivered him to the tormentors, till he should pay all that was due unto him. So likewise shall my heavenly Father do also unto you, if ye from your hearts forgive not every one his brother their trespasses. •

¶ And he said unto his disciples, Therefore I say unto you, Take no thought for your life, what ye shall eat; neither for the body, what ye shall put on. The life is more than meat, and the body *is more* than raiment. Consider the ravens: [F]or they neither sow nor reap; which neither have storehouse nor barn; and God feedeth them: [H]ow much more are ye better than the fowls? And which of you with taking thought can add to his stature one cubit? If ye then be not able to do that thing which is least, why take ye thought for the rest? Consider the lilies how they grow: [T]hey toil not, they spin not; and yet I say unto you, that Solomon in all his glory was not arrayed like one of these. If then God so clothe the grass, which is today in the field and tomorrow is cast into the oven; how much more *will he clothe* you, O ye of little faith? And seek not ye what ye shall eat, or what ye shall drink, neither be ye of

MATTHEW	MARK	LUKE	JOHN

doubtful mind. For all these things do the nations of the world seek after: [A]nd your Father knoweth that you have need of these things.

¶ But rather seek ye the kingdom of God; and all these things shall be added unto you. Fear not, little flock; for it is your Father's good pleasure to give you the kingdom. Sell that ye have, and give alms; provide yourselves bags which wax not old, a treasure in the heavens that faileth not, where no thief approacheth, neither moth corrupteth. For where your treasure is, there will your heart be also. Let your loins be girded about, and *your* lights burning; [a]nd ye yourselves like unto men that wait for their lord, when he will return from the wedding; that when he cometh and knocketh, they may open unto him immediately. Blessed *are* those servants, whom the lord when he commeth shall find watching: [V]erily I say unto you, that he shall gird himself, and make them to sit down to meat, and will come forth and serve them. And if he shall come in the second watch, or come in the third watch, and find *them* so, blessed are those servants. And this know, that if the goodman of the house had known what hour the thief would come, he would have watched, and not have suffered his house to be broken through. Be ye therefore ready also: [F]or the Son of man cometh at an hour when ye think not.

¶ Then Peter said unto him, Lord, speakest thou this parable unto us, or even to all? And the Lord said, Who then is that faithful and wise steward, whom *his* lord shall make ruler over his household, to give *them their* portion of meat in due season? Blessed *is* that servant, whom his lord when he cometh shall find so doing. Of a truth I say unto you, that he will make him ruler over all that he hath. But and if that servant say in his heart, My lord delayeth his coming; and shall begin to beat the menservants and maidens, and to eat and drink, and be drunken; [t]he lord of that servant will come in a day when he looketh not for *him*, and at an hour when he is not aware, and will cut him in sunder, and will appoint him his portion with the unbelievers. And that servant, which knew his lord's will, and prepared not *himself*, neither did according to his will, shall be beaten with many *stripes*. But he that knew not, and did commit things worthy of stripes, shall be beaten with few *stripes*. For unto whom-

MATTHEW	MARK	LUKE	JOHN

soever much is given, of him shall be much required: [A]nd to whom men have committed much, of him they will ask the more.

¶ I am come to send fire on the earth; and what will I, if it be already kindled? But I have a baptism to be baptized with; and how am I straitened till it be accomplished! Suppose ye that I am come to give peace on earth? I tell you, Nay; but rather division: For from henceforth there shall be five in one house divided, three against two, and two against three. The father shall be divided against the son, and the son against the father; the mother against the daughter, and the daughter against the mother; the mother in law against her daughter in law, and the daughter in law against her mother in law.

¶ And he said also to the people, When ye see a cloud rise out of the west, straighway ye say, There cometh a shower; [A]nd so it is. And when *ye see* the south wind blow, ye say, There will be heat; [A]nd it cometh to pass. *Ye* hypocrites, ye can discern the face of the sky and of the earth; but how is it that ye do not discern this time? Yea, and why even of yourselves judge ye not what is right?

¶ When thou goest with thine adversary to the magistrate, *as thou art* in the way, give diligence that thou mayest be delivered from him; lest he hale thee to the judge, and the judge deliver thee to the officer, and the officer cast thee into prison. I tell thee, thou shalt not depart thence, till thou hast paid the very last mite.

AΩ

Chapter 12

Among My
Disciples

Isaiah 8:16

Redaction: Among My Disciples

MATTHEW	MARK	LUKE	JOHN

MATTHEW	MARK	LUKE	JOHN

- Until the Time Come -

Matt • Mark • Luke 13:01-35 • John

¶ T[here] were present at that season some that told him of the Galilæans, whose blood Pilate had mingled with their sacrifices. And Jesus answering said unto them, Suppose ye that these Galilaeans were sinners above all the Galilaeans, because they suffered such things? I tell you, Nay: but, except ye repent, ye shall all likewise perish. Or those eighteen, upon whom the tower in Siloam fell, and slew them, think ye that they were sinners above all men that dwell in Jerusalem? I tell you, Nay: [B]ut, except ye repent, ye shall all likewise perish.

¶ He spake also this parable; A certain *man* had a fig tree planted in his vineyard; and he came and sought fruit thereon, and found none. Then said he unto the dresser of his vineyard, Behold, these three years I come seeking fruit on this fig tree, and find none: [C]ut it down; why cumbereth it the ground? And he answering said unto him, Lord, let it alone this year also, till I shall dig about it, and dung *it*: And if it bear fruit, *well*: [A]nd if not, *then* after that thou shalt cut it down. And he was teaching in one of the synagogues on the sabbath.

¶ And, behold, there was a woman which had a spirit of infirmity eighteen years, and was bowed together, and could in no wise lift up *herself*. And when Jesus saw her, he called *her to him*, and said unto her, Woman, thou art loosed from thine infirmity. And he laid *his* hands on her: [A]nd immediately she was made straight, and glorified God. And the ruler of the synagogue answered with indignation, because that Jesus had healed on the sabbath day, and said unto the people, There are six days in which men ought to work: [I]n them therefore come and be healed, and not on the sabbath day. The Lord then answered him, and said, *Thou* hypocrite, doth not each one of you on the sabbath loose his ox or *his* ass from the stall, and lead *him* away to watering? And ought not this woman being a daughter of Abraham, whom Satan hath bound, lo, these eighteen years, be loosed from this bond on

MATTHEW	MARK	LUKE	JOHN

the sabbath day? And when he had said these things, all his adversaries were ashamed: [A]nd all the people rejoiced, for all the glorious things that were done by him.

¶ Then said he, Unto what is the kingdom of God like? and whereunto shall I resemble it? It is like a grain of mustard seed, which a man took, and cast into his garden; and it grew, and waxed a great tree; and the fowls of the air lodged in the branches of it. And again he said, Whereunto shall I liken the kingdom of God? It is like leaven, which a woman took and hid in three measures of meal, till the whole was leavened. And he went through the cities and villages, teaching, and journeying toward Jerusalem. Then said one unto him, Lord, are there few that be saved? And he said unto them,

---

¶ Strive to enter in at the strait gate: [F]or many, I say unto you, will seek to enter in, and shall not be able. When once the master of the house is risen up, and hath shut to the door, and ye begin to stand without, and to knock at the door, saying, Lord, Lord, open unto us; and he shall answer and say unto you, I know you not whence ye are: Then shall ye begin to say, We have eaten and drunk in thy presence, and thou hast taught in our streets. But he shall say, I tell you, I know you not whence ye are; depart from me, all *ye* workers of iniquity. There shall be weeping and gnashing of teeth, when ye shall see Abraham, and Isaac, and Jacob, and all the prophets, in the kingdom of God, and you *yourselves* thrust out. And they shall come from the east, and *from* the west, and from the north, and *from* the south, and shall sit down in the kingdom of God. And, behold, there are last which shall be first, and there are first which shall be last.

¶ The same day there came certain of the Pharisees, saying unto him, Get thee out, and depart hence: [F]or Herod will kill thee. And he said unto them, Go ye, and tell that fox, Behold, I cast out devils, and I do cures to day and to morrow, and the third *day*, I shall be perfected. Nevertheless I must walk to day, and to morrow, and the *day* following: [F]or it cannot be that a prophet perish out of Jerusalem. O Jerusalem, Jerusalem, which killest the prophets, and stonest them that are sent unto thee; how often would I have gathered thy children together, as a hen *doth gather* her brood under *her*

MATTHEW	MARK	LUKE	JOHN

wings, and ye would not! Behold, your house is left unto you desolate: [A]nd verily I say unto you, Ye shall not see me, until *the time* come when ye shall say, Blessed *is* he that cometh in the name of the Lord.

Ω

Redaction: Among My Disciples

MATTHEW	MARK	LUKE	JOHN

MATTHEW	MARK	LUKE	JOHN

- The Master of the House -

Matt • Mark • Luke 14:01-35 • John

¶ And it came to pass, as he went into the house of one of the chief Pharisees to eat bread on the sabbath day, that they watched him. And behold there was a certain man before him which had the dropsy. And Jesus answering spake unto the lawyers and Pharisees, saying, Is it lawful to heal on the sabbath day? And they held their peace. And he took *him*, and healed him, and let him go; [a]nd answered them, saying, Which of you shall have an ass or an ox fallen into a pit, and will not straightway pull him out on the sabbath day? And they could not answer him again to these things.

¶ And he put forth a parable to those which were bidden, when he marked how they chose out the chief rooms; saying unto them, When thou art bidden of any *man* to a wedding, sit not down in the highest room; lest a more honorable man than thou be bidden of him; [a]nd he that bade thee and him come and say to thee, Give this man place; [A]nd thou begin with shame to take the lowest room. But when thou art bidden, go and sit down in the lowest room; that when he that bade thee cometh, he may say unto thee, Friend, go up higher: [T]hen shalt thou have worship in the presence of them that sit at meat with thee. For whosoever exalteth himself shall be abased; and he that humbleth himself shall be exalted.

¶ Then said he also to him that bade him, When thou makest a dinner or a supper, call not thy friends, nor thy brethren, neither thy kinsmen, nor *thy* rich neighbors; lest they also bid thee again, and a recompense be made thee. But when thou makest a feast, call the poor, the maimed, the lame, the blind: And thou shalt be blessed; for they can not recompense thee: [F]or thou shalt be recompensed at the resurrection of the just.

¶ And when one of them that sat at meat with him heard these things, he said unto him, Blessed *is* he that shall eat bread in the kingdom of God. Then said he unto him, A certain man made a great supper, and bade many: And sent his servant at supper time to say to them that were bidden, Come;

MATTHEW	MARK	LUKE	JOHN

for all things are now ready. And they all with one *consent* began to make excuse. The first said unto him, I have bought a piece of ground, and I must needs go and see it: I pray thee have me excused. And another said, I have bought five yoke of oxen, and I go to prove them: I pray thee have me excused. And another said, I have married a wife, and therefore I can not come. So that servant came, and shewed his Lord these things. Then the master of the house being angry said to his servant, Go out quickly into the streets and lanes of the city, and bring in hither the poor, and the maimed, and the halt, and the blind. And the servant said, Lord, it is done as thou hast commanded, and yet there is room. And the lord said unto the servant, Go out into the highways and hedges, and compel *them* to come in, that my house may be filled. For I say unto you, That none of those men which were bidden shall taste of my supper.

¶ And there went great multitudes with him: [A]nd he turned, and said unto them, If any *man* come to me, and hate not his father, and mother, and wife, and children, and brethren, and sisters, yea, and his own life also, he can not be my disciple. And whosoever doth not bear his cross, and come after me, cannot be my disciple. For which of you, intending to build a tower, sitteth not down first, and counteth the cost, whether he have *sufficient* to finish *it*? Lest haply, after he hath laid the foundation, and is not able to finish *it*, all that behold *it* begin to mock him, [s]aying, This man began to build, and was not able to finish. Or what king, going to make war against another king, sitteth not down first, and consulteth whether he be able with ten thousand to meet him that cometh against him with twenty thousand? Or else, while the other is yet a great way off, he sendeth an ambassage, and desireth conditions of peace. So likewise, whosoever he be of you that forsaketh not all that he hath, he cannot be my disciple.

¶ Salt is good: [B]ut if the salt have lost his savour, wherewith shall it be seasoned? It is neither fit for the land, nor yet for he dunghill; *but* men cast it out. He that hath ears to hear, let him hear.

Ω

MATTHEW	MARK	LUKE	JOHN

- The True Riches -

Matt • Mark • Luke 15:01-16:18 • John

¶ Then drew near unto him all the publicans and sinners for to hear him. And the Pharisees and scribes murmured, saying, This man receiveth sinners, and eateth with them.

¶ And he spake this parable unto them, saying, What man of you, having an hundred sheep, if he loose one of them, doth not leave the ninety and nine in the wilderness, and go after that which is lost, until he find it? And when he hath found *it*, he layeth *it* on his shoulders, rejoicing. And when he cometh home, he calleth together *his* friends, and neighbours, saying unto them, Rejoice with me; for I have found my sheep which was lost. I say unto you, that likewise joy shall be in heaven over one sinner that repenteth, more than over ninety and nine just persons, which need no repentance.

¶ Either what woman having ten pieces of silver, if she lose one piece, doth not light a candle, and sweep the house, and seek diligently till she find *it*? And when she hath found *it*, she calleth *her* friends and neighbours together, saying, Rejoice with me; for I have found the piece which I had lost. Likewise, I say unto you, there is joy in the presence of the angels of God over one sinner that repenteth.

¶ And he said, A certain man had two sons: And the younger of them said to *his* father, Father, give me the portion of goods that falleth *to me*. And he divided unto them *his* living. And not many days after, the younger son gathered all together, and took his journey into a far country, and there wasted his substance with riotous living. And when he had spent all, there arose a mighty famine in that land; and he began to be in want. And he went and joined himself to a citizen of that country; and he sent him into his fields to feed swine. And he would fain have filled his belly with the husks that the swine did eat: [A]nd no man gave unto him. And when he came to himself, he said, How many hired servants of my father's have bread enough and to spare, and I perish with hunger! I will arise and go to my father, and will say unto him, Father I have sinned against heaven, and before thee, [a]nd am no more worthy

MATTHEW	MARK	LUKE	JOHN

to be called thy son: [M]ake me as one of thy hired servants. And he arose and came to his father. But when he was yet a great way off, his father saw him, and had compassion, and ran, and fell on his neck, and kissed him. And the son said unto him, Father, I have sinned against heaven, and in thy sight, and am no more worthy to be called thy son. But the father said to his servants, Bring forth the best robe, and put *it* on him; and put a ring on his hand, and shoes on *his* feet: And bring hither the fatted calf, and kill *it*; and let us eat, and be merry: For this my son was dead, and is alive again; he was lost, and is found. And they began to be merry. Now his elder son was in the field: [A]nd as he came and drew nigh to the house, he heard musick and dancing. And he called one of the servants, and asked what these things meant. And he said unto him, Thy brother is come; and thy father hath killed the fatted calf, because he hath received him safe and sound. And he was angry, and would not go in: [T]herefore came his father out, and intreated him. And he answering said to *his* father, Lo, these many years do I serve thee, neither transgressed I at any time thy commandment: [A]nd yet thou never gavest me a kid, that I might make merry with my friends: But as soon as this thy son was come, which hath devoured thy living with harlots, thou hast killed for him the fatted calf. And he said unto him, Son, thou art ever with me, and all that I have is thine. It was meet that we should make merry, and be glad: [F]or this thy brother was dead, and is alive again; and was lost, and is found.

¶ And he said also unto his disciples, There was a certain rich man, which had a steward; and the same was accused unto him that he had wasted his goods. And he called him, and said unto him, How is it that I hear this of thee? [G]ive an account of thy stewardship; for thou mayest be no longer steward. Then the steward said within himself, What shall I do? for my lord taketh away from me the stewardship: I cannot dig; to beg I am ashamed. I am resolved what to do, that, when I am put out of the stewardship, they may receive me into their houses. So he called everyone of his lord's debtors *unto him*, and said unto the first, How much owest thou unto my lord? And he said, a hundred measures of oil. And he said unto him, Take thy bill, and sit down quickly, and write fifty. Then said he to another, And how much owest thou? And he said, An hundred measures of wheat. And he said unto him, Take

MATTHEW	MARK	LUKE	JOHN

thy bill, and write fourscore. And the lord commended the unjust steward, because he had done wisely: [F]or the children of this world are in their generation wiser than the children of light. And I say unto you, Make to yourselves friends of the mammon of unrighteousness; that, when ye fail, they may receive you into everlasting habitations. He that is faithful in that which is least is faithful also in much: [A]nd he that is unjust in the least is unjust also in much. If therefore ye have not been faithful in the unrighteous mammon, who will commit to your trust the true *riches*? And if ye have not been faithful in that which is another man's, who shall give you that which is your own?

¶ No servant can serve two masters: [F]or either he will hate the one, and love the other; or else he will hold to the one, and despise the other. Ye cannot serve God and mammon. And the Pharisees also, who were covetous, heard all these things: [A]nd they derided him. And he said unto them, Ye are they which justify yourselves before men; but God knoweth your hearts: [F]or that which is highly esteemed among men is abomination in the sight of God. The law and the prophets *were* until John: [S]ince that time the kingdom of God is preached, and every man presseth into it. And it is easier for heaven and earth to pass, than one tittle of the law to fail. Whosoever putteth away his wife, and marrieth another, committeth adultery: [A]nd whosoever marrieth her that is put away from *her* husband committeth adultery.

AΩ

Redaction: Among My Disciples

MATTHEW	MARK	LUKE	JOHN

Chapter 13

We Shall Live in His Sight

Hosea 6:01-03

Redaction: We Shall Live in His Sight

MATTHEW	MARK	LUKE	JOHN

MATTHEW	MARK	LUKE	JOHN

- Lazarus is Dead -

Matt • Mark • Luke 16:19-17:19-37 • John 11:01-16

¶ N[ow] a certain *man* was sick, *named* Lazarus, of Bethany, the town of Mary and her sister Martha. (It was *that* Mary which anointed the Lord with ointment, and wiped his feet with her hair, whose brother Lazarus was sick.) Therefore his sisters sent unto him, saying, Lord, behold, he whom thou lovest is sick. When Jesus heard *that*, he said, This sickness is not unto death, but for the glory of God, that the Son of God might be glorified thereby. Now Jesus loved Martha, and her sister, and Lazarus. When he had heard therefore that he was sick, he abode two days still in the same place where he was. Then after that saith he to *his* disciples, Let us go into Judea again. *His* disciples say unto him, Master, the Jews of late sought to stone thee; and goest thou thither again? Jesus answered, Are there not twelve hours in the day? If any man walk in the day, he stumbleth not, because he seeth the light of this world. But if a man walk in the night, he stumbleth, because there is no light in him. These things said he: •

¶ There was a certain rich man, which was clothed in purple and fine linen, and fared sumptuously every day: And there was a certain beggar named Lazarus, which was laid at his gate, full of sores, And desiring to be fed with the crumbs which fell from the rich man's table: [M]ore over the dogs came and licked his sores. And it came to pass, that the beggar died, and was carried by the angels into Abraham's Bosom: [T]he rich man also died, and was buried; [a]nd in hell he lift up his eyes, being in torments, and seeth Abraham afar off, and Lazarus in his bosom. And he cried and said, Father Abraham, have mercy on me, and send Lazarus, that he may dip the tip of his finger in water, and cool my tongue; for I am tormented in this flame. But Abraham said, Son, remember that thou in thy lifetime receivest thy good things, and likewise Lazarus evil things: [B]ut now he is comforted, and thou art tormented. And beside all this, between us and you there is a great gulf fixed: [S]o that they which would pass from hence to you cannot; neither can they pass to us, that *would come* from thence. Then he said, I pray thee therefore, father, that thou wouldest send him to my father's house: For I have five brethren; that he may testify unto them, lest they also come into this place of torment. Abraham saith

MATTHEW	MARK	LUKE	JOHN

unto him, They have Moses and the prophets; let them hear them. And he said, Nay, father Abraham: [B]ut if one went unto them from the dead, they will repent. And he said unto him, If they hear not Moses and the prophets, neither will they be persuaded, though one arose from the dead. •

¶ [A]nd after that he saith unto them, Our friend Lazarus sleepeth; but I go, that I may wake him out of sleep. Then said his disciples, Lord, if he sleep, he shall do well. Howbeit Jesus spake of his death: [B]ut they thought that he had spoken of taking of rest in sleep. Then said Jesus unto them plainly, Lazarus is dead. And I am glad for your sakes that I was not there, to the intent ye may believe; nevertheless let us go unto him. Then said Thomas, which is called Didymus, unto his fellow disciples, Let us also go, that we may die with him. •

¶ T[hen] said he unto the disciples, It is impossible but that offenses will come: [B]ut woe *unto him*, through whom they come! It were better for him that a millstone were hanged about his neck, and he cast into the sea, than that he should offend one of these little ones.

¶ Take heed to yourselves: If thy brother trespass against thee, rebuke him; and if he repent, forgive him. And if he trespass against thee seven times in a day, and seven times in a day turn again unto thee, saying, I repent; [T]hou shalt forgive him. And the apostles said unto the Lord, Increase our faith. And the Lord said, If ye had faith as a grain of mustard seed, ye might say unto this sycamine tree, Be thou plucked up by the root, and be thou planted in the sea; and it should obey you. But which of you, having a servant plowing or feeding cattle, will say unto him by and by, when he is come from the field, Go and sit down to meat? And will not rather say unto him, Make ready wherewith I may sup, and gird thyself, and serve me, till I have eaten and drunken; and afterward thou shalt eat and drink? Doth he thank that servant because he did the things that were commanded him? I trow not. So likewise ye, when ye shall have done all those things which are commanded you, say, We are unprofitable servants: [W]e have done that which was our duty to do. •

Ω

MATTHEW	MARK	LUKE	JOHN

- Beyond Jordan -

Matt 19:01-15 • Mark 10:01-16 • Luke 17:20-18:17 • John

¶ And it came to pass, • when Jesus had finished these sayings, • as he went to Jerusalem, that he passed through the midst of Samaria and Galilee. • A[nd] he arose from thence, and • he departed from Galilee, and came into the coasts of Judæa {beyond / by} the farther side of Jordan: [A]nd the people resort unto him again; and as he was wont, he taught them again. • And great multitudes followed him; and he healed them there. • And as he entered into a certain village, there met him ten men that were lepers, which stood afar off: And they lifted up *their* voices, and said, Jesus, Master, have mercy on us. And when he saw *them*, he said unto them, Go shew yourselves unto the priests. And it came to pass, that, as they went, they were cleansed. And one of them, when he saw that he was healed, turned back, and with a loud voice glorified God, And fell down on *his* face at his feet, giving him thanks: [A]nd he was a Samaritan. And Jesus answering said, Were there not ten cleansed? but where are the nine? There are not found that returned to give glory to God, save this stranger. And he said unto him, Arise go thy way: Thy faith hath made thee whole. •

¶ The Pharisees also came unto him, tempting him, • and asked him, • saying unto him, Is it lawful for a man to put away his wife for every cause? And he answered and said unto them, Have ye not read, that he which made *them* at the beginning made them male and female, [a]nd said, For this cause shall a man leave father and mother, and shall cleave to his wife: [A]nd they twain shall be one flesh? Wherefore they are no more twain, but one flesh. What therefore God hath joined together, let not man put assunder. They say unto him, Why did Moses then command to give a writing of divorcement, and to put her away? • And he answered and said unto them, What did Moses command you? And they said, Moses suffered to write a bill of divorcement, and to put *her* away. And Jesus answered and said unto them, • Moses {because of / [f]or} the hardness of your • hearts suffered you to put away your wives: • [H]e wrote you this precept. But from the beginning of the creation • it was not so. • God made them male and female. For this cause shall man leave his father and mother, and cleave

MATTHEW	MARK	LUKE	JOHN

to his wife; [a]nd they twain shall be one flesh: [S]o then they are no more twain, but one flesh. What therefore God hath joined together, let not man put asunder. • And I say unto you, Whosoever shall put away his wife, except *it* be for fornication, and shall marry another, commiteth adultery: [A]nd whoso marrieth her which is put away doth commit adultery. • And in the house his disciples asked him again of the same *matter*. And he saith unto them, Whosoever shall put away his wife, and marry another, commiteth adultery against her. And if a woman shall put away her husband, and be married to another, she commiteth adultery. •

¶ His disciples say unto him, If the case of the man be so with *his* wife, it is not good to marry. But he said unto them, All *men* cannot receive this saying, save *they* to whom it is given. For there are some eunuchs, which were so born from *their* mother's womb: [A]nd there are some eunuchs, which were made eunuchs of men: [A]nd there be eunuchs, which have made themselves eunuchs for the kingdom of heaven's sake. He that is able to receive *it*, let him receive *it*. •

¶ And when he was demanded of the Pharisees, when the Kingdom of God should come, he answered them and said, The kingdom of God cometh not with observation: Neither shall they say, Lo here! or, lo there! for, behold, the kingdom of God is within you. And he said unto the disciples, The days will come, when ye shall desire to see one of the days of the Son of man, and ye shall not see *it*. And they shall say to you, See here; or, see there: [G]o not after *them*, nor follow *them*. For as the lightning, that lighteneth out of the one *part* under heaven, shineth unto the other *part* under heaven; so shall also the Son of man be in his day. But first must he suffer many things, and be rejected of this generation. And as it was in the days of Noe, so shall it be also in the days of the Son of man. They did eat, they drank, they married wives, they were given in marriage, until the day that Noe entered into the ark, and the flood came, and destroyed them all. Likewise also as it was in the days of Lot; they did eat, they drank, they bought, they sold, they planted, they builded; [b]ut the same day that Lot went out of Sodom it rained fire and brimstone from heaven, and destroyed *them* all. Even thus shall it be in the day when the Son of man is revealed. In that day, he which shall be upon the house top, and his stuff in

MATTHEW	MARK	LUKE	JOHN

the house, let him not come down to take it away: [A]nd he that is in he field, let him likewise not return

back. Remember Lot's wife. Whosoever shall seek to save his life shall lose it; and whosoever shall lose

his life shall preserve it. I tell you, in that night there shall be two *men* in one bed; the one shall be

taken, and the other shall be left. Two *women* shall be grinding togehter; the one shall be taken, and

the other left. Two men shall be in the field; the one shall be taken, and the other left. And they

answered and said unto him, Where, Lord? And he said unto them, Wheresoever the body *is*, thither

will the eagles be gathered together.

¶ And he spake a parable unto them *to this end*, that men ought always to pray, and not to faint;

[s]aying, There was in a city a judge, which feared not God, neither regarded man: And there was a

widow in that city; and she came unto him, saying, Avenge me of mine adversary. And he would not for

a while: [B]ut afterward he said within himself, Though I fear not God, nor regard man; [y]et because

this widow troubleth me, I will avenge her, lest by her continual coming she weary me. And the Lord

said, Hear what the unjust judge saith. And shall not God avenge his own elect, which cry day and night

unto him, though he bear long with them? I tell you that he will avenge them speedily. Nevertheless

when the Son of man cometh, shall he find faith on the earth? And he spake this parable unto certain

which trusted in themselves that they were righteous, and despised others: Two men went up into the

temple to pray; the one a Pharisee, and the other a publican. The Pharisee stood and prayed thus with

himself, God, I thank thee, that I am not as other men *are*, extortioners, unjust, adulterers, or even as

this publican. I fast twice in the week, I give tithes of all that I possess. And the publican, standing afar

off, would not lift up so much as *his* eyes unto heaven, but smote upon his breast, saying, God be

merciful to me a sinner. I tell you, this man went down to his house justified *rather* than the other: [F]or

every one that exalteth himself shall be abased; and he that humbleth himself shall be exalted. •

¶ Then were brought unto him little children, • [a]nd they brought unto him also infants, • that

he should {touch / put *his* hands on} them, and pray: • [B]ut when *his* disciples saw *it*, they rebuked

them • that brought *them*. But when Jesus saw *it*, he was much displeased, • But Jesus called them unto

Redaction: We Shall Live in His Sight

MATTHEW	MARK	LUKE	JOHN

him, and said, • unto them, Suffer the little children to come unto me, and forbid them not: • [F]or of

such is the kingdom of {heaven. / God.} Verily I say unto you, Whosoever shall not receive the

kingdom of God as a little child he shall {not/in no wise} enter therein. • And he took them up in his

arms, and {put / laid} *his* hands on them, • and blessed them • and departed thence. •

Ω

MATTHEW	MARK	LUKE	JOHN

- A Ransom for Many -

Matt 19:16-20:28 • Mark 10:17-45 • Luke 18:18-34 • John

¶ And when he was gone forth into the way, • behold, • there came one running, • a certain ruler • and kneeled to him, and asked him, • saying, Good Master, what good thing shall I do, that I may {have / inherit} eternal life? And Jesus said unto him, Why callest thou me good? • *[T]here is* none good {but / save} one, *that is*, God. [B]ut if thou wilt enter into life, keep the commandments. He saith unto him, Which? Jesus said, Thou knowest the commandments, Thou shalt do no murder, {Thou shalt / Do} not commit adultery, • {Thou shalt / Do} not steal, • {Thou shalt / Do} not bear false witness, Defraud not, • Honor thy father and *thy* mother: [A]nd, Thou shalt love thy neighbor as thyself. The young man • answered and said unto him, Master, all these have I {observed / kept} from my youth up: [W]hat lack I yet? • Now when Jesus heard these things, • beholding him loved him, and said unto him, • [Y]et • [o]ne thing thou lackest: • Jesus said unto him, If thou wilt be perfect, • go thy way, • *and* sell {that / whatsoever / all that} thou hast, and {distribute / give} to the poor, and thou shalt have treasure in heaven: [A]nd come, take up the cross, and follow me. • But when the young man heard that saying, • he was sad at that saying, [a]nd and went away {grieved / sorrowful}: [F]or he had great possessions. • [F]or he was very rich.

¶ And when Jesus saw that he was very sorrowful, • Jesus looked round about, • [t]hen said Jesus unto his disciples, Verily I say unto you, that a rich man shall hardly enter into the kingdom of heaven. • How hardly shall they that have riches enter into the kingdom of God! And the disciples were astonished at his words. But Jesus answereth again, and saith unto them, Children, how hard is it for them that trust in riches to enter into the kingdom of God! • And again I say unto you, It is easier for a camel to go through the eye of a needle, than for a rich man to enter into the kingdom of God. When his disciples heard *it*, they were exceedingly amazed, • And they were astonished out of measure, saying among themselves, Who then can be saved? And Jesus looking upon them • beheld *them*, and said unto them, • The things which are impossible with men are possible with God. • With men this is impossible;

MATTHEW	MARK	LUKE	JOHN

• but not with God: [F]or with God all things are possible. •

¶ Then answered Peter and • began to say unto him, Lo, • Behold we have {forsaken / left} all, and have • followed thee; what shall we have therefore? And Jesus answered and said, unto them, Verily I say unto you, That ye which have followed me, in the regeneration when the Son of man shall sit in the throne of his glory, ye also shall sit upon twelve thrones, judging the twelve tribes of Israel. • {There is no man / And every one} that hath {forsaken / left} • houses, or brethren, or sisters, or father, or mother, or wife, or children, or lands, • for the kingdom of God's sake, • for my name's sake, • and the gospel's, • [w]ho shall not receive manifold more in this present time, • [b]ut he shall receive an hundred fold now in this time, houses, and brethren and sisters, and mothers, and children, and lands, with persecutions; and in the world to come • shall inherit {everlasting / eternal} life. • But many *that are* first shall be last; and the last *shall be* first.

¶ For the kingdom of heaven is like unto a man *that is* an householder, which went out early in the morning to hire labourers into his vineyard. And when he had agreed with the labourers for a penny a day, he sent them into his vineyard. And he went out about the third hour, and saw others standing idle in the marketplace, And he said unto them; Go ye also into the vineyard, and whatsoever is right I will give you. And they went their way. Again he went about the sixth and ninth hour, and did likewise. And about the eleventh hour he went out, and found others standing idle, and saith unto them, Why stand ye here all the day idle?

¶ They say unto him, Because no man hath hired us. He saith unto them, Go ye also into the vineyard; and whatsoever is right, *that* shall ye receive. So when the even was come, the lord of the vineyard saith unto his steward, Call the labourers, and give them *their* hire, beginning from the last unto the first. And when they came that *were hired* about the eleventh hour, they received every man a penny. But when the first came, they supposed that they should have received more; and they likewise received every man a penny. And when they had received *it*, they murmured against the goodman of

MATTHEW	MARK	LUKE	JOHN

the house, [s]aying, These last have wrought *but* one hour, and thou hast made them equal unto us, which have borne the burden and the heat of the day. But he answered one of them, and said, Friend, I do thee no wrong: [D]idst not thou agree with me for a penny? Take *that* thine *is*, and go thy way: I will give unto this last, even as unto thee. Is it not lawful for me to do what I will with my own? Is thine eye evil, because I am good? So the last shall be first, and the first last: [F]or many be called, but few chosen. •

¶ And they were in the way going up to Jerusalem; and Jesus went before them: [A]nd they were amazed; and as they followed, they were afraid. • And Jesus going up to Jerusalem • took *unto him* the • twelve disciples apart in the way, • and began to tell them what things should happen unto him, • and said unto them, Behold, we go up to Jerusalem; and the Son of man shall be {betrayed / delivered} unto the chief priests, and unto the scribes; and they shall condemn him to death, • and all things that are written by the prophets concerning the Son of man shall be accomplished. For he shall be delivered unto the Gentiles, and shall be mocked, and spitefully entreated, and {spitted on / shall spit upon him,} and shall {kill him: / crucify *him*; / put him to death:} and the third day he shall rise again. And they understood none of these things: [A]nd this saying was hid from them, neither knew they the things which were spoken. • Then came to him the mother of Zebedee's children with her sons, worshipping *him*, and desiring a certain thing of him. • And James and John, the sons of Zebedee, come unto him saying, Master, we would that thou shouldest do for us whatsoever we shall desire. • And he said unto her, • [a]nd he said unto them, • {What wilt thou / What would ye} that I should do for you? • She saith unto him, Grant that these my two sons may sit, the one on thy right hand, and the other on the left, in thy kingdom. • They said unto him, Grant us that we may sit, one on thy right hand, and the other on thy left hand, in thy glory. • But Jesus answered and said • unto them, • Ye know not what ye ask. Are ye able to drink of the cup that I shall drink of, and to be baptized with the baptism that I am baptized with? They say unto him, We are able. • And Jesus said unto them, Ye shall indeed drink of the cup that I drink of; and with the baptism that I am baptized withal ye shall be baptized: But to sit on my right

MATTHEW	MARK	LUKE	JOHN

hand and on my left hand is not mine to give; • but *it shall be given to them* for whom it is prepared of my Father. • And when the ten heard *it*, they began to be much displeased with James and John. • [T]hey were moved with indignation against the two brethren. • But Jesus called them *to* him, and saith unto them, • Ye know that the princes • which are accounted to rule over the Gentiles exercise {lordship / dominion} over them, and {they that are great / their great ones} exercise authority upon them. • But it shall not be so among you: [B]ut whosoever will be great among you, let him be your minister; [a]nd whosoever will be chief among you, let him be your servant: • And whosoever of you will be the chiefest, shall be servant of all. • Even as the Son of man came not to be ministered unto, but to minister, and to give his life a ransom for many. •

Ω

MATTHEW	MARK	LUKE	JOHN

- Jericho -

Matt 20:29-34 • Mark 10:46-52 • Luke 18:35-19:27 • John

¶ And it came to pass, that as he was come nigh unto Jericho, a certain blind man sat by the way side begging: And hearing the multitude pass by, he asked what it meant. And they told him that Jesus of Nazareth passeth by. And he cried, saying, Jesus, *thou* Son of David, have mercy on me. And they which went before rebuked him, that he should hold his peace: [B]ut he cried so much the more, *Thou* Son of David, have mercy on me. And Jesus stood, and commanded him to be brought unto him: [A]nd when he was come near, he asked him, [s]aying, What wilt thou that I should do unto thee? And he said, Lord, that I may receive my sight. And Jesus said unto him, Receive thy sight: [T]hy faith hath saved thee. And immediately he received his sight, and followed him, glorifying God: [A]nd all the people, when they saw *it*, gave praise unto God. •

¶ And they came to Jericho: • [and] *Jesus* entered and passed through Jericho. And, behold, *there was* a man named Zacchaeus, which was the chief among the publicans, and he was rich. And he sought to see Jesus who he was; and could not for the press, because he was little of stature. And he ran before, and climbed up into a sycomore tree to see him: [F]or he was to pass that *way*. And when Jesus came to the place, he looked up, and saw him, and said unto him, Zacchaeus, make haste, and come down; for to day I must abide at thy house. And he made haste, and came down, and received him joyfully. And when they saw *it*, they all murmured, saying, That he was gone to be guest with a man that is a sinner. And Zacchaeus stood, and said unto the Lord; Behold, Lord, the half of my goods I give to the poor; and if I have taken any thing from any man by false accusation, I restore *him* fourfold. And Jesus said unto him, This day is salvation come to this house, forsomuch as he also is a son of Abraham. For the Son of man is come to seek and to save that which was lost. And as they heard these things, he added and spake a parable, because he was nigh to Jerusalem, and because they thought that the kingdom of God should immediately appear. He said therefore, A certain nobleman went into a far country to receive for himself a kingdom, and to return. And he called his ten servants, and delivered

MATTHEW	MARK	LUKE	JOHN

them ten pounds, and said unto them, Occupy till I come. But his citizens hated him, and sent a message after him, saying, We will not have this *man* to reign over us. And it came to pass, that when he was returned, having received the kingdom, then he commanded these servants to be called unto him, to whom he had given the money, that he might know how much every man had gained by trading. Then came the first, saying, Lord thy pound hath gained ten pounds. And he said unto him, Well, thou good servant: Because thou hast been faithful in a very little, have thou authority over ten cities. And the second came, saying, Lord, thy pound hath gained five pounds. And he said likewise to him, Be thou also over five cities. And another came, saying, Lord, behold, *here is* thy pound, which I have kept laid up in a napkin: For I feared thee, because thou art a austere man: [T]hou takest up that thou layedst not down, and reapest that thou didst not sow. And he saith unto him, Out of thine own mouth will I judge thee, *thou* wicked servant. Thou knewest that I was an austere man, taking up that I laid not down, and reaping that I did not sow: Wherefore then gavest not thou my money into the bank, that at my coming I might have required mine own with usury? And he said unto them that stood by, Take from him the pound, and give *it* to him that hath ten pounds. (And they said unto him, Lord, he hath ten pounds.) For I say unto you, That unto every one which hath shall be given; and from him that hath not, even that he hath shall be taken away from him. But those mine enemies, which would not that I should reign over them, bring hither, and slay *them* before me. • And as {he went out / they departed} from Jericho, • with his disciples and a {great number of people / great multitude} followed him.

¶ And, behold, two blind men sitting by the wayside, • blind Bartimaeus, the son of Timaeus, sat by the wayside begging. And when {he / they} heard that it was Jesus of Nazareth, • passed by, • he began to cry out, and say, Jesus, *thou* Son of David, have mercy on me. • Have mercy on us, O Lord, *thou* Son of David. • And many charged him that he should hold his peace: • And the multitude rebuked them, because they should hold their peace: • [B]ut he cried the more a great deal, • saying, Have mercy on us, O Lord, *thou* Son of David. And Jesus stood still, and • commanded • them, • to be called. And they call the blind man, saying unto him, Be of good comfort, rise; he calleth thee. And he, casting

MATTHEW	MARK	LUKE	JOHN

away his garment, rose, and came to Jesus. And Jesus answered and said unto him, What wilt thou that I should do unto thee? The blind man said unto him, Lord, that {I might receive my sight. / our eyes may be opened.} So Jesus had compassion *on them*, and touched their eyes: • And Jesus said unto him, Go thy way; thy faith hath made thee whole. • [A]nd immediately their eyes received sight, and they followed • Jesus in the way.

Ω

Redaction: We Shall Live in His Sight

MATTHEW	MARK	LUKE	JOHN

MATTHEW	MARK	LUKE	JOHN

- Lazarus Come Forth -

Matt 21:01-11 • Mark 11:01-11 • Luke 19:28-29 • John 11:17-46

¶ And when he had thus spoken, he went before, ascending up to Jerusalem. • Then • it came to pass, • when {Jesus came, / he was come / they came / they drew} nigh unto Jerusalem, and were come • nigh to Bethphage and Bethany, at the mount called the mount of Olives, • he found that he [*Lazarus*] had lain in the grave four days already. Now Bethany was nigh unto Jerusalem, about fifteen furlongs off: And many of the Jews came to Martha and Mary, to comfort them concerning their brother. Then Martha, as soon as she heard that Jesus was coming, went and met him: [B]ut Mary sat still in the house. Then said Martha unto Jesus, Lord, if thou hadst been here, my brother had not died. But I know, that even now, whatsoever thou wilt ask of God, God will give it thee. Jesus saith unto her, Thy brother shall rise again. Martha saith unto him, I know that he shall rise again in the resurrection at the last day. Jesus said unto her, I am the resurrection, and the life: [H]e that believeth in me, though he were dead, yet shall he live: And whoever liveth and believeth in me shall never die. Believest thou this? She saith unto him, Yea, Lord: I believe that thou art the Christ, the Son of God, which should come into the world. And when she had so said, she went her way, and called Mary her sister secretly, saying, The Master is come, and calleth for thee. As soon as she heard that, she arose quickly, and came unto him. Now Jesus was not yet come into the town, but was in that place where Martha met him. The Jews then which were with her in the house, and comforted her, when they saw Mary, that she rose up hastily and went out, followed her, saying, She goeth unto the grave to weep there. Then when Mary was come where Jesus was, and saw him, she fell down at his feet, saying unto him, Lord, if thou hadst been here, my brother had not died. When Jesus therefore saw her weeping, and the Jews also weeping which came with her, he groaned in the spirit, and was troubled, And said, Where have ye laid him? They said unto him, Lord, come and see. Jesus wept. Then said the Jews, Behold how he loved him! And some of them said, Could not this man, which opened the eyes of the blind, have caused that even this man should not have died? Jesus therefore again groaning in himself cometh to the grave. It

MATTHEW	MARK	LUKE	JOHN

was a cave, and a stone laid upon it. Jesus said, Take ye away the stone. Martha the sister of him that

was dead, saith unto him, Lord, by this time he stinketh: [F]or he hath been *dead* four days. Jesus saith

unto her, Said I not unto thee, that, if thou wouldest believe, thou shouldest see the glory of God? Then

they took away the stone *from the place* where the dead was laid. And Jesus lifted *up* his eyes, and said,

Father, I thank thee that thou hast heard me. And I knew that thou hearest me always: [B]ut because of

the people which stand by I said *it*, that they may believe that thou hast sent me. And when he thus had

spoken, he cried with a loud voice, Lazarus, come forth. And he that was dead came forth, bound hand

and foot with graveclothes: [A]nd his face was bound about with a napkin. Jesus saith unto them, Loose

him, and let him go. Then many of the Jews which came to Mary, and had seen the things which Jesus

did, believed on him. But some of them went their ways to the Pharisees, and told them what things

Jesus had done.

ΑΩ

Chapter 14

THY KING COMETH

Zechariah 9:09

Redaction: Thy King Cometh

MATTHEW	MARK	LUKE	JOHN

MATTHEW	MARK	LUKE	JOHN

- Hosanna in the Highest -

Matt 21:01-11 • Mark 11:01-11 • Luke 19:29-44 • John

¶ [T]hen sent Jesus • forth two of his disciples, • [s]aying unto them, • Go ye • your way into the village over against you: • [I]n the which • straightway • at your entering • as soon as ye be entered into it, • ye shall find an ass tied, and a colt with her: • [W]hereon yet never man sat: • [L]oose *them,* and bring *them* • *hither* • unto me. And if any *man* • {ask / say ought unto} you, • Why do ye • {this / loose him}? [T]hus shall ye say unto him, Because the Lord have need of • them; [A]and straightway he will send them • hither. • All this was done, that it might be fulfilled which was spoken by the prophet, saying, Tell ye the daughter of Sion, Behold, thy King cometh unto thee, meek, and sitting upon an ass, and a colt the foal of an ass. And the disciples • that were sent went their way, • and found the colt tied • even as he had said unto them • by the door without in a place where two ways met; • and did as Jesus commanded them, • and they loose him. • And as they were loosing the colt, the owners thereof said unto them, Why loose ye the colt? • And certain of them that stood there said unto them, What do ye loosing the colt? And they said unto them even as Jesus had commanded: • The Lord hath need of him. • [A]nd they let them go. And they brought • the ass, and the colt • to Jesus: [A]nd they cast • and put • their {garments / clothes} • upon {the colt / them}, • {and they set Jesus thereon. / and he sat upon him.} • And as he went, • a very great multitude spread their {garments / clothes} in the way. • And others cut down branches from • off • the trees, and strawed *them* in the way. • And when he was come nigh, even now at the descent of the mount of Olives, the whole multitude of the disciples began to rejoice and praise God with a loud voice for all the mighty works that they had seen; • [a]nd the multitudes that went before, and • they • that followed, cried, saying, Hosanna to the Son of David: Blessed {*is* he / *be* the King} that cometh in the name of the Lord: [P]eace in heaven, and glory in the highest. • Blessed be the kingdom of our father David, that cometh in the name of the Lord: - Hosanna in the highest. - • And some of the Pharisees from among the multitude said unto him, Master, rebuke thy disciples. And he answered and said unto them, I tell you that, if these should hold their peace, the stones would immediately cry out.

MATTHEW	MARK	LUKE	JOHN

¶ And when he was come near, he beheld the city, and wept over it, [s]aying, If thou hadst known, even thou, at least in this thy day, the things *which belong* unto thy peace! [B]ut now they are hid from thine eyes. For the days shall come upon thee, that thine enemies shall cast a trench about thee, and compass thee round, and keep thee in on every side, [a]nd shall lay thee even with the ground, and thy children within thee; and they shall not leave in thee one stone upon another; because thou knewest not the time of thy visitation. • And when he was come into Jerusalem, • and into the temple • all the city was moved, saying, Who is this? And the multitude said, This is Jesus the prophet of Nazareth of Galilee. • [A]nd when he had looked round about upon all things, and now the eventide was come, he went out unto Bethany with the twelve.

Ω

MATTHEW	MARK	LUKE	JOHN

- The House of Prayer -

Matt 21:12-32 • Mark 11:12-26-12:01 • Luke 19:45-20:08 • John

¶ And on the morrow, when they were come from Bethany, he was hungry: And seeing a fig tree afar off having leaves, he came, if haply he might find any thing thereon: [A]nd when he came to it, he found nothing but leaves; for the time of figs was not *yet*. And Jesus answered and said unto it, No man eat fruit of thee hereafter for ever. And his disciples heard *it*. And they come to Jerusalem: • And Jesus went into the temple of God, • and began to cast out them that sold therein, and them that bought • in the temple, and overthrew the tables of the money changers, and the seats of them that sold doves, • And would not suffer that any man should carry *any* vessel through the temple. And he taught, saying unto them, Is it not written, My house shall be called of all nations - the house of prayer -? • And said unto them, It is written, My house shall be called the house of prayer; [B]ut ye have made it a den of thieves. • And he taught daily in the temple. But the chief priests and the scribes and the chief of the people sought {to / how they might} destroy him: [F]or they feared him, • [a]nd could not find what they might do: [F]or all the people were very attentive to hear him • because all the people was astonished at his doctrine. • And the blind and the lame came to him in the temple; and he healed them. And when the chief priests and scribes saw the wonderful things that he did, and the children crying in the temple, and saying, Hosanna to the Son of David; [T]hey were sore displeased, [a]nd said unto him, Hearest thou what these say? And Jesus saith unto them, Yea; have ye never read, Out of the mouth of babes and sucklings thou hast perfected praise? •

¶ And when even was come, • he left them, and went out of the city into Bethany; and he lodged there. Now in the morning as he returned into the city, he hungered. And when he saw a fig tree in the way, he came to it, and found nothing thereon, but leaves only, and said unto it, Let no fruit grow on thee hence forward for ever. And presently the fig tree withered away! And when the disciples • as they passed by, • saw *it*, • they saw the fig tree dried up from the roots • they marvelled, saying, How soon is the fig tree withered away! • And Peter calling to remembrance saith unto him,

MATTHEW	MARK	LUKE	JOHN

Master, behold, the fig tree which thou cursedst is withered away. And Jesus answering saith unto them, Have faith in God. • Verily I say unto you, If ye have faith, and doubt not, ye shall not only do this *which is done* to the fig tree, but also {if ye / [t]hat whosoever} will say unto this mountain, Be thou removed, and be thou cast into the sea; [A]nd shall not doubt in his heart, but shall believe that those things which he saith shall come to pass; he shall have whatsoever he saith[,] • it shall be done. • Therefore I say unto you, • all • [w]hat things soever ye desire, • ye shall ask in prayer, • when ye pray • believing, • that • ye shall receive • *them*, and ye shall have *them*. And when ye stand praying, forgive, if ye have ought against any: [T]hat your Father also which is in heaven may forgive you your trespasses. But if ye do not forgive, neither will your Father which is in heaven forgive your trespasses.

¶ A[nd] it came to pass, *that* on one of those days, • they come again to Jerusalem: • And when he was come into the temple, • as he taught the people in the temple, and preached the gospel, • as he was walking in the temple, there come to him the chief priests, and the scribes, and the elders • of the people • [a]nd spake unto him, saying, Tell us, by what authority doest thou these things? • [A]nd who • is he that • gave thee this authority to do these things? And Jesus answered and said unto them, I will also ask of you one question, • which if ye tell • and answer me, • I in the like wise will tell you by what authority I do these things. The baptism of John, whence was it? [F]rom heaven, or of men? • [A]nswer me. And they reasoned with themselves, saying, • If we shall say, From heaven; [H]e will say unto us, Why did ye not then believe him? But if we shall say, Of men; {[W]e fear / [T]hey feared}: • [A]ll the people will stone us: [F]or they be persuaded that John was a prophet. • [F]or all *men* • {hold / counted} John, that he was a prophet indeed. And they answered and said unto Jesus, We cannot tell • whence *it was*. • And Jesus answering saith unto them, Neither do I tell you by what authority I do these things.

¶ And he began to speak unto them by parables. • But what think ye? A *certain* man had two sons; and he came to the first, and said, Son, go work today in my vineyard. He answered and said, I will not: But afterward he repented, and went. And he came to the second, and said likewise. And he answered and said, I *go*, sir: [A]nd went not. Whether of them twain did the will of *his* father? They say

MATTHEW	MARK	LUKE	JOHN

unto him, The first. Jesus saith unto them, Verily I say unto you, [t]hat [T]he publicans and the harlots go into the kingdom of God before you. For John came unto you in the way of righteousness, and ye believed him not: [B]ut the publicans and harlots believed him: [A]nd ye, when ye had seen *it*, repented not afterward, that ye might believe him.

Ω

Redaction: Thy King Cometh

MATTHEW	MARK	LUKE	JOHN

MATTHEW	MARK	LUKE	JOHN

- The Head of the Corner -

Matt 21:33-22:14 • Mark 12:01-12 • Luke 20:09-19 • John

¶ Hear another parable: • Then began he to speak to the people this parable; • There was a certain • {man / householder}, which planted a vineyard, • and set an hedge about *it*, • and digged a wine press in it, • *for* the winefat, and built a tower, and let it {out / forth} • to husbandmen, • and went into a far country for a long time. • And at the season • when the time of the fruit drew near, he sent his servants to the husbandmen, that they should give • that they might receive • from the husbandmen of the • fruits • of the vineyard. • And the husbandmen took • [a]nd they caught • his servants, and beat one, • and sent *him* away empty. And again he sent unto them another servant; and at him they cast stones, and wounded him in the head, • and they beat him also, and entreated *him* shamefully, and sent *him* away empty • shamefully handled. • And again he sent a third: [A]nd they wounded him also, and cast *him* out. • And again he sent another; and him they killed • and stoned another. Again, he sent • many • other servants more than the first: [A]nd they did unto them likewise • beating some, and killing some. • Then said the lord of the vineyard, What shall I do? • But last of all • [h]aving yet therefore one son, his wellbeloved, • he sent unto them his son, saying, • I will send my beloved son: [I]t may be they will reverence • {my son / *him*} when they see him. • But when the husbandman saw the son, • those husbandmen • reasoned among themselves, saying, This is the heir: [C]ome, let us kill him, • and let us seize on his inheritance • that the inheritance {may / shall} • be ours. So they • caught him, • took him, • and cast *him* out of the vineyard, • and {killed / slew} *him*. When the lord therefore of the vineyard cometh, what • therefore shall the • Lord of the vineyard do • unto those husbandmen? They say unto him, • [H]e will come and • miserably destroy those wicked • husbandmen, {and will give / and will let out} {his / *the*} • vineyard unto other husbandmen, which shall render unto him the fruits in their seasons. • [(Jesus said)] He shall come and destroy these husbandmen, and shall give the vineyard to others. And when they heard *it*, they said, God forbid. And he beheld them, and • Jesus saith unto them, • What is this then that is written, • [d]id you never read in the scriptures, • this scripture; • The stone

MATTHEW	MARK	LUKE	JOHN

which the builders rejected, the same is become - the head of the corner -: • This was the Lord's doing, and it is marvellous in our eyes? • Therefore say I unto you, The kingdom of God shall be taken from you, and given to a nation bringing forth the fruits thereof. • Whosoever shall fall upon {that / this} stone shall be broken: [B]ut on whomsoever it shall fall, it will grind him to powder.

¶ And when the chief priests • and the scribes • and Pharisees had heard his parables, they perceived that he spake of them. But • the same hour • when they sought to lay {hands / hold} • on him, they feared the {multitude, / people} • because they took him for a prophet • for they {knew / perceived} that he had spoken this parable against them. •

¶ And Jesus answered and spake unto them again by parables, and said, The kingdom of heaven is like unto a certain king, which made a marriage for his son, [a]nd sent forth his servants to call them that were bidden to the wedding: [A]nd they would not come. Again, he sent forth other servants, saying, Tell them which are bidden, Behold, I have prepared my dinner: [M]y oxen and *my* fatlings *are* killed, and all things *are* ready: [C]ome unto the marriage. But they made light of *it*, and went their ways, one to his farm, another to his merchandise: And the remnant took his servants, and entreated *them* spitefully, and slew *them*. But when the king heard *thereof*, he was wroth: [A]nd he sent forth his armies, and destroyed those murderers, and burned up their city. Then saith he to his servants, The wedding is ready, but they which were bidden were not worthy. Go ye therefore into the highways, and as many as ye shall find, bid to the marriage. So those servants went out into the highways, and gathered together all as many as they found, both bad and good: [A]nd the wedding was furnished with guests.

¶ And when the king came in to see the guests, he saw there a man which had not on a wedding garment: And he saith unto him, Friend, how camest thou in hither not having a wedding garment? And he was speechless. Then said the king to the servants, Bind him hand and foot, and take

MATTHEW	MARK	LUKE	JOHN

him away, and cast *him* into outer darkness; there shall be weeping and gnashing of teeth. For many are called, but few *are* chosen. •

Ω

Redaction: Thy King Cometh

MATTHEW	MARK	LUKE	JOHN

MATTHEW	MARK	LUKE	JOHN

- That One Man Should Die -

Matt 22:15-23:12 • Mark 12:12-39 • Luke 20:20-46 • John 11:47-53

¶ Then went the Pharisees, • and they left him, and went their way. • Then gathered the chief priests and the Pharisees a council, and said, What do we? [F]or this man doeth many miracles. If we let him thus alone, all *men* will believe on him: [A]nd the Romans shall come and take away both our place and nation. And one of them *named* Caiaphas, being the high priest that same year, said unto them, Ye know nothing at all, [n]or consider that it is expedient for us, that one man should die for the people, and that the whole nation perish not. And this spake he not of himself: [B]ut being high priest that year, he prophesied that Jesus should die for that nation; [a]nd not for that nation only, but that also he should gather together in one the children of God that were scattered abroad. Then from that day forth they took counsel together • how they might entangle him in *his* talk • for to put him to death. •

¶ And they watched *him*, and sent forth spies, • unto him certain of the Pharisees • their disciples with the herodians, • which should feign themselves just men, that they might take hold of his words, • to catch him in *his* words. • [T]hat so they might deliver him unto the power and authority of the governor. • And when they were come, • they asked him, saying, • unto him, • Master, we know that thou art true, • that thou sayest and teachest rightly, • the way of God in truth, neither carest thou for any *man:* [F]or thou {regardest / acceptest} • not the person of • *any* • men • but teachest the way of God truly: • Tell us therefore, What thinkest thou? • Is it lawful for us to give tribute unto Cæsar, or {no / not?} • Shall we give, or shall we not give? But he, knowing their hypocrisy, • Jesus perceived their {wickedness / craftiness}, and said unto them, • Why tempt ye me, *ye* hypocrites? Shew me the tribute money. • [B]ring me a penny, that I may see *it.* • And they brought unto him a penny. And he saith unto them, Whose *is* this image and superscription? • Whose image and superscription hath it? They answered and said • unto him, Cæsar's. • Then • Jesus answering said unto them, • Render therefore unto Cæsar the things which {are / be} • Cæsar's; and unto God the things {that are / which be} • God's.

Redaction: Thy King Cometh

MATTHEW	MARK	LUKE	JOHN

When they had heard *these words*, • they could not take hold of his words before the people: [A]nd
they marvelled at • {him / his answer}, and held their peace • and left him, and went their way. •

¶ Then • [t]he same day came • unto him • certain of the Sadducees, which {deny that there is
any / say there is no} resurrection; and they asked him, saying, • Master, Moses {said, / wrote unto us,}
If any man's brother die, having a wife, • and leave *his* wife *behind him*, and {leave no / having no / he
die without} children, that his brother should {take / marry} his wife, and raise up seed unto his
brother. Now there were with us • therefore • seven brethren: [A]nd the first, when he had
{married/took} a wife, {died without children / dying left no seed / and, deceased, having no issue,}
[and] left his wife unto his brother: Likewise the second also, • took her to wife, • neither left he any
seed: • and he died childless. And the third • likewise • took her; and in like manner the seven also: •
[H]ad her, • and they • left no {seed / children}, • unto the seventh • and died. Last of all the woman died
also. Therefore in the resurrection • when they shall rise, whose wife • of them {is she / shall she be} • of
the seven? • [F]or {the seven / they} all had her • to wife. And Jesus answering said unto them, Ye do
err, • [d]o ye not therefore err, because ye know not the scriptures, neither the power of God? • The
children of this world marry, and are given in marriage: • For in the resurrection • they which shall be
accounted worthy to obtain that world, and the resurrecttion from the dead, • when they shall rise from
the dead, they neither marry, nor are given in marriage; but are as the angels • of God • which are in
heaven. • Neither can they die anymore: [F]or they are equal unto the angels; and are the children of
God, being the children of the resurrection. Now • as touching the resurrection of the dead, • that the
dead are raised, even Moses shewed at the bush, when he calleth the Lord the God of Abraham, and
the God of Isaac, and the God of Jacob. • [H]ave ye not read in the book of Moses, • that which was
spoken unto you by God, • how in the bush God spake unto him, saying, I *am* the God of Abraham, and
the God of Isaac, and the God of Jacob? • For he is not a God of the dead, • but the God of the living:
[Y]e therefore do greatly err. • And when the multitude heard *this*, they were astonished at his
doctrine.

MATTHEW	MARK	LUKE	JOHN

¶ But when the Pharisees had heard that he had put the Sadducees to silence, they were gathered together. Then one of {them / the scribes} • *which was* a lawyer, • came, and having heard them reasoning together, and perceiving that he had answered them well, asked him, • *a question*, tempting him, and saying, Master, which *is* the • first • great • commandment of all • in the law? • And Jesus answered • unto him, • The first of all the commandments *is*, Hear, O Israel; The Lord our God is one Lord: And thou shalt love the Lord thy God with all thy heart, and with all thy soul, and with all thy mind, and with all thy strength: • This is the first and great commandment. And the second *is* like unto it, • *namely* this, • Thou shalt love thy neighbor as thy self. • There is none other commandment greater than these. • On these two commandments hang all the law and the prophets. •

¶ Then certain of the scribes answering said, Master, thou hast well said. • And the scribe said unto him, Well, Master, thou hast said the truth: [F]or there is one God; and their is none other but he: And to love him with all the heart, and with all the understanding, and with all the soul, and with all the strength, and to love *his* neighbor as himself, is more than all whole burnt offerings and sacrifices. And when Jesus saw that he answered discreetly, he said unto him, Thou art not far from the kingdom of God. And no man after that durst ask him *any question* • *at all.* •

¶ While the Pharisees were gathered together, Jesus asked them, [s]aying, What think ye of Christ? [W]hose son is he? They say unto him, *The Son* of David. • And Jesus answered and said, • unto them, • while he taught in the temple, How say the {scribes / they} • that Christ is {the Son of David? / David's son?} • How then doth David in spirit call him Lord, • For David himself • saith in the book of Psalms, • by the Holy Ghost, The LORD • said unto my Lord, Sit thou on my right hand, • till I make thine enemies thy footstool? If David {then / therefore} himself calleth him Lord; {and whence / how} is he then his son? • And the common people heard him gladly. • And no man was able to answer him a word, neither durst any *man* from that day forth ask him any more *questions.*

MATTHEW	MARK	LUKE	JOHN

¶ T[hen] spake Jesus • [a]nd he said unto them in his doctrine, • to the multitude, and to his disciples, • in the audience of all the people • [s]aying, The scribes and the Pharisees sit in Moses' seat: All therefore whatsoever they bid you observe, *that* observe and do; but • [b]eware of the scribes, • do not ye after their works: [F]or they say, and do not. For they bind heavy burdens and grievous to be borne, and lay *them* on men's shoulders; but they *themselves* will not move them with one of their fingers. But all their works they do for to be seen of men: [T]hey make broad their phylacteries, and enlarge the borders of their garments, • which {love / desire} {to walk / go} in long {clothing / robes,} and love {greetings / salutations} in the marketplaces, And the {chief / highest} seats in the synagogues, and the {chief / uppermost} rooms at feasts: • [A]nd to be called of men, Rabbi, Rabbi. But be not ye called Rabbi: [F]or one is your Master, *even* Christ; and all ye are brethren. And call no *man* your father upon the earth: [F]or one is your Father, which is in heaven. Neither be ye called masters: [F]or one is your master, *even* Christ. But he that is greatest among you shall be your servant. And whosoever shall exalt himself shall be abased; and he that shall humble himself shall be exalted.

Ω

MATTHEW	MARK	LUKE	JOHN

- The Measure of Your Fathers -

Matt 23:13-39 • Mark 12:40 • Luke 20:47 • John 11:54

¶ But woe unto you, scribes and Pharisees, hypocrites! [F]or ye shut up the kingdom of heaven against men: [F]or ye neither go in *yourselves*, neither suffer ye them that are entering to go in. Woe unto you, scribes and Pharisees, hypocrites! {[F]or ye / Which} devour widows' houses, and for a pretense make long prayers: {[T]hese / [T]he same / [Y]e} shall receive the greater damnation. Woe unto you, scribes and Pharisees, hypocrites! [F]or ye compass sea and land to make one proselyte, and when he is made, ye make him twofold more the child of hell than yourselves. Woe unto you, *ye* blind guides, which say, Whosoever shall swear by the temple, it is nothing; but whosoever shall swear by the gold of the temple, he is a debtor! *Ye* fools and blind: [F]or whether is greater, the gold, or the temple that sactifeth the gold? And, Whosoever shall swear by the altar, it is nothing; but whosoever shall sweareth by the gift that is upon it, he is guilty. *Ye* fools and blind: [F]or whether *is* greater, the gift, or the altar that sactifieth the gift? Whoso therefore shall swear by the altar, sweareth by it, and by all things thereon. And whoso shall swear by the temple, sweareth by it, and by him that dwelleth therein. And he that shall swear by heaven, sweareth by the throne of God, and by him that sitteth thereon. Woe unto you, scribes and Pharisees, hypocrites! [F]or ye pay tithe of mint and anise and cummin, and have omitted the weightier *matters* of the law, judgment, mercy, and faith: [T]hese ought ye to have done, and not to leave the other undone. *Ye* blind guides, which strain at a gnat, and swallow a camel. Woe unto you, scribes and Pharisees, hypocrites! [F]or ye make clean the outside of the cup and of the platter, but within they are full of extortion and excess. *Thou* blind Pharisee, cleanse first that *which is* within the cup and platter, that the outside of them may be clean also. Woe unto you, scribes and Pharisees, hypocrites! [F]or ye are like unto whited sepulchers, which indeed appear beautiful outward, but are within full of dead *men's* bones, and of all uncleaness. Even so ye also outwardly appear righteous unto men, but within ye are full of hypocrisy and iniquity. Woe unto you, scribes and Pharisees, hypocrites! [B]ecause ye build the tombs of the prophets, and garnish the

MATTHEW	MARK	LUKE	JOHN

sepulchers of the righteous, [a]nd say, If we had been in the days of our fathers, we would not have been partakers with them in the blood of the prophets. Wherefore ye be witnesses unto yourselves, that ye are the children of them which killed the prophets. Fill ye up then the measure of your fathers. *Ye* serpents, *ye* generation of vipers, how can ye escape the damnation of hell? Wherefore, behold, I send unto you prophets, and wise men, and scribes: [A]nd *some* of them ye shall kill and crucify; and *some* of them shall ye scourge in your synagogues, and persecute *them* from city to city: That upon you may come all the righteous blood shed upon the earth, from the blood of righteous Abel unto the blood of Zacharias son of Barachias, whom ye slew between the temple and the altar. Verily I say unto you, All these things shall come upon this generation. O Jerusalem, Jerusalem, *thou* that killest the prophets, and stonest them which are sent unto thee, how often would I have gathered thy children together, even as a hen gathereth her chickens under *her* wings, and ye would not! Behold, your house is left unto you desolate. For I say unto you, Ye shall not see me henceforth, till ye shall say, Blessed *is* he that cometh in the name of the Lord. • Jesus therefore walked no more openly among the Jews; but went thence unto a country near to the wilderness, into a city called Ephraim, and there continued with his disciples.

AΩ

Chapter 15

THE TIME
OF TROUBLE

Psalm 27:05

Redaction: The Time of Trouble

MATTHEW	MARK	LUKE	JOHN

MATTHEW	MARK	LUKE	JOHN

- The Beginning of Sorrows -

Matt 24:01-28 • Mark 12:41-13:23 • Luke 21:01-24 • John 11:55-12:01

¶ And the Jews' Passover was nigh at hand: [A]nd many went out of the country up to Jerusalem before the passover, to purify themselves. Then sought they for Jesus, and spake among themselves, as they stood in the temple, What think ye, that he will not come to the feast? Now both the chief priests and the Pharisees had given a commandment, that, if any man knew where he were, he should shew *it*, that they might take him. •

¶ And Jesus sat over against the treasury, • [a]nd he looked up, • and beheld how the people cast money into the treasury: • [A]nd saw the rich men casting their gifts into the treasury. • [A]nd many that were rich cast in much. • And he saw also • there came a certain poor widow, and she {threw / casting} • in • thither • two mites, which make a farthing. And he called *unto him* his disciples, and saith unto them, Verily • Of a truth I say unto you, that this poor widow hath cast in more • than all they which have cast into the treasury: • For all of these • {did / have} of their abundance cast in unto the offerings of God, • but she of her {want / penury} • did cast in all that she had, *even* all her living. •

¶ And Jesus went out, and departed from the temple: • And as some spake of the temple, how it was adorned with goodly stones and gifts, • his disciples came to *him* for to shew him the buildings of the temple. • And as he went out of the temple, one of his disciples saith unto him, Master, see what manner of stones and what buildings *are here!* And Jesus answering said unto him, Seest thou these great buildings? • See ye not all these things? • *As for* these things which ye behold, the days will come, in the which • verily I say unto you, There shall not be left here one stone upon another, that shall not be thrown down. •

¶ T[hen] Jesus six days before the passover came to Bethany, where Lazarus was which had been dead, whom he raised from the dead. • And as he sat upon the mount of Olives over against the temple, • the disciples • Peter and James and John and Andrew • came unto him privately, • [a]nd they

MATTHEW	MARK	LUKE	JOHN

asked him, saying, Master, but • [t]ell us, • when shall these things be? [And what sign *will there be* • of thy coming, and of the end of the world • when all these things shall {be fulfilled? / come to pass?} • And Jesus answered and said unto them, • Take heed that ye be not deceived: • {[T]hat no / [L]est any} • man deceive you. For many shall come in my name, saying, I am Christ; • and the time draweth near: • [A]nd shall deceive many. • [G]o ye not therefore after them. But when ye shall hear of wars • and rumors of wars, • and commotions, • see that ye be not troubled: • [B]e not terrified: • [F]or all *these* • *such* • things must first come to pass; but the end {*is* not / *shall* not *be*} yet • by and by. Then said he unto them, • For nation shall rise against nation, and kingdom against kingdom: • And great earthquakes shall be in divers places, and famines, and pestilences; and fearful sights • and troubles: • [A]nd great signs shall there be from heaven. • All these *are* the beginning of sorrows. •

¶ But take heed to yourselves: • [B]efore all these, they shall lay their hands on you, and persecute *you,* • [F]or they shall deliver you up to councils; and in the synagogues ye shall be beaten: • Then shall they deliver you up • into prisons, • to be afflicted, • and ye shall be brought before rulers and kings for my sake, • and shall kill you: [A]nd ye shall be hated of all nations for my name's sake. • And it shall turn to you for a testimony • against them. And the gospel must first be published among all nations. • Settle *it* therefore in your hearts, not to meditate before what ye shall answer: • But when they shall lead *you,* and deliver you up, take no thought beforehand what ye shall speak, neither do ye premeditate: • For I will give you a mouth and wisdom, which all your adversaries shall not be able to gainsay nor resist. • [B]ut whatsoever shall be given you in that hour, that speak ye: [F]or it is not ye that speak, but the Holy Ghost. • And then shall many be offended, and shall betray one another, and shall hate one another. • And ye shall be betrayed both by parents, and brethren, and kinfolks, and friends; • [n]ow the brother shall betray the brother to death, and the father the son; and children shall rise up against *their* parents, • and *some* of you shall they cause to be put to death. • And many false prophets shall rise, and shall deceive many. And because iniquity shall abound, the love of many shall wax cold. • And ye shall be hated of all *men* for my name's sake. But there shall not an hair of your head

MATTHEW	MARK	LUKE	JOHN

perish. • But he that shall endure unto the end, the same shall be saved. • In your patience possess ye your souls. • And this gospel of the kingdom shall be preached in allthe world for a witness unto all nations; and then shall the end come. •

¶ But • [w]hen ye therefore shall see the abomination of desolation, spoken of by Daniel the prophet, • standing • in the holy place, • where it ought not, (let him • whoso • that readeth understand,) • And when ye shall see Jerusalem compassed with armies, then know that the desolation thereof is nigh. Then let them which are in Judæa flee • into the mountains: • [A]nd let them which are in the midst of it depart out; • [a]nd let him that is on the housetop not {go / come} • down into the house, neither enter *therein*, to take anything out of his house: •

¶ Neither let him which is in the field return back • again for to take up his {garment / clothes} • and let not them that are in the countries enter thereinto. For these be the days of vengeance, that all things which are written may be fulfilled. {But / And} woe unto them that are with child, and to them that give suck in those days! But pray ye that your flight be not in the winter, neither on the sabbath day: For then • *in* those days shall be • great {tribulation / affliction}, • such as was not since the beginning • of the creation • of the world • which God created unto • this time, no, {nor / neither} • ever shall be. • [F]or there shall be great distress in the land, and wrath upon this people. And they shall fall by the edge of the sword, and shall be lead away captive into all nations: [A]nd Jerusalem shall be trodden down of the Gentiles, until the times of the gentiles be fulfilled. • And except that the Lord had shortened those days, • there should no flesh be saved: • [B]ut for the elect's sake, whom he hath chosen, he hath shortened the days. • Then if any man shall say unto you, Lo, here *is* Christ, • or, lo, *he is* there; believe *him* not: • For there shall arise false Christs, and false prophets, and shall shew great signs and wonders; • to seduce, • insomuch that • if *it were* possible, • they shall deceive • even • the very elect. • But take ye heed: [B]ehold, I have fortold you • before • all things. • Wherefore if they shall say unto you, Behold, he is in the desert; go not forth, behold, *he is* in the secret chambers; believe *it*

MATTHEW	MARK	LUKE	JOHN

not. For as the lightning cometh out of the east, and shineth even unto the west; so shall also the coming of the Son of man be. For wheresoever the carcase is, there will the eagles be gathered together. •

Ω

MATTHEW	MARK	LUKE	JOHN

- After the Tribulation -

Matt 24:29-51 • Mark 13:24-37 • Luke 21:25-38 • John

¶ But in those days, • [i]mmediately after {the / that} • tribulation of those days • there shall be signs in the sun, and in the moon, and in the stars; • the sun be darkened, and the moon shall not give her light, and the stars • of heaven • shall fall from heaven, • [a]nd upon the earth distress of nations, with perplexity; the sea and the waves roaring; [m]en's hearts failing them for fear, and for looking after those things which are coming on the earth: [F]or the powers • that are {in / of} the heavens shall be shaken: And then shall appear the sign of the Son of man in heaven: [A]nd then shall all the tribes of the earth mourn, and • then shall they see the Son of man coming in the clouds • of heaven • with great power and glory. And then shall he send his angels, • with the great sound of a trumpet, and they shall gather together his elect from the four winds, • from the uttermost part of the earth to the uttermost part of heaven • from one end of heaven to the other. • And when these things begin to come to pass, then look up, and lift up your heads; for your redemption draweth nigh. • Now learn a parable of the fig tree; • And he spake to them a parable; Behold the fig tree, • [w]hen {his / her} • branch is yet tender, • and all the trees; [w]hen they now shoot • and putteth forth leaves, • ye see and know of your own selves that summer is now {nigh / near} • at hand. • So likewise ye, when ye shall see all these things, • come to pass, know ye that the kingdom of God is {nigh / near} • at hand • *even* at the doors. • Verily I say unto you, that this generation shall not pass, till all these things be {done / fulfilled}. Heaven and earth shall pass away, but my words shall not pass away. •

¶ But of that day and *that* hour knoweth no man, no, not the angels • of heaven, • which are in heaven, neither the Son, but {the / my} Father only. But as the days of Noe *were*, so shall also the coming of the Son of man be. For as in the days that were before the flood they were eating and drinking, marrying and giving in marriage, until the day that Noe entered into the ark, [a]nd knew not until the flood came, and took them all away; so shall also the coming of the Son of man be. Then shall two be in the field; the one shall be taken, and the other left. Two *women shall be* grinding at the mill;

MATTHEW	MARK	LUKE	JOHN

the one shall be taken, and the other left. • And take heed to yourselves, • watch and pray: • [L]est at any time your hearts be overcharged with surfeiting, and drunkeness, and cares of this life, and *so* that day come upon you unawares • for ye know not when the time is. • For as a snare shall it come on all them that dwell on the face of the whole earth. • *For the Son of man is* as a man taking a far journey, who left his house, and gave authority to his servants, and to everyman his work, and commanded the porter to watch.

¶ Watch ye therefore: • [A]nd pray always, that ye may be accounted worthy to escape all these things that shall come to pass, and to stand before the Son of man. • [F]or ye know not • what hour • when • your Lord • the master of the house • {doth come / cometh} at even, or at midnight, or at the cockcrowing, or in the morning: Lest coming suddenly he find you sleeping. And what I say unto you I say unto all, Watch. • But know this, that if the goodman of the house had known in what watch the thief would come, he would have watched, and would not have suffered his house to be broken up. Therefore be ye also ready: [F]or in such an hour as ye think not the Son of man cometh. Who then is a faithful and wise servant, whom his lord hath made ruler over his household, to give them meat in due season? Blessed *is* that servant, whom his lord when he cometh shall find so doing. Verily I say unto you, [t]hat he shall make him ruler over all his goods. But and if that evil servant shall say in his evil heart, My lord delayeth his coming; [a]nd shall begin to smite *his* fellowservants, and to eat and drink with the drunken; [t]he lord of that servant shall come in a day when he looketh not for *him*, and in an hour that he is not aware of, [a]nd shall cut him asunder, and appoint *him* his portion with the hypocrites: [T]here shall be weeping and gnashing of teeth. • And in the day time he was teaching in the temple; and at night he went out, and abode in the mount that is called *the mount* of Olives. And all the people came early in the morning to him in the temple, for to hear him. •

Ω

MATTHEW	MARK	LUKE	JOHN

- The Son of Man Cometh -

Matt 25:01-46 • Mark • Luke • John

¶ T[hen] shall the kingdom of heaven be likened unto ten virgins, which took their lamps, and went forth to meet the bridegroom. And five of them were wise, and five *were* foolish. They that *were* foolish took their lamps, and took no oil with them: But the wise took oil in their vessels with their lamps. While the bridegroom tarried, they all slumbered and slept. And at midnight there was a cry made, Behold the bridegroom cometh; go ye out to meet him. Then all those virgins arose, and trimmed their lamps. And the foolish said unto the wise, Give us of your oil; for our lamps are gone out. But the wise answered, saying, *Not so*; lest there be not enough for us and you: [B]ut go ye rather to them that sell, and buy for yourselves. And while they went to buy, the bridegroom came; and they that were ready went in with him to the marriage: [A]nd the door was shut. Afterward came also the other virgins, saying, Lord, Lord, open to us. But he answered and said, Verily I say unto you, I know you not. Watch therefore, for ye know neither the day nor the hour wherein the Son of man cometh.

¶ For *the kingdom of heaven is* as a man traveling into a far country, *who* called his own servants, and delivered unto them his goods. And unto one he gave five talents, to another two, and to another one; to every man according to his severalability; and straight way took his journey. Then he that had received the five talents went and traded with the same, and made *them* other five talents. And likewise he that *had received* two, he also gained other two. But he that had received one went and digged in the earth, and hid his lord's money. After a long time the lord of those servants cometh, and reckoneth with them. And so he that had received five talents came and brought other five talents, saying, Lord, thou deliveredst unto me five talents: [B]ehold, I have gained beside them five talents more. His lord said unto him, Well done, *thou* good and faithful servant: [T]hou hast been faithful over a few things, I will make thee ruler over many things: [E]nter thou into the joy of thy lord. He also that had received two talents came and said, Lord, thou deliveredst unto me two talents: [B]ehold, I have gained two other talents beside them. His lord said unto him, Well done, good and faithful servant; thou

MATTHEW	MARK	LUKE	JOHN

hast been faithful over a few things, I will make thee ruler over many things: [E]nter thou into the joy of

thy lord. Then he which had received the one talent came and said, Lord, I knew thee that thou art an

hard man, reaping where thou hast not sown, and gathering where thou hast not strawed: And I was

afraid, and went and hid thy talent in the earth: [L]o, *there* thou hast *that is* thine. His lord answered and

said unto him, *Thou* wicked and slothful servant, thou knewest that I reap where I sowed not, and

gather where I have not strawed: Thou oghtest therefore to have put my money to the exchangers, and

then at my coming I should have received mine own with usury. Take therefore the talent from him,

and give *it* unto him which hath ten talents. For unto everyone that hath shall be given, and he shall

have abundance: [B]ut from him that hath not shall be taken away even that which he hath. And cast ye

the unprofitable servant into outer darkness: [T]here shall be weeping and gnashing of teeth.

¶ When the Son of man shall come in his glory, and all the holy angels with him, then shall he

sit upon the throne of his glory: And before him shall be gathered all nations: [A]nd he shall separate

them one from another, as a shepherd divideth *his* sheep from the goats: And he shall set the sheep on

his right hand, but the goats on the left. Then shall the King say unto them on his right hand, Come ye

blessed of my Father, inherit the kingdom prepared for you from the foundation of the world: For I was

an hungered, and ye gave me meat: I was thirsty, and ye gave me drink: I was a stranger, and ye took

me in: Naked, and ye clothed me: I was sick, and ye visited me: I was in prison, and ye came unto me.

Then shall the righteous answer him, saying, Lord, when saw we thee an hungered, and fed *thee*? or

thirsty, and gave *thee* drink? When saw we thee a stranger, and took *thee* in? or naked, and clothed

thee? Or when saw we thee sick, or in prison, and came unto thee? And the King shall answer and say

unto them, Verily I say unto you, Inasmuch as ye have done *it* unto one of the least of these my

brethren, ye have done *it* unto me. Then shall he say also unto them on the left hand, Depart from me,

ye cursed, into everlasting fire, prepared for the devil and his angels: For I was an hungered, and ye

gave me no meat: I was thirsty, and ye gave me no drink: I was a stranger, and ye took me not in:

naked, and ye clothed me not: sick, and in prison, and ye visited me not. Then shall they also answer

MATTHEW	MARK	LUKE	JOHN

him, saying, Lord, when saw we thee an hungered, or athirst, or a stranger, or naked, or sick, or in prison, and did not minister unto thee? Then shall he answer them, saying, Verily I say unto you, Inasmuch as ye did *it* not to one of the least of these, ye did *it* not to me. And these shall go away into ever lasting punishment: [B]ut the righteous into life eternal. •

Ω

Redaction: The Time of Trouble

MATTHEW	MARK	LUKE	JOHN

MATTHEW	MARK	LUKE	JOHN

- Judas Iscariot, Simon's Son -

Matt 26:01-16 • Mark 14:01-11 • Luke 22:01-06 • John 12:02-50

¶ Now the feast of unleavened bread drew nigh, which is called the Passover. • After two days was *the feast of* the Passover, and of unleavened bread: • A[nd] it came to pass, when Jesus had finished all these sayings, he said unto his disciples, Ye know that after two days is *the feast of* the passover, and the Son of man is betrayed to be crucified. Then assembled together the chief priests, and the scribes, and the elders of the people, unto the palace of the chief priest, who was called Caiaphas, • and the chief priests and the scribes sought • [a]nd consulted {that / how} they might take • Jesus by {subtility, / craft,} and {put *him* to death / kill *him*.} But they said, Not on the feast *day*, [L]est there be an uproar among the people • for they feared the people. •

¶ Now when Jesus {was / being} • in Bethany, in the house of Simon the leper, • [t]here they made him a supper; and Martha served: [B]ut Lazarus was one of them that sat at the table with him. • [A]s he sat at meat, • [t]here came unto him a woman[.] • Then took Mary • having an alabaster box of • a pound of • very precious ointment • of spikenard • very costly, • and she break the box, • and poured it on his head, as he sat *at meat* • and anointed the feet of Jesus, and wiped his feet with her hair: [A]nd the house was filled with the odour of the ointment. • But when his disciples saw *it*, • there were some that had indignation within themselves, • saying, To what purpose *is* this waste? • [A]nd said, Why was this waste of the ointment made? • Then saith one of his disciples, Judas Iscariot, Simon's *son*, which should betray him, Why was not this ointment sold for three hundred pence, and given to the poor? • For this ointment might have been sold for much, • more than three hundred pence, and have been given to the poor. And they murmured against her. • This he said, not that he cared for the poor; but because he was a thief, and had the bag, and bare what was put therein. • When Jesus understood *it*, • [t]hen Jesus • said unto them, • Let her alone; why trouble ye • the woman? [F]or she hath wrought a good work upon me. • [A]gainst the day of my burying hath she kept this. • For ye have the poor with you always, and whensoever ye will ye may do them good: [B]ut me ye have not always. She hath done

MATTHEW	MARK	LUKE	JOHN

what she could: • For in that she hath poured this ointment on my body, • she • {did *it* / is come aforehand} to anoint my body {to the burying / for my burial.} • Verily I say unto you, Wheresoever this gospel shall be preached throughout the whole world, • *there* shall also this, that this woman hath done, {be told / spoken} • for a memorial of her. • Much people of the Jews therefore knew that he was there: [A]nd they came not for Jesus sake only, but that they might see Lazarus also, whom he had raised from the dead. •

¶ Then entered Satan into Judas surnamed Iscariot, being of the number of the twelve. And he went his way, and communed with the chief priests and captains, how he might betray him unto them. • And said *unto them*, What will ye give me, and I will deliver him unto you? • And when they heard *it*, they were glad, and promised to give him money. • And they covenanted with him for thirty pieces of silver. • And he promised, [a]nd from that time he sought opportunity • how he might conveniently betray him • unto them in the absence of the multitude. • But the chief priests consulted that they might put Lazarus also to death; [b]ecause that by reason of him many of the Jews went away, and believed on Jesus.

¶ On the next day much people that were come to the feast, when they heard that Jesus was coming to Jerusalem, [t]ook branches of Palm trees, and went forth to meet him, and cried, Hosanna: Blessed *is* the King of Israel that cometh in the name of the Lord. And Jesus, when he had found a young ass, sat thereon; as it is written, Fear not, daughter of Sion: [B]ehold, thy King cometh, sitting on an ass's colt. These things understood not his disciples at the first: [B]ut when Jesus was glorified, then remembered they that these things were written of him, and *that* they had done these things unto him. The people therefore that was with him when he called Lazarus out of the grave, and raised him from the dead, bare record. For this cause the people also met him, for that they heard that he had done this miracle. The Pharisees therefore said among themselves, Perceive ye how ye prevail nothing? Behold, the world is gone after him.

MATTHEW	MARK	LUKE	JOHN

¶ And there were certain Greeks among them that came up to worship at the feast: The same came therefore to Philip, which was of Bethsaida, of Galilee, and desired him, saying, Sir, we would see Jesus. Philip cometh and telleth Andrew: [A]nd again Andrew and Philip tell Jesus.

¶ And Jesus answered them, saying, The hour is come, that the Son of man should be glorified. Verily, Verily, I say unto you, Except a corn of wheat fall into the ground and die, it abideth alone: [B]ut if it die, it bringeth forth much fruit. He that loveth his life shall lose it; and he that hateth his life in this world shall keep it unto life eternal. If any man serve me, let him follow me; and where I am, there shall also my servant be: [I]f any man serve me, him will *my* Father honour. Now is my soul troubled; and what shall I say? Father save me from this hour: [B]ut for this cause came I unto this hour. Father, glorify thy name. Then came there a voice from heaven, *saying*, I have both glorified *it*, and will glorify *it* again. The people therefore, that stood by, and heard *it*, said that it thundered: [O]thers said, An angel spake to him. Jesus answered and said, This voice came not because of me, but for your sakes. Now is the judgment of this world: [N]ow shall the prince of this world be cast out. And I, if I be lifted up from the earth, will draw all *men* unto me. This he said, signifying what death he should die. The people answered him, We have heard out of the law that Christ abideth for ever: [A]nd how sayest thou, The Son of man must be lifted up? [W]ho is this Son of man? Then Jesus said unto them, Yet a little while is the light with you. Walk while ye have the light, lest darkness come upon you: [F]or he that walketh in darkness knoweth not whither he goeth. While ye have light, believe in the light, that ye may be the children of the light. These things spake Jesus, and departed, and did hide himself from them.

¶ But though he had done so many miracles before them, yet they believed not on him: That the saying of Esaias the prophet might be fulfilled, which he spake, Lord, who hath believed our report? and to whom hath the arm of the Lord been revealed? Therefore they could not believe, because that Esaias said again, He hath blinded their eyes, and hardened their heart; that they should not see with *their* eyes, nor understand with *their* heart, and be converted, and I should heal them. These things said Esaias, when he saw his glory, and spake of him.

MATTHEW	MARK	LUKE	JOHN

¶ Nevertheless among the chief rulers also many believed on him; but because of the Pharisees they did not confess *him*, lest they should be put out of the synagogue: For they loved the praise of men more than the praise of God. Jesus cried and said, He that believeth on me, believeth not on me, but on him that sent me. And he that seeth me seeth him that sent me. I am come a light into the world, that whosoever believeth on me should not abide in darkness. And if any man hear my words, and believe not, I judge him not: [F]or I came not to judge the world, but to save the world. He that rejecteth me, and receiveth not my words, hath one that judgeth him: [T]he word that I have spoken, the same shall judge him in the last day. For I have not spoken of myself; but the Father which sent me, he gave me a commandment, what I should say, and what I should speak. And I know that his commandment is life everlasting: [W]hatsoever I speak therefore, even as the Father said unto me, so I speak.

ΑΩ

Chapter 16

THE COVENANT
WITH MANY

Daniel 9:27

Redaction: The Covenant with Many

MATTHEW	MARK	LUKE	JOHN

MATTHEW	MARK	LUKE	JOHN

- A Large Upper Room -

Matt 26:17-29 • Mark 14:12-25 • Luke 22:7-30 • John 13:01-35

¶ Then came the • first *day* of the *feast of* unleavened bread • {when they killed the passover, / when the passover must be killed.} • [T]he disciples came to Jesus, • [a]nd he sent Peter and John, saying, Go and prepare us the passover, that we may eat. • [H]is disciples said unto him, Where wilt thou that we go and prepare • for thee • that thou mayest eat the passover? And he sendeth forth [*these*] two of his disciples, and saith unto them, Go ye into the city, and • [b]ehold, when ye are entered into the city, • there shall meet you • such a man, • bearing a pitcher of water: [F]ollow him. And wheresoever he shall go in, • follow him into the house where he entereth in. And ye shall say unto the good man of the house, The Master saith unto thee, • My time is at hand; I will keep the passover at thy house with my disciples. • Where is the guestchamber, where I shall eat the passover with my disciples? • And he will shew you a large upper room furnished *and* prepared: [T]here make ready for us. And his disciples went forth, and came into the city, and found as he had said unto them: • And the disciples did as Jesus had appointed them; • and they made ready the passover. •

¶ Now • when even was come, • he cometh with the twelve • before the feast of the passover, when Jesus knew that his hour was come that he should depart out of this world unto the Father, having loved his own which were in the world, he loved them unto the end. • [H]e sat down, and the twelve apostles with him. • And as they sat and did eat, Jesus said, • unto them, With desire I have desired to eat this passover with you before I suffer: For I say unto you I will not anymore eat thereof, until it be fulfilled in the kingdom of God. And he took the cup, and gave thanks, and said, Take this, and divide *it* among yourselves: For I say unto you, I will not drink of the fruit of the vine, until the kingdom of God shall come. And he took bread, and gave thanks, and brake *it*, and gave unto them, saying, This is my body which is given for you: [T]his do in remembrance of me. Likewise also the cup after supper, saying, This cup *is* the new testament in my blood, which is shed for you. •

MATTHEW	MARK	LUKE	JOHN

¶ And supper being ended, the devil having now put into the heart of Judas Iscariot, Simon's *son*, to betray him; Jesus knowing that the Father had given all things into his hands, and that he was come from God, and went to God; He riseth from supper, and laid aside his garments; and took a towel, and girded himself. After that he poureth water into a bason, and began to wash the disciples' feet, and to wipe *them* with the towel wherewith he was girded. Then cometh he to Simon Peter: [A]nd Peter saith unto him, Lord, dost thou wash my feet? Jesus answered and said unto him, What I do thou knowest not now; but thou shalt know hereafter. Peter saith unto him, Thou shalt never wash my feet. Jesus answered him, If I wash thee not, thou hast no part with me. Simon Peter saith unto him, Lord, not my feet only, but also *my* hands and *my* head. Jesus saith to him, He that is washed needeth not save to wash *his* feet, but is clean every whit: [A]nd ye are clean, but not all. For he knew who should betray him; therefore said he, Ye are not all clean. So after he had washed there feet, and had taken his garments, and was set down again, he said unto them, Know ye what I have done to you? Ye call me Master and Lord: [A]nd ye say well; for *so* I am. If I then, *your* Lord and Master, have washed your feet; ye also ought to wash one another's feet. For I have given you an example, that ye should do as I have done to you. Verily, Verily I say unto you, The servant is not greater than his lord; neither he that is sent greater than he that sent him. If ye know these things, happy are ye if ye do them.

¶ I speak not of you all: I know whom I have chosen: but that the scripture may be fulfilled, He that eateth bread with me hath lifted up his heel against me. Now I tell you before it come, that, when it is come to pass, ye may believe that I am *he*. Verily, verily, I say unto you, He that receiveth whomsoever I send receiveth me; and he that receiveth me receiveth him that sent me.

¶ When Jesus had thus said, he was troubled in spirit, and testified, and said, • But, behold, the hand of him that betrayeth me *is* with me on the table. • Verily, verily, I say unto you, that one of you • which eateth with me • shall betray me. Then the disciples looked one

MATTHEW	MARK	LUKE	JOHN

on another, doubting of whom he spake. • And they began to be • exceeding sorrowful, and begin every one of them to say unto him, • one by one, • Lord, • *Is* it I? And another *said, Is* it I? • Now there was leaning on Jesus' bosom one of his disciples, whom Jesus loved. Simon Peter therefore beckoned to him, that he should ask who it should be of whom he spake. He then lying on Jesus' breast saith unto him, Lord, who is it? Jesus answered, • and said unto them, *It is* one of the twelve, that dippeth • *his* hand with me in the dish, • [h]e it is, to whom I shall give a sop, when I have dipped *it[;]* • the same shall betray me. • And truly the Son of man • indeed goeth, • as it was determined: • [A]s it is written of him: • [B]ut woe unto that man by whom the Son of man is betrayed! [I]t had been good for that man if he had • {never / not} been born. • And they began to inquire among themselves, which of them it was that should do this thing. • And when he had dipped the sop, he gave *it* to Judas Iscariot, *the son* of Simon. • Then Judas, which betrayed him, answered and said, Master, is it I? He said unto him, Thou hast said. • And after the sop Satan entered into him. Then said Jesus unto him, That thou doest, do quickly. Now no man at the table knew for what intent he spake this unto him. For some *of them* thought, because Judas had the bag, that Jesus had said unto him, Buy *those things* that we have need of against the feast; [O]r, that he should give something to the poor. He then having received the sop went immediately out: [A]nd it was night. •

¶ And there was also a strife among them, which of them should be accounted the greatest. And he said unto them, The kings of the Gentiles exercise lordship over them; and they that exercise authority upon them are called benefactors. But ye *shall* not *be* so: [B]ut he that is greatest among you, let him be as the younger; and he that is chief, as he that doth serve. For whether *is* greater, he that sitteth at meat, or he that serveth? [I]s not he that sitteth at meat? [B]ut I am among you as he that serveth. Ye are they which have continued with me in my temptations. And I appoint unto you a kingdom, as my Father hath appointed unto me; [t]hat ye may eat and drink at my table in my kingdom, and sit on thrones judging the twelve tribes of Israel. •

MATTHEW	MARK	LUKE	JOHN

¶ Therefore, when he was gone out, Jesus said, Now is the Son of man glorified, and God is glorified in him. If God be glorified in him, God shall also glorify him in himself, and shall straightway glorify him. Little children, yet a little while I am with you. Ye shall seek me: [A]nd as I said unto the Jews, Whither I go, ye can not come; so now I say to you. A new commandment I give unto you, That ye love one another; as I have loved you, that ye also love one another. By this shall all *men* know that ye are my disciples, if ye have love one to another. •

¶ And as they were eating, Jesus took bread, and blessed *it*, and break *it*, and gave *it* to the disciples, and said, Take, eat; this is my body. • And he took the cup, and when he had given thanks, he gave *it* to them: • saying, Drink ye all of it; • [A]nd they all drank of it. And he said unto them, • For this is my blood of the new testament, which is shed for many for the remission of sins. But • [v]erily I say unto you, • I will not drink henceforth of this fruit of the vine, until that day when I drink it new with you in my Father's Kingdom • the kingdom of God.

Ω

MATTHEW	MARK	LUKE	JOHN

- To the Mount of Olives -

Matt 26:30-35 • Mark 14:26-31 • Luke 22:31-39 • John 13:36-14

¶ And when they had sung an hymn, they went out into the mount of Olives. • Then saith Jesus unto them, All ye shall be offended because of me this night: [F]or it is written, I will smite the shepherd, and the sheep of the flock shall be scattered abroad. But after I am risen again, I will go before you into Galilee. • But • Peter answered and said unto him, • Although • all *men* shall be offended because of thee, *yet* will I never be offended. • And the Lord said, Simon, Simon, behold, Satan hath desired *to have* you, that he may sift *you* as wheat: But I have prayed for thee, that thy faith fail not: [A]nd when thou art converted, strengthen thy brethren.•

¶ Simon Peter said unto him, Lord, whither goest thou? Jesus answered him, Whither I go, thou canst not follow me now; but thou shalt follow me afterwards. Peter said unto him, Lord, why cannot I follow thee now? • Lord, I am ready to go with thee, both into prison, and to death. • I will lay down my life for thy sake. Jesus answered him, • [a]nd he said • unto him, Wilt thou lay down thy life for my sake? Verily, verily, I {say / tell} • unto thee, • Peter, That this day, *even* in this night, the cock shall not crow twice, this day, before that thou {hast denied me thrice / shalt thrice deny} that thou knowest me. • But • Peter • spake the more vehemently, • said unto him, Though I should die with thee, yet will I not deny thee. Likewise also said all the disciples. • And he said unto them, When I sent you without purse, and scrip, and shoes, lacked ye anything? And they said, Nothing. Then he said unto them, But now, he that hath a purse, let him take *it*, and likewise *his* scrip: [A]nd he that hath no sword, let him sell his garment, and buy one. For I say unto you, that this that is written must yet be accomplished in me, And he was reckoned among the transgressors: [F]or the things concerning me have an end. And they said, Lord, behold, here *are* two swords. And he said unto them, It is enough.

¶ And he came out, and went, as he was wont, to the mount of Olives; and his disciples also followed him. • L[et] not your heart be troubled: [Y]e believe in God, believe also in me. In my Father's

MATTHEW	MARK	LUKE	JOHN

house are many mansions: [I]f *it were* not *so*, I would have told you. I go to prepare a place for you. And if I go and prepare a place for you, I will come again, and receive you unto myself; that where I am, *there* ye may be also. And whither I go ye know, and the way ye know. Thomas saith unto him, Lord, we know not whither thou goest; and how can we know the way? Jesus saith unto him, I am the way, the truth, and the life: [N]o man cometh unto the Father, but by me. If ye had known me, ye should have known my Father also: [A]nd from hence forth ye know him, and have seen him. Philip saith unto him, Lord, shew us the Father, and it sufficeth us. Jesus saith unto him, Have I been so long time with you, and yet hast thou not known me, Philip? [H]e that hath seen me hath seen the Father; and how sayest thou *then*, Shew us the Father? Believest thou not that I am in the Father, and the Father in me? [T]he words that I speak unto you I speak not of myself: [B]ut the Father that dwelleth in me, he doeth the works. Believe me that I *am* in the Father, and the Father in me: [O]r else believe me for the very works' sake. Verily, Verily, I say unto you, [h]e that believeth on me, the works that I do shall he do also; and greater *works* than these shall he do; because I go unto my Father. And whatsoever ye shall ask in my name, that will I do, that the Father may be glorified in the Son. If ye shall ask anything in my name, I will do *it*.

¶ If ye love me, keep my commandments. And I will pray the Father, and he shall give you another Comforter, that he may abide with you forever; *[e]ven* the Spirit of truth; whom the world cannot receive, because it seeth him not, neither knoweth him: [B]ut ye know him; for he dwelleth with you, and shall be in you. I will not leave you comfortless: I will come to you. Yet a little while, and the world seeth me no more; but ye see me: [B]ecause I live, ye shall live also. At that day ye shall know that I *am* in my Father, and ye in me, and I in you. He that hath my commandments, and keepeth them, he it is that loveth me: [A]nd he that loveth me shall be loved of my Father, and I will love him, and will manifest myself to him. Judas saith unto him, not Iscariot, Lord, how is it that thou wilt manifest thyself unto us, and not unto the world. Jesus answered and said unto him, If a man love me, he will keep my words: [A]nd my Father will love him, and we will come unto him, and make our abode with him. He

MATTHEW	MARK	LUKE	JOHN

that loveth me not keepeth not my sayings: [A]nd the word which ye hear is not mine, but the Father's which sent me. These things have I spoken unto you, being *yet* present with you. But the Comforter, *which is* the Holy Ghost, whom the Father will send in my name, he shall teach you all things, and bring all things to your remembrance, whatsoever I have said unto you. Peace I leave with you, my peace I give unto you: [N]ot as the world giveth, give I unto you. Let not your heart be troubled, neither let it be afraid. Ye have heard how I said unto you, I go away, and come *again* unto you. If ye loved me, ye would rejoice, because I said, I go unto the Father: [F]or my Father is greater than I. And now I have told you before it come to pass, that, when it is come to pass, ye might believe. Hereafter I will not talk much with you: [F]or the prince of this world cometh, and hath nothing in me. But that the world may know that I love the Father; and as the Father gave me commandment, even so I do. Arise, let us go hence.

Ω

Redaction: The Covenant with Many

MATTHEW	MARK	LUKE	JOHN

MATTHEW	MARK	LUKE	JOHN

- Ye Are My Friends -

Matt • Mark • Luke • John 15:01-16:33

¶ I AM the true vine, and my Father is the husbandman. Every branch in me that beareth not fruit he taketh away: [A]nd every *branch* that beareth fruit, he purgeth it, that it may bring forth more fruit. Now ye are clean through the word which I have spoken unto you. Abide in me, and I in you. As the branch cannot bear fruit of itself, except it abide in the vine; no more can ye, except ye abide in me. I am the vine, ye *are* the branches: He that abideth in me, and I in him, the same bringeth forth much fruit: [F]or without me ye can do nothing. If a man abide not in me, he is cast forth as a branch, and is withered; and men gather them, and cast *them* into the fire, and they are burned. If ye abide in me, and my words abide in you, ye shall ask what ye will, and it shall be done unto you. Herein is my Father glorified, that ye bear much fruit; so shall ye be my disciples. As the Father hath loved me, so have I loved you: [C]ontinue ye in my love. If ye keep my commandments, ye shall abide in my love; even as I have kept my Father's commandments, and abide in his love. These things have I spoken unto you, that my joy might remain in you, and *that* your joy might be full. This is my commandment, That ye love one another, as I have loved you. Greater love hath no man than this, that a man lay down his life for his friends. Ye are my friends, if ye do whatsoever I command you. Henceforth I call you not servants; for the servant knoweth not what his lord doeth: [B]ut I have called you friends; for all things that I have heard of my Father I have made known unto you. Ye have not chosen me, but I have chosen you, and ordained you, that ye should go and bring forth fruit, and *that* your fruit should remain: [T]hat whatsoever ye shall ask of the Father in my name, he may give it you. These things I command you, that ye love one another. If the world hate you, ye know that it hated me before *it hated* you. If ye were of the world, the world would love his own: [B]ut because ye are not of the world, but I have chosen you out of the world, therefore the world hateth you. Remember the word that I said unto you, The servant is not greater than his lord. If they have persecuted me, they will also persecute you; if they have kept my saying, they will keep yours also. But all these things will they do unto you for my name's sake,

MATTHEW	MARK	LUKE	JOHN

because they know not him that sent me. If I had not come and spoken unto them, they had not had sin: [B]ut now they have no cloke for their sin. He that hateth me hateth my Father also. If I had not done among them the works which none other man did, they had not had sin: [B]ut now have they both seen and hated both me and my Father. But *this cometh to pass*, that the word might be fulfilled that is written in their law, They hated me without a cause. But when the Comforter is come, whom I will send unto you from the Father, *even* the Spirit of truth, which proceedeth from the Father, he shall testify of me: And ye also shall bear witness, because ye have been with me from the beginning.

¶ T[hese] things have I spoken unto you, that ye should not be offended. They shall put you out of the synagogues: [Y]ea, the time cometh, that whosoever killeth you will think that he doeth God service. And these things will they do unto you, because they have not known the Father, nor me. But these things have I told you, that when the time shall come, ye may remember that I told you of them. And these things I said not unto you at the beginning, because I was with you. But now I go my way to him that sent me; and none of you asketh me, Whither goest thou? But because I have said these things unto you, sorrow hath filled your heart. Nevertheless I tell you the truth; [i]t is expedient for you that I go away: [F]or if I go not away, the Comforter will not come unto you; but if I depart, I will send him unto you. And when he is come, he will reprove the world of sin, and of righteousness, and of judgment: Of sin, because they believe not on me; Of righteousness, because I go to my Father, and ye see me no more; [o]f judgment, because the prince of this world is judged. I have yet many things to say unto you, but ye cannot bear them now. Howbeit when he, the Spirit of truth, is come, he will guide you into all truth: [F]or he shall not speak of himself; but whatsoever he shall hear, *that* shall he speak: [A]nd he will shew you things to come. He shall glorify me: [F]or he shall receive of mine, and shall shew *it* unto you. All things that the Father hath are mine: [T]herefore said I, that he shall take of mine, and shall shew *it* unto you. A little while, and ye shall not see me: [A]nd again, a little while, and ye shall see me, because I go to the Father. Then said *some* of his disciples among themselves, What is this that he saith unto us, A little while, and ye shall not see me: [A]nd again, a little while, and ye shall

MATTHEW	MARK	LUKE	JOHN

see me: [A]nd, Because I go to the Father? They said therefore, What is this that he saith, A little while? [W]e cannot tell what he saith. Now Jesus knew that they were desirous to ask him, and said unto them, Do ye inquire among yourselves of that I said, A little while, and ye shall not see me: [A]nd again, a little while, and ye shall see me? Verily, verily, I say unto you, That ye shall weep and lament, but the world shall rejoice: [A]nd ye shall be sorrowful, but your sorrow shall be turned into joy. A woman when she is in travail hath sorrow, because her hour is come: [B]ut as soon as she is delivered of the child, she remembers no more the anguish, for joy that a man is born into the world. And ye now therefore have sorrow: [B]ut I will see you again, and your heart shall rejoice, and your joy no man taketh from you. And in that day ye shall ask me nothing. Verily, verily, I say unto you, Whatsoever ye shall ask the Father in my name, he will give *it* you. Hitherto have ye asked nothing in my name: [A]sk, and ye shall receive, that your joy may be full. These things have I spoken unto you in proverbs: [B]ut the time cometh, when I shall no more speak unto you in proverbs, but I shall shew you plainly of the Father. At that day ye shall ask in my name: [A]nd I say not unto you, that I will pray the Father for you: For the Father himself loveth you, because ye have loved me, and have believed that I came out from God. I came forth from the Father, and am come into the world: [A]gain, I leave the world, and go to the Father. His disciples said unto him, Lo, now speakest thou plainly, and speakest no proverb. Now are we sure that thou knowest all things, and needest not that any man should ask thee: [B]y this we believe that thou comest forth from God. Jesus answered them, Do ye now believe? Behold, the hour cometh, yea, is now come, that ye shall be scattered, every man to his own, and shall leave me alone: [A]nd yet I am not alone, because the Father is with me. These things I have spoken unto you, that in me ye might have peace. In the world ye shall have tribulation: [B]ut be of good cheer; I have overcome the world.

Ω

Redaction: The Covenant with Many

MATTHEW	MARK	LUKE	JOHN

MATTHEW	MARK	LUKE	JOHN

- That the World May Know -

Matt • Mark • Luke • John 17:1-53

¶ T[hese] words spake Jesus, and lifted up his eyes to heaven, and said, Father, the hour is come; glorify thy Son, that thy Son also may glorify thee: As thou has given him power over all flesh, that he should give eternal life to as many as thou hast given him. And this is life eternal, that they might know thee the only true God, and Jesus Christ, whom thou hast sent. I have glorified thee on the earth: I have finished the work which thou gavest me to do. And now, O Father, glorify thou me with thine own self with the glory which I had with thee before the world was. I have manifested thy name unto the men which thou gavest me out of the world: [T]hine they were, and thou gavest them me; and they have kept thy word. Now they have known that all things whatsoever thou hast given me are of thee. For I have given unto them the words which thou gavest me; and they have received *them*, and have known surely that I came out from thee, and they have believed that thou didst send me. I pray for them: I pray not for the world, but for them which thou hast given me; for they are thine. And all mine are thine, and thine are mine; and I am glorified in them. And now I am no more in the world, but these are in the world, and I come to thee. Holy Father, keep through thine own name those whom thou hast given me, that they may be one, as we *are*. While I was with them in the world, I kept them in thy name: [T]hose that thou gavest me I have kept, and none of them is lost, but the son of perdition; that the scripture might be fulfilled. And now come I to thee; and these things I speak in the world, that they might have my joy fulfilled in themselves. I have given them thy word; and the world hath hated them, because they are not of the world, even as I am not of the world. I pray not that thou shouldest take them out of the world, but that thou shouldest keep them from the evil. They are not of the world, even as I am not of the world. Sanctify them through thy truth: [T]hy word is truth. As thou hast sent me into the world, even so have I also sent them into the world. And for their sakes I sanctify myself, that they also might be sanctified through the truth. Neither pray I for these alone, but for them also which shall believe on me through their word; [t]hat they also may be one; as thou Father, *art* in me, and I in thee,

Redaction: The Covenant with Many

MATTHEW	MARK	LUKE	JOHN

that they also may be one in us: [T]hat the world may believe that thou hast sent me. And the glory which thou gavest me I have given them; that they may be one, even as we are one: I in them and thou in me, that they may be made perfect in one; and that the world may know that thou hast sent me, and hast loved them, as thou hast loved me. Father, I will that they also, whom thou hast given me, be with me where I am; that they may behold my glory, which thou hast given me: [F]or thou lovedst me before the foundation of he world. O righteous Father, the world hath not known thee: [B]ut I have known thee, and these have known that thou hast sent me. And I have declared unto them thy name, and will declare it: [T]hat the love wherewith thou hast loved me may be in them, and I in them.

Ω

MATTHEW	MARK	LUKE	JOHN

- A Place Called Gethsemane -

Matt 26:36-56 • Mark 14:32-52 • Luke 22:40-53 • John 18:01-11

¶ W[hen] Jesus had spoken these words, he went forth with his disciples over the brook Cedron, where was a garden, • Then cometh Jesus with them into a place • {which was named / called} Gethsemane, • [a]nd when he was at the place, • into the which he entered, and his disciples • he saith • unto • his disciples, Sit ye here, while I shall • go and pray yonder. • And Judas also, which betrayed him, knew the place: [F]or Jesus oft times resorted thither with his disciples. • And he took with him Peter and the two sons of Zebedee, • James and John, and began to be sore amazed, and • sorrowful and very heavy. Then saith he unto them, My soul is exceeding sorrowful, even unto death: [T]arry ye here, and watch with me. • And he went forward a little • further, and fell • on the ground, • on his face, and prayed, • that, if it were possible, the hour might pass from him. And he said, • O my • Abba, Father, all things *are* possible unto thee; • if it be possible, let this cup pass from me: • [T]ake away this cup from me: [N]evertheless not {what / as} I will, but {as / what} thou *wilt.* • And he cometh unto the disciples, and finds them asleep, • and saith unto Peter, Simon, sleepest thou? • What, could ye not watch with me one hour? • Watch ye and pray, {lest ye enter / that ye enter not} into temptation: [T]he spirit {indeed / truly} is {ready / willing} but the flesh *is* weak. He went away again the second time, • was withdrawn from them about a stone's cast, and kneeled down • and prayed, • and spake the same words. • Saying, Father if thou be willing, remove this cup from me: [N]evertheless • O my Father, if this cup may not pass away from me, except I drink it, • not my will, but thine • will • be done. And there appeared an angel unto him from heaven, strengthening him. And being in an agony he prayed more earnestly: [A]nd his sweat was as it were great drops of blood falling down to the ground. And when he was rose up from prayer, • he returned, • And he came • to his disciples, • and found them asleep again • for sorrow, • (for there eyes were heavy,) • [a]nd said unto them, Why sleep ye? [R]ise and pray, lest ye enter into temptation. • [N]either wist they what to answer him. • And he left them, and went away again, and prayed the third time, saying the same words. Then cometh he to his disciples, • the third

MATTHEW	MARK	LUKE	JOHN

time, and saith unto them, Sleep on now, and take *your* rest: • [B]ehold, • it is enough, the hour is come •

at hand, and • behold, the Son of man is betrayed into the hands of sinners. Rise up, • let us be going: •

[L]o, • behold he is at hand that doth betray me. •

¶ And immediately, while he yet spake, • lo, • behold • Judas, one of the twelve, • then, having

received • with him • a band *of men* and officers • a great multitude with swords and staves, • from the

chief priests and Pharisees, • and the scribes and the elders • of the people • cometh thither with

lanterns and torches and weapons. Jesus therefore, knowing all things that should come upon him,

went forth, and said unto them, Whom seek ye? They answered him, Jesus of Nazareth. Jesus saith unto

them, I am *he*. And Judas also, which betrayed him, stood with them. As soon then as he had said unto

them, I am *he*, they went backward, and fell to the ground. Then asked he them again, Whom seek ye?

And they said, Jesus of Nazareth. Jesus answered, I have told you that I am *he*: [I]f therefore ye seek me,

let these go their way: That the saying might be fulfilled, which he spake, Of them which thou gavest

me have I lost none. • And he that betrayed him had given them a {token, / sign} • saying, Whomsoever

I shall kiss, that same is he; take him, • hold him fast • and lead *him* away safely. • And forthwith • as

soon as he was come, he goeth straightway to • Jesus, and said, Hail, master[.] • [A]nd kissed him. •

¶ And Jesus said unto him, Friend, wherefore art thou come? • Judas, betrayest thou the Son of

man with a kiss? • Then came they, and laid • their • hands on Jesus, and took him. • When they which

were about him saw what would follow, they said unto him, Lord, shall we smite with the sword? •

¶ And, behold, • [t]hen Simon Peter • one of them which were with Jesus • that stood by •

stretched out *his* hand, • having a sword • drew his sword, and struck • and smote the high priest's

servant, and cut off his right ear. The servant's name was Malchus. Then said Jesus unto Peter, • Put up

again thy sword • into {the sheath: / his place} [F]or all they that take the sword shall perish with the

sword. • Suffer ye thus far. • [T]he cup which my Father hath given me, shall I not drink it? • And he

touched his ear, and healed him. • Thinkest thou that I cannot now pray to my Father, and he shall

MATTHEW	MARK	LUKE	JOHN

presently give me more than twelve legions of angels? But how then shall the scriptures be fulfilled, that thus it must be? In that same hour • Jesus answered and said unto • the multitudes, • the chief priests, and captains of the temple, and the elders, which were come to him, • Are ye come out as against a thief with swords and staves for to take me? • When • I sat daily with you teaching in the temple, • ye stretched forth no hands against me: • [A]nd ye laid no hold on me • and ye took me not: [B]ut the scriptures must be fulfilled • this is your hour, and the power of darkness. • [A]ll of this was done, that the scriptures of the prophets might be fulfilled. Then all the disciples forsook him, and fled. • And there followed him a certain young man, having a linen cloth cast about *his* naked *body*; and the young men laid hold on him: And he left the linen cloth, and fled from them naked.

AΩ

Redaction: The Covenant with Many

MATTHEW	MARK	LUKE	JOHN

Chapter 17

THE LORD'S PASSOVER

Exodus 12:10-12

Redaction: The Lord's Passover

MATTHEW	MARK	LUKE	JOHN

MATTHEW	MARK	LUKE	JOHN

- Before the Cock Crow -

Matt 26:57-27:01 • Mark 14:53-15:01• Luke 22:54-71 • John 18:12-27

¶ Then the band and the captain and officers of the Jews • that had laid hold on Jesus • took Jesus, and bound him, • [a]nd they led Jesus away • to Caiaphas the high priest, • and brought him into the high priest's house • where • with him were assembled all the chief priests and the elders and the scribes. • And lead him away to Annas first; for he was father in law to Caiaphas, which was the high priest that same year. Now Caiaphas was he, which gave counsel to the Jews, that it was expedient that one man should die for the people.

¶ And Simon Peter followed Jesus • afar off unto the high priest's palace, • and *so did* another disciple: [T]hat disciple was known unto the high priest, and went in with Jesus into the palace of the high priest. But Peter stood at the door without. Then went out that other disciple, which was known unto the high priest, and spake unto her that kept the door, and {brought in Peter / went in,} • even into the palace of the high priest: • Then saith the damsel that kept the door unto Peter, Art not thou also *one* of this man's disciples? He saith, I am not. And the servants and officers stood there, who • when they had {kindled / made} a fire of coals • in the midst of the hall, • for it was cold: [A]nd they warmed themselves: • [A]nd were set down together, • and Peter stood with them, • and he sat • down among them • with the servants, and warmed himself at the fire • to see the end. •

¶ The high priest then asked Jesus of his disciples, and of his doctrine. Jesus answered him, I spake openly to the world; I ever taught in the synagogue, and in the temple, whither the Jews always resort; and in secret have I said nothing. Why askest thou me? Ask them which heard me, what I have said unto them: [B]ehold, they know what I said. And when he had thus spoken, one of the officers which stood by struck Jesus with the palm of his hand, saying, Answerest thou the high priest so? Jesus answered him, If I have spoken evil, bear witness of the evil: [B]ut if well, why smitest thou me? Now Annas had sent him bound unto Caiaphas the high priest. • And the chief priests and • elders, and all

MATTHEW	MARK	LUKE	JOHN

the council, sought • for • false witness against Jesus, to put him to death; [b]ut found none: [Y]ea

though many false witnesses came, *yet* found they none. • For many bare false witness against him, but

their witness agreed not together. • At the last • there {arose / came} • certain, • two false witnesses, •

and bare false witness against him, saying, We heard him say, I will destroy this temple that is made

with hands, and within three days I will build another made without hands. • And said, This *fellow* said, I

am able to destroy the temple of God and build it in three days. • But neither so did their witness agree

together. • And the high priest arose, and • stood up in the midst, and asked Jesus, saying, Answerest

thou nothing? [W]hat is it which these witness against thee? But he held his peace, and answered

nothing. Again the high priest asked him, and said unto him, Art thou the Christ, the Son of the Blessed?

• But Jesus held his peace. And the high priest answered and said unto him, I adjure thee by the living

God, that thou tell us whether thou be the Christ, the Son of God. Jesus saith unto him, Thou hast said: • I

am: • [N]evertheless I say unto you, Hereafter, shall you see the Son of man sitting on the right hand of

power, and coming in the clouds of heaven. Then the high priest rent his clothes, saying, He hath

spoken blasphemy; what further need have we of witnesses? [B]ehold, now ye have heard {his / the} •

blasphemy. What think ye? They answered • and they all condemned him • and said, He is guilty of

death. Then • some began to spit {on him, / in his face,} • and to cover his face, and to buffet him, and to

say unto him, Prophesy: [A]nd the {servants / others} {smote / did strike} him with the palms of their

hands. • Saying, Prophesy unto us, thou Christ, [w]ho is he that smote thee?

¶ Now • as Peter {was / sat} without • beneath in the palace, there cometh {one of the maids / a

certain maid / a damsel} • of the high priest: • [A]nd came unto him, • beheld him as he sat by the fire, •

[a]nd Simon Peter stood and warmed himself. • And when she saw Peter warming himself, she •

earnestly looked upon him, and said, This man was also with him. • [S]aying, Thou also was with Jesus •

of Nazareth of Galilee. • They said therefore unto him, Art not thou also *one* of his disciples? • And he

denied him, • before *them* all, saying, • Woman I know him not. • I know not • neither understand I what

thou sayest. • And he went out into the porch; and the cock crew. And • another *maid* • saw him again,

and began to say to them that stood by • there, • This is *one* of them. • This *fellow* was also with Jesus of

MATTHEW	MARK	LUKE	JOHN

Nazareth. • And after a little while another saw him, and said, Thou art also of them. And Peter • denied it, and • said, Man I am not. • And again he denied with an oath, I do not know the man. • And a little after, • about the space of one hour after • came unto him they that stood by, and said • again to Peter, Surely thou art *one* of them: • [F]or thy speech betrayeth thee • for thou art a Galilæean, and thy speech agreeth *thereto.* • [A]nother confidently affirmed, saying, Of a truth this *fellow* also was with him: [F]or he is a Galilæan. • One of the servants of the high priest, being *his* kinsman whose ear Peter cut off, saith, Did not I see thee in the garden with him? • Then began he to curse and to swear, *saying,* • I know not this man of whom ye speak. • Peter then denied again: • And Peter said, Man, I know not what thou sayest. And immediately, while he yet spake, • the second time the cock crew. • And the Lord turned, and looked upon Peter. And Peter remembered the word of the Lord • Jesus, • how he had said unto him, • Before the cock crow twice, thou shalt deny me thrice. And when he thought thereon, • Peter went out, and wept bitterly.

¶ And the men that held Jesus mocked him, and smote *him.* And when they had blindfolded him, they struck him on the face, and asked him, saying, Prophesy, who is it that smote thee? And many other things blasphemously spake they against him. •

¶ And straightway • [w]hen the morning was come, • as soon as it was day, • all the chief priests • with the elders • of the people • and scribes and the whole council, • came together, • held a consultation • against Jesus to put him to death: • [A]nd led him into their council, saying, Art thou the Christ? [T]ell us. And he said unto them, If I tell you, ye will not believe: And if I also ask *you,* ye will not answer me, nor let *me* go. Hereafter shall the Son of man sit on the right hand of the power of God. Then said they all, Art thou then the Son of God? And he said unto them, Ye say that I am. And they said, What need we any further witness? [F]or we ourselves have heard of his own mouth.

Ω

Redaction: The Lord's Passover

MATTHEW	MARK	LUKE	JOHN

MATTHEW	MARK	LUKE	JOHN

- The King of the Jews -

Matt 27:02-31 • Mark 15:01-20 • Luke 23:01-25 • John 18:28-19:16

¶ And the whole multitude of them arose, • [a]nd when they had bound him, • [t]hen lead they Jesus • and carried *him* away, • from Caiaphas unto the hall of judgment: • [A]nd delivered him to Pontius Pilate the governor.

¶ Then Judas, which had betrayed him, when he saw that he was condemned, repented himself, and brought again the thirty pieces of silver to the chief priests and elders, [s]aying, I have sinned in that I have betrayed the innocent blood. And they said, What *is that* to us? [S]ee thou *to that.* And he cast down the pieces of silver in the temple, and departed, and went and hanged himself. And the chief priests took the silver pieces, and said, It is not lawful for to put them into the treasury, because it is the price of blood. And they took counsel, and bought with them the potter's field, to bury strangers in. Wherefore that field was called, The field of blood, unto this day. Then was fulfilled that which was spoken by Jeremy the prophet, saying, And they took the thirty pieces of silver, the price of him that was valued, whom they of the children of Israel did value; [a]nd gave them for the potter's field as the Lord appointed me. • [A]nd it was early; and they themselves went not into the judgment hall, lest they should be defiled; but that they may eat the passover. Pilate then went out unto them, and said, What accusation bring ye against this man? They answered and said unto him, If he were not a malefactor, we would not have delivered him up unto thee. Then said Pilate unto them, Take ye him, and judge him according to your law. The Jews therefore said unto him, It is not lawful for us to put any man to death: That the saying of Jesus might be fulfilled, which he spake, signifying what death he should die. • And they began to accuse him, saying, We found this *fellow* perverting the nation, and forbidding to give tribute to Cæsar, saying that he himself is Christ a King. • Then Pilate entered into the judgment hall again, and called Jesus, • And Jesus stood before the governor: • And Pilate • the governor asked him, saying, • unto him, Art thou the King of the Jews? Jesus answered him, Sayest thou this thing of thyself, or did others tell it thee of me? Pilate answered, Am I a Jew? Thine own nation and

MATTHEW	MARK	LUKE	JOHN

the chief priests have delivered thee unto me: [W]hat hast thou done? Jesus answered, My kingdom is not of this world: [I]f my kingdom were of this world, then would my servants fight, that I should not be delivered to the Jews: [B]ut now is my kingdom not from hence. Pilate therefore said unto him, Art thou a king then? Jesus answered • him and said, • Thou sayest that I am a king. To this end was I born, and for this cause came I into the world, that I should bear witness unto the truth. Everyone that is of the truth heareth my voice. Pilate saith unto him, What is truth? And when he had said this, he went out again unto the Jews, • [t]hen said Pilate to the chief priests and *to* the people, I find no fault in this man. • I find in him no fault *at all*. • And when he was accused • of many things • of the chief priests and elders, he answered nothing. Then said Pilate unto him, Hearest thou not how many things they witness against thee? • And Pilate asked him again, saying, Answerest thou nothing? [B]ehold how many things they witness against thee. But Jesus yet answered nothing; • to never a word; insomuch that • Pilate • the governor marvelled greatly. • And they were the more fierce, saying, He stirreth up the people, teaching throughout all Jewry, beginning from Galilee to this place. When Pilate heard of Galilee, he asked whether the man were a Galilæean. And as soon as he knew that he belonged unto Herod's jurisdiction, he sent him to Herod, who himself also was at Jerusalem at that time.

¶ And when Herod saw Jesus, he was exceeding glad: [F]or he was desirous to see him of a long *season*, because he had heard many things of him; and he hoped to have seen some miracle done by him.

¶ Then he questioned with him in many words; but he answered him nothing. And the chief priests and scribes stood and vehemently accused him. And Herod with his men of war set him at naught, and mocked *him*, and arrayed him in a gorgeous robe, and sent him again to Pilate.

¶ And the same day Pilate and Herod were made friends together, for before they were at enmity between themselves. •

Ω

MATTHEW	MARK	LUKE	JOHN

- Crucify Him -

Matt 27:15-32 • Mark 15:06-21 • Luke 13:20-26 • John18:39-19:17

¶ Now at *that* feast the governor was wont to release unto the people • one prisoner, whomever they desired. • And they had then • one • a notable prisoner, • named Barabbas, *which* lay bound with them that *had* made insurrection with him, who had committed murder in the insurrection. • Therefore • Pilate, when he had called together the chief priests and the rulers and the people, • when they were gathered together, • [s]aid unto them, Ye have brought this man unto me, as one that perverteth the people: [A]nd behold, I, having examined *him* before you, have found no fault in this man touching those things whereof ye accuse him: No, nor yet Herod: [F]or I sent you to him; and, lo, nothing worthy of death is done unto him. I will therefore chastise him, and release *him*. (For of necessity he must release one unto them at the feast.) • And the multitude crying aloud began to desire *him to do* as he had ever done unto them. But Pilate answered them, saying, • unto them, • But ye have a custom, that I should release unto you one at the passover: • Whom will ye • therefore • that I release unto you? Barabbas, or Jesus which is called Christ • the King of the Jews? • For he knew that the chief priests had delivered him for envy. •

¶ When he was set down on the judgment seat, his wife sent unto him, saying, Have thou nothing to do with that just man: [F]or I have suffered many things this day in a dream because of him. But the chief priests and elders {persuaded / moved} • the {multitude / people} • that they should ask Barabbas, • that he should rather release Barabbas unto them • and destroy Jesus. The governor answered and said unto them, Whether of the twain will ye that I release unto you? They said, Barabbas. • And they cried out all at once, saying, Away with this *man*, and release unto us Barabbas: • Then cried they all again, saying, Not this man, but Barabbas. Now Barabbas was a robber. • (Who for a certain sedition made in the city, and for murder, was cast into prison.) Pilate therefore, willing to release Jesus, • answered and {said / spake} • again unto them, What will ye then that I shall do • with Jesus which is called Christ • *unto him* whom ye call the King of the Jews? • But they • all • cried, saying,

MATTHEW	MARK	LUKE	JOHN

• unto him, Let him be crucified. • And they cried out again, • Crucify *him*, crucify him. • Then Pilate •

the governor said, • unto them the third time, Why, what evil hath he done? I have found no cause of

death in him: I will therefore chastise him, and let *him* go. And they were instant with loud voices, • And

they cried out the more exceedingly, • requiring that he might be crucified • saying, Let him be

crucified. • Crucify him. • And the voices of them and of the chief priests prevailed. •

¶ When Pilate saw that he could prevail nothing, but *that* rather a tumult was made, he took

water, and washed *his* hands before the multitude, saying, I am innocent of the blood of this just

person: [S]ee ye *to it*. Then answered all the people, and said, His blood *be* on us, and on our children.

• And Pilate gave sentence that it should be as they required. •

¶ And *so* Pilate, willing to content the people, released Barabbas unto them, • him that for

sedition and murder was cast into prison, whom they had desired; but • [t]hen Pilate therefore took

Jesus, • and when he had scourged Jesus, • he delivered Jesus to their will • to be crucified. Then the

soldiers of the governor took Jesus • [a]nd the soldiers led him away • into the common hall, • called

Prætorium; and they call together • and gathered unto him the whole band of *soldiers*. And they

stripped him, and • they • {put on / clothed} him with • a • {purple / scarlet} robe. • And the soldiers •

when they had platted a crown of thorns, they put *it* • {about / upon} his head, and a reed in his right

hand: [A]nd they bowed the knee before him, • [a]nd began to salute • and mocked him, saying, Hail,

King of the Jews! And they spit upon him, and took the reed, and smote him on the head • [a]nd they

smote him with their hands • and bowing *their* knees worshiped him. • Pilate therefore went forth again,

and saith unto them, Behold, I bring him forth to you, that ye may know that I find no fault in him. Then

came Jesus forth, wearing the crown of thorns, and the purple robe. And *Pilate* saith unto them, Behold

the man! When the chief priests therefore and officers saw him, they cried out, saying, Crucify *him*,

crucify *him*. Pilate saith unto them, Take ye him, and crucify *him*: [F]or I find no fault in him. The Jews

answered him, We have a law, and by our law he ought to die, because he made himself the Son of

God.

MATTHEW	MARK	LUKE	JOHN

¶ When Pilate therefore heard that saying, he was the more afraid; [a]nd went again into the judgment hall, and saith unto Jesus, Whence art thou? But Jesus gave him no answer. Then saith Pilate unto him, Speakest thou not unto me? [K]nowest thou not that I have power to crucify thee, and have power to release thee? Jesus answered, Thou couldest have no power *at all* against me, except it were given thee from above: [T]herefore he that delivered me unto thee hath the greater sin. And from thenceforth Pilate sought to release him: [B]ut the Jews cried out, saying, If thou let this man go, thou art not Cæsar's friend: [W]hosoever maketh himself a king speaketh against Cæsar.

¶ When Pilate therefore heard that saying, he brought Jesus forth, and sat down in the judgment seat in a place that is called the Pavement, but in the Hebrew, Gabbatha. And it was the preparation of the passover, and about the sixth hour: [A]nd he saith unto the Jews, Behold your King! But they cried out, Away with *him*, away with *him*, crucify him. Pilate saith unto them, [S]hall I crucify your King? The chief priests answered, We have no king but Cæsar. • And {when / after} • they had mocked him, they took off the purple • robe • and put his own {clothes / raiment} • on him, • [t]hen delivered he him therefore unto them to be crucified. And they took Jesus and led *him* {away / out} to crucify him. • And he bearing his cross went forth • [a]nd as they {led him away, / came out,} they {found / laid hold upon} • [a]nd they compel {one / a man} of Cyrene, Simon by name: • [A] Cyrenian, who passed by, coming out of the country, the father of Alexander and Rufus, • him they compelled and on him they laid the cross, • to bear his cross • that he might bear *it* after Jesus.

Ω

Redaction: The Lord's Passover

MATTHEW	MARK	LUKE	JOHN

MATTHEW	MARK	LUKE	JOHN

- Golgotha -

Matt 27:33-54 • Mark 15:22-39 • Luke 23:27-48 • John19:17-30

¶ And there followed him a great company of people, and of women, which also bewailed and lamented him. But Jesus turning unto them said, Daughters of Jerusalem, weep not for me, but weep for yourselves, and for your children. For, behold the days are coming, in the which they shall say, Blessed *are* the barren, and the wombs that never bare, and the paps that never gave suck. Then shall they begin to say to the mountains, Fall on us; and to the hills, Cover us. For if they do these things in a green tree, what shall be done in the dry? And there were also two other, malefactors, led with him to be put to death. • And when they were come • they bring him unto • the place which is called Calvary • being interpreted, The place of a skull • which is called in the Hebrew Golgotha: •

¶ They gave him • wine • vinegar to drink mingled with {gall / myrrh}: [B]ut he received *it* not • and when he had tasted *thereof*, he would not drink. And • {there / [w]here} they crucified him, • and the • two other • malefactors • with him, on either side, • one on the right hand, and the other on the left • and Jesus in the midst. • Then said Jesus, Father, forgive them; for they no not what they do. •

¶ And Pilate wrote a title, and put *it* on the cross. And the writing was, [Jesus of Nazareth the King of the Jews.] This title then read many of the Jews: [F]or the place where Jesus was crucified was nigh to the city: [A]nd it was written in Hebrew, *and* Greek, *and* Latin. Then said the chief priests of the Jews to Pilate, Write not, The King of the Jews; but that he said, I am King of the Jews. Pilate answered, What I have written I have written.

¶ Then the soldiers, when they had crucified Jesus, took his garments, • And they parted his raiment, • and made four parts, to every soldier a part; • casting lots upon them, what every man should take. • [A]nd also *his* coat: [N]ow the coat was without seam, woven from the top throughout. They said therefore among themselves, Let us not rend it, but cast lots for it, whose it shall be: [T]hat the scripture might be fulfilled, • which was spoken by the prophet, • which saith, [T]hey parted my {raiment /

Redaction: The Lord's Passover

MATTHEW	MARK	LUKE	JOHN

garments} • among them, and {for / upon} • my vesture they did cast lots. These things therefore the soldiers did. • And sitting down they watched him there; • [a]nd it was the third hour, and they crucified him. • And the people stood beholding. And the rulers also with them derided *him,* saying, He saved others; let him save himself, if he be Christ, the chosen of God. And the soldiers also mocked him, coming to him, and offering him vinegar, [a]nd saying, If thou be the king of the Jews, save thyself. • And set up over his head • also was written • the superscription of his accusation • in letters of Greek, and Latin, and Hebrew, • [This is Jesus • the King of the Jews]. And with him they crucify • there • two thieves; the one on his right hand, and the other on his left. And the scripture was fulfilled, which saith, And he was numbered with the transgressors. •

¶ And they that passed by {reviled / railed on} • him, wagging their heads, • and saying, Ah, thou that destroyest the temple, and buildest *it* in three days, • save thyself. If thou be the Son of God, • come down from the cross. Likewise also the chief priests mocking • *him,* with the scribes and elders, said • among themselves[*,*] • He saved others; himself he cannot save. • Let Christ the King of Israel • [i]f he be the King of Israel, let him {now come down / descend now} from the cross, that we may see • and we will believe him. He trusted in God; let him deliver him now, if he will have him: [F]or he said, I am the Son of God. The thieves also, which were crucified with him, {cast the same in his teeth / reviled him.} •

¶ Now there stood by the cross of Jesus his mother, and his mother's sister, Mary the *wife* of Cleophas, and Mary Magdalene. When Jesus therefore saw his mother, and the disciple standing by, whom he loved, he saith unto his mother, Woman, behold thy son! Then saith he to the disciple, Behold thy mother! And from that hour that disciple took her unto his own *home.* •

¶ And one of the malefactors which were hanged railed on him, saying, If thou be Christ, save thyself and us. But the other answering rebuked him, saying, Dost not thou fear God, seeing thou art in the same condemnation? And we indeed justly; for we receive the due reward of our deeds: [B]ut this man hath done nothing amiss. And he said unto Jesus, Lord, remember me when thou comest into thy kingdom. And Jesus said unto him, Verily I say unto thee, To day shalt thou be with me in paradise. •

MATTHEW	MARK	LUKE	JOHN

Now • when • it was about the sixth hour, • there was • a darkness over {all the earth / the whole land} until the ninth hour. And at • about the ninth hour Jesus cried with a loud voice, • saying, {Eloi, Eloi, / Eli, Eli} lama sabachthani? • [W]hich is, • to say, • being interpreted, My God, My God, why hast thou forsaken me? And some of them that stood by • there, when they heard *that* • said, Behold, • [t]his *man* calleth for Elias. •

¶ After this, Jesus knowing that all things were now accomplished, that the scripture might be fulfilled, saith, I thirst. Now there was set a vessel full of vinegar: • And straightway one of them ran, and took a sponge, and filled *it* • full of vinegar, • and put *it* upon • a • hyssop • reed, • and put *it* to his mouth • and gave him to drink • saying, Let alone; let us see whether Elias will come to take him down. • When Jesus therefore had received the vinegar, • The rest said, Let be, let us see whether Elias will come to save him. • And the sun was darkened, and the veil of the temple was rent in the midst.

¶ And when Jesus had cried with a loud voice, he said, Father, into thy hands I commend my spirit: • And • Jesus, when he had cried again with a loud voice, • he said, It is finished: [A]nd he bowed his head, • and having said thus, he {gave / yielded} • up the ghost. • And, behold, the veil of the temple was rent in twain from the top to the bottom; and the earth did quake, and the rocks rent; [a]nd the graves were opened; and many bodies of the saints which slept arose, [a]nd came out of the graves after his resurrection, and went into the holy city, and appeared unto many. •

¶ Now when the Centurion • which stood over against him, • saw what was done, • that he so cried out, and gave up the ghost, • he glorified God, saying, Certainly this was a righteous man. • Truly this man was the Son of God. • [A]nd they that were with him, watching Jesus, saw the earthquake, and those things that were done, they feared greatly, saying, Truly this was the Son of God. • And all the people that came together to that sight, beholding the things which were done, smote their breasts, and returned. •

Ω

Redaction: The Lord's Passover

MATTHEW	MARK	LUKE	JOHN

MATTHEW	MARK	LUKE	JOHN

- The Body of Jesus -

Matt 27:55-66 • Mark 15:40-47 • Luke 23:49-56 • John 19:31-42

¶ The Jews therefore, because it was the preparation, that the bodies should not remain upon the cross on the sabbath day, (for the sabbath day was an high day,) besought Pilate that their legs might be broken, and *that* they might be taken away. Then came the soldiers, and break the legs of the first, and of the other which was crucified with him. But when they came to Jesus, and saw that he was dead already, they break not his legs: But one of the soldiers with a spear pierced his side, and forthwith came there out blood and water. And he that saw *it* bare record, and his record is true: [A]nd he knoweth that he saith true, that ye might believe. For these things were done, that the scripture should be fulfilled, A bone of him shall not be broken. And again another scripture saith, [T]hey shall look on him whom they pierced. • And all his acquaintance, and the • many • women that followed • Jesus from Galilee, ministering unto him: • [L]ooking on • stood afar off, beholding these things. • Among • whom was Mary Magdalene, and Mary the mother of James the less and of Joses, and Salome • the mother of Zebedee's children. • (Who also, when he was in Galilee, followed him, and ministered unto him;) and many other women which came up with him unto Jerusalem.

¶ And now when the even was come, because it was the preparation, that is, the day before the sabbath, • And after this • behold, • there came a rich man of Arimathæa, named Joseph, • an honourable counseller, • a good man, and a just: • [W]ho also himself • being a disciple of Jesus, but secretly for fear of the Jews, • (The same had not consented to the counsel and deed of them;) he was of Arimathæa, a city of the Jews: [W]ho also himself waited for the kingdom of God. This *man* • came, and went in boldly • unto Pilate, • besought Pilate • and {begged / {craved} • the body of Jesus. • [T]hat he might take away the body of Jesus: • And Pilate marvelled if he were already dead: [A]nd calling *unto him* the centurion, he asked him whether he had been any while dead. And when he knew *it* of the centurion, he gave the body to Joseph. • Then Pilate commanded the body to be delivered. • And Pilate gave *him* leave. He came therefore, and took the body of Jesus. • And he bought fine linen, • [a]nd

MATTHEW	MARK	LUKE	JOHN

there came also Nicodemus, which at the first came to Jesus by night, and brought a mixture of myrrh and aloes, about an hundred pound *weight*. Then took they the body of Jesus • down, • [a]nd Joseph had taken the body, • and wound • and wrapped it in • a clean linen cloth, • with the spices, as the manner of the Jews is to bury. Now in the place where in he was crucified there was a garden; and in the garden a new sepulchre, • and laid him in • his own new tomb, which he had hewn out in the {rock: / stone} • [W]herein was never man • before • yet laid. • [A]nd he rolled a great stone to the door of the sepulchre, and departed. • There laid they Jesus therefore because of • that day was • the Jews' preparation *day;* for the sepulchre was nigh at hand • and the sabbath drew on. And the women also, which came with him from Galilee, followed after, • there was Mary Magdalene, and the other Mary, • *the mother* of Joses • sitting over against the sepulcher • and beheld the sepulchre, • where • and how his body was laid. And they returned, and prepared spices and ointments; and rested the sabbath day according to the commandment. •

¶ Now the next day, that followed the day of the preparation, the chief priests and Pharisees came together unto Pilate, [s]aying, Sir, we remember that that deceiver said, while he was yet alive, After three days I will rise again. Command therefore that the sepulchre be made sure until the third day, lest his disciples come by night, and steal him away, and say unto the people, He is risen from the dead: [S]o that the last error shall be worse than the first. Pilate said unto them, Ye have a watch: [G]o your way, make *it* as sure as ye can. So they went, and made the sepulchre sure, sealing the stone, and setting a watch.

ΑΩ

Chapter 18

The Sun of Righteousness

Malachi 4:02

Redaction: The Sun of Righteousness

MATTHEW	MARK	LUKE	JOHN

MATTHEW	MARK	LUKE	JOHN

- He is Risen -

Matt 28:01-15 • Mark 16:01-11 • Luke 24:01-12 • John 20:01-18

¶ In the end • when the sabbath was past, Mary Magdalene, and Mary the *mother* of James, and Salome, had bought sweet spices, that they might come and anoint him. •

¶ Now • as it began to dawn {toward / upon} the first *day* of the week, very early in the morning, • came Mary Magdalene and the other Mary • unto the sepulchre, bringing the spices which they had prepared, and certain *others* with them • to see the sepulchre • when it was yet dark, • at the rising of the sun. And they said among themselves, Who shall roll us away the stone from the door of the sepulchre? • And, behold, there was a great earthquake: [F]or the angel of the Lord descended from heaven, and came and rolled back the stone from the door, and sat upon it. His countenance was like lightning, and his raiment white as snow: And for fear of him the keepers did shake, and became as dead *men*. • And when they looked, • unto the sepulchre, • they saw that • the stone • was • {rolled / taken} • away from the sepulchre. • [F]or it was very great. • And they entered • into the sepulchre, • and found not the body of the Lord Jesus. • [T]hey saw a young man sitting on the right side, clothed in a long white garment; • [a]nd it came to pass, as they were much perplexed there about, behold, two men stood by them in shining garments: And as they were afraid, and bowed down *their* faces to the earth, • the angel answered and said unto the women, Fear not ye: for I know that ye seek • Jesus of Nazareth, which was crucified: • [T]hey said unto them, Why seek ye the living among the dead? • He is not here: [F]or he is risen, as he said. Come, see the place where the Lord lay. • [B]ehold the place where they laid him. • [R]emember how he spake unto you when he was yet in Galilee, Saying, The Son of man must be delivered into the hands of sinful men, and be crucified, and the third day rise again. And they remembered his words[.] • But go your way • quickly, and tell his disciples • and Peter • that he is risen from the dead; and, behold, he goeth before you into Galilee; there shall ye see him: • [A]s he said unto you. • [L]o, I have told you. • And they went out quickly, and fled from the sepulchre; • with fear and great joy; • for they trembled and were amazed: [N]either said they anything to any *man*; for

MATTHEW	MARK	LUKE	JOHN

they were afraid • and did run to bring his disciples word. • And returned from the sepulchre, • [t]hen she runneth and cometh to Simon Peter, and to the other disciple, whom Jesus loved, and saith unto them, They have taken away the Lord out of the sepulchre, and we know not where they have laid him. • [A]nd told all these things unto the eleven, and to all the rest. It was Mary Magdalene, and Joanna, and Mary *the mother* of James, and other *women that were* with them, which told these things unto the apostles. And their words seemed to them as idle tales, and they believed them not. Then arose Peter, • Peter therefore went forth, and that other disciple, • and ran • and came • unto • the sepulchre. So they ran both together: [A]nd the other disciple did out run Peter, and came first to the sepulchre. And he stooping down, *and looking in,* saw the linen clothes lying; yet went he not in. Then cometh Simon Peter following him, and went into the sepulchre, • and stooping down, he beheld the linen clothes laid by themselves, • [a]nd the napkin, that was about his head, not lying with the linen clothes, but wrapped together in a place by itself. • [A]nd departed, wondering in himself at that which was come to pass. • Then went in also that other disciple, which came first to the sepulchre, and he saw, and believed. For as yet they knew not the scripture, that he must rise again from the dead. Then the disciples went away again unto their own home.

¶ But Mary stood without at the sepulchre weeping: [A]nd as she wept, she stooped down, *and looked* into the sepulchre, And seeth two angels in white sitting, the one at the head, and the other at the feet, where the body of Jesus had lain. And they say unto her, Woman, why weepest thou? She saith unto them, Because they have taken away my Lord, and I know not where they have laid him. And when she had thus said, she turned herself back, and saw Jesus standing, and knew not that it was Jesus. •

¶ Now when *Jesus* was risen early the first *day* of the week, he appeared first to Mary Magdalene, out of whom he had cast seven devils. • Jesus saith unto her, Woman, why weepest thou? [W]hom seekest thou? She, supposing him to be the gardener, saith unto him, Sir, if thou hast borne him hence, tell me where thou hast laid him, and I will take him away. Jesus saith unto her, Mary. She

MATTHEW	MARK	LUKE	JOHN

turned herself, and saith unto him, Rabboni; [W]hich is to say, Master. Jesus saith unto her, Touch me not; for I am not yet ascended to my Father: [B]ut go to my brethren, and say unto them, I ascend unto my Father, and your Father; and *to* my God, and your God. •

¶ And as they went to tell his disciples, behold, Jesus met them, saying, All hail. And they came and held him by the feet and worshipped him. Then said Jesus unto them, Be not afraid: [G]o tell my brethren that they go into Galilee, and there shall they see me.

¶ Now when they were going, behold some of the watch came into the city, and shewed unto the chief priests all the things that were done. And when they were assembled with the elders, and had taken counsel, they gave large money unto the soldiers, [s]aying, Say ye, His disciples came by night, and stole him *away* while we slept. And if this come to the governor's ears, we will persuade him, and secure you. So they took the money, and did as they were taught: [A]nd this saying is commonly reported among the Jews until this day. •

¶ Mary Magdalene came and told the disciples • that had been with him, as they mourned and wept • that she had seen the Lord, and *that* he had spoken these things unto her. • And they, when they had heard that he was alive, and had been seen of her, believed not.

Ω

Redaction: The Sun of Righteousness

MATTHEW	MARK	LUKE	JOHN

MATTHEW	MARK	LUKE	JOHN

- To a Village Called Emmaus -

Matt • Mark 16:12 • Luke 24:13-32 • John

¶ After that he appeared in another form unto two of them, as they walked, and went into the country. • And, behold, two of them went that same day to a village called Emmaus, which was from Jerusalem about three score furlongs. And they talked together of all these things which had happened. And it came to pass, that, while they communed *together* and reasoned, Jesus himself drew near, and went with them. But their eyes were holden that they should not know him. And he said unto them, What manner of communications are these that ye have one to another, as ye walk, and are sad? And the one of them, whose name was Cleopas, answering said unto him, Art thou only a stranger in Jerusalem, and hast not known the things which are come to pass there in these days? And he said unto them, What things? And they said unto him, Concerning Jesus of Nazareth, which was a prophet mighty in deed and word before God and all the people: And how [T]he chief priests and our rulers delivered him to be condemned to death, and have crucified him. But we trusted that it had been he which should have redeemed Israel: [A]nd beside all this, [T]oday is the third day since these things were done. Yea, and certain women also of our company made us astonished, which were early at the sepulchre; [a]nd when they found not his body, they came, saying, that they had also seen a vision of angels, which said that he was alive. And certain of them which were with us went to the sepulchre, and found *it* even so as the women had said: [B]ut him they saw not. Then he said unto them, O fools, and slow of heart to believe all that the prophets have spoken: Ought not Christ to have suffered these things, and to enter into his glory? And beginning at Moses and all the prophets, he expounded unto them in all the scriptures the things concerning himself. And they drew nigh unto the village, whither they went: [A]nd he made as though he would have gone further. But they constrained him, saying, Abide with us: [F]or it is toward evening, and the day is far spent. And he went in to tarry with them. And it came to pass, as he sat at meat with them, he took bread, and blessed *it*, and brake, and gave to them. And their eyes were opened, and they knew him; and he vanished out of their sight. And they said one to another, Did not our heart burn within us, while he talked with us by the way, and while he opened to

Redaction: The Sun of Righteousness

MATTHEW	MARK	LUKE	JOHN

us the scriptures? And they rose up • [a]nd they went • the same hour, and returned to Jerusalem, and found the eleven gathered together, and them that were with them, [s]aying, The Lord is risen indeed, and hath appeared to Simon. And they told what things were done in the way, and how he was known of them in breaking of bread • unto the residue: [N]either believed they them. •

Ω

MATTHEW	MARK	LUKE	JOHN

- Peace Be unto You -

Matt 28:16-18 • Mark 16:14 • Luke 24:36-49 • John 20:18-31

¶ Then the same day at evening, being the first *day* of the week, when the doors were shut where the disciples were assembled for fear of the Jews, • [a]nd as they thus spake, • came Jesus • himself • and stood in the midst • of them, and saith unto them, Peace *be* unto you. But they were terrified and affrighted, and supposed that they had seen a spirit. And he said unto them, Why are ye troubled? [A]nd why do thoughts arise in your hearts? Behold my hands and my feet, that it is I myself: [H]andle me, and see; for a spirit hath not flesh and bones, as ye see me have. And when he had thus spoken, he shewed • unto them *his* hands and his side • and *his* feet. • Then were the disciples glad, when they saw the Lord. • And while they yet believed not for joy, and wondered, he said unto them, Have ye here any meat? And they gave him a piece of a broiled fish, and of an honeycomb. And he took *it*, and did eat before them. And he said unto them, These *are* the words which I spake unto you, while I was yet with you, that all things must be fulfilled, which were written in the law of Moses, and *in* the prophets, and *in* the psalms, concerning me. • Then said Jesus to them again, Peace *be* unto you: [A]s *my* Father hath sent me, even so send I you. And when he had said this, he breathed on *them*, and saith unto them, Receive ye the Holy Ghost: • Then opened he their understanding, that they might understand the scriptures, [a]nd said unto them, Thus it is written, and thus it behoved Christ to suffer, and to rise from the dead the third day: And that repentance and remission of sins should be preached in his name among all nations, beginning at Jerusalem. • Whose soever sins ye remit, they are remitted unto them; *and* whose soever *sins* ye retain, they are retained. • And ye are witnesses of these things.

¶ And, behold, I send the promise of my Father upon you: [B]ut tarry ye in the city of Jerusalem, until ye be endued with power from on high. • But Thomas, one of the twelve, called Didymus, was not with them when Jesus came. The other disciples therefore said unto him, We have seen the Lord. But he said unto them, Except I shall see in his hands the print of the nails, and put my finger into the print of the nails, and thrust my hand into his side, I will not believe.

MATTHEW	MARK	LUKE	JOHN

¶ And after eight days again his disciples were within, and Thomas with them: • Afterward he appeared unto the eleven as they sat at meat, • *then* came Jesus, the doors being shut, and stood in the midst, and said, Peace *be* unto you. Then saith he to Thomas, Reach hither thy finger, and behold my hands; and reach hither thy hand, and thrust *it* into my side: [A]nd be not faithless, but believing. And Thomas answered and said unto him, My Lord and my God. Jesus saith unto him, Thomas, because thou hast seen me, thou hast believed: [B]lessed *are* they that have not seen, and *yet* have believed. • [A]nd upbraided them with their unbelief and hardness of heart, because they believed not them that had seen him after he was risen. •

¶ Then the eleven disciples went away into Galilee, into a mountain where Jesus had appointed them. And when they saw him, they worshipped him: [B]ut some doubted. And Jesus came and spake unto them, saying, All power is given unto me in heaven and in earth. •

¶ And many other signs truly did Jesus in the presence of his disciples, which are not written in this book: But these are written, that ye might believe that Jesus is the Christ, the Son of God; and that believing ye might have life through his name.

Ω

MATTHEW	MARK	LUKE	JOHN

- Go Ye into All the World -

Matt 28:19-20 • Mark 16:15-20 • Luke 24:50-53 • John 21:01-25

¶ A[fter] these things Jesus shewed himself again to the disciples at the sea of Tiberias; and on this wise shewed he *himself*. There were together Simon Peter, and Thomas called Didymus, and Nathanael of Cana in Galilee, and the *sons* of Zebedee, and two other of his disciples. Simon Peter saith unto them, I go a fishing. They say unto him, We also go with thee. They went forth, and entered into a ship immediately; and that night they caught nothing. But when the morning was now come, Jesus stood on the shore: [B]ut the disciples knew not that it was Jesus. Then Jesus saith unto them, Children, have ye any meat? They answered him, No. And he said unto them, Cast the net on the right side of the ship, and ye shall find. They cast therefore, and now they were not able to draw it for the multitude of fishes. Therefore that disciple whom Jesus loved saith unto Peter, It is the Lord. Now when Simon Peter heard that it was the Lord, he girt *his* fisher's coat *unto him*, (for he was naked,) and did cast himelf into the sea. And the other disciples came in a little ship; (for they were not far from land, but as it were two hundred cubits,) dragging the net with fishes. As soon then as they were come to land, they saw a fire of coals there, and fish laid thereon, and bread. Jesus saith unto them, Bring of the fish which ye have now caught. Simon Peter went up, and drew the net to land full of great fishes, an hundred and fifty and three: and for all there were so many, yet was not the net broken. Jesus saith unto them, Come *and* dine. And none of the disciples durst ask him, Who art thou? [K]nowing that it was the Lord. Jesus then cometh, and taketh bread, and giveth them, and fish likewise. This is now the third time that Jesus shewed himself to his disciples, after that he was risen from the dead.

¶ So when they had dined, Jesus saith to Simon Peter, Simon, *son* of Jonas, lovest thou me more than these? He saith unto him, Yea, Lord; thou knowest that I love thee. He saith unto him, Feed my lambs. He saith to him again the second time, Simon, *son* of Jonas, lovest thou me? He saith unto him, Yea, Lord; thou knowest that I love thee. He saith unto him, Feed my sheep. He saith unto him the third time, Simon, *son* of Jonas, lovest thou me? Peter was grieved because he said unto him the third time,

MATTHEW	MARK	LUKE	JOHN

Lovest thou me? And he said unto him, Lord, thou knowest all things; thou knowest that I love thee. Jesus saith unto him, Feed my sheep. Verily, verily, I say unto thee, When thou wast young, thou girdedst thyself, and walkedst whither thou wouldest: [B]ut when thou shalt be old, thou shalt stretch forth thy hands, and another shall gird thee, and carry *thee* whither thou wouldest not. This spake he, signifying by what death he should glorify God. And when he had spoken this, he saith unto him, Follow me. Then Peter, turning about, seeth the disciple whom Jesus loved following; which also leaned on his breast at supper, and said, Lord, which is he that betrayeth thee? Peter seeing him saith to Jesus, Lord, and what *shall* this man *do*? Jesus saith unto him, If I will that he tarry till I come, what *is that* to thee? [F]ollow thou me. Then went this saying abroad among the brethren, that that disciple should not die: yet Jesus said not unto him, He shall not die; but, If I will that he tarry till I come, what *is that* to thee? This is the disciple which testifieth of these things, and wrote these things: [A]nd we know that his testimony is true. •

––

¶ And he lead them out as far as to Bethany, and he lifted up his hands, and blessed them. • And he said unto them, • Go ye therefore, • into all the world, • and teach all nations, • and preach the gospel to every creature. • [B]aptizing them in the name of the Father, and of the Son, and of the Holy Ghost: Teaching them to observe all things whatsoever I have commanded you: • He that believeth and is baptized shall be saved; but he that believeth not shall be damned. And these signs shall follow them that believe; In my name shall they cast out devils; they shall speak with new tongues; They shall take up serpents; and if they drink any deadly thing, it shall not hurt them; they shall lay hands on the sick, and they shall recover. •

––

¶ [A]nd, lo, I am with you alway, *even* unto the end of the world. • So then • it came to pass, • after the Lord had spoken unto them, • while he blessed them, he was parted from them, • received • and carried up into heaven • and sat on the right hand of God. • And they worshipped him, and returned to Jerusalem with great joy: And were continually in the temple, praising and blessing God. • And they went forth, and preached everywhere, the Lord working with *them*, and confirming the word

MATTHEW	MARK	LUKE	JOHN

with signs following. • And there are also many other things which Jesus did, the which, if they should be written every one, I suppose that even the world itself could not contain the books that should be written. Amen.

AΩ

AMEN.

www.ingramcontent.com/pod-product-compliance
Lightning Source LLC
Chambersburg PA
CBHW030414100426
42812CB00028B/2952/J